Contemporary S Plays for Higher English and Drama

Anne Gifford and Jane Robertson

Hodder & Stoughton

A MEMBER OF THE HODDER HEADLINE GROUP

Orders: please contact Bookpoint Ltd, 130 Milton Park, Abingdon, Oxon OX14 4SB. Telephone: (44) 01235 827720. Fax: (44) 01235 400454. Lines are open from 9.00 – 6.00, Monday to Saturday, with a 24 hour message answering service. Email address: orders@bookpoint.co.uk

British Library Cataloguing in Publication Data
A catalogue record for this title is available from the British Library

ISBN 0 340 80321 5

Published by Hodder & Stoughton Educational Scotland
First Published 2002
Impression number   10 9 8 7 6 5 4 3 2 1
Year   2007 2006 2005 2004 2003 2002

Cover photo by Douglas McBride. Theatre Babel's production of Liz Lochhead's *Medea* premiered at the Old Fruitmarket, Glasgow in March 2000. Part of *Greeks*, it is one of a trilogy of modern versions of classical texts commissioned by Theatre Babel with support from the Scottish Arts Council (National Lottery Fund) and Tramway.

Typeset by Dorchester Typesetting Group Ltd, Dorchester, Dorset, England.
Printed in Great Britain for Hodder & Stoughton Educational, a division of Hodder Headline Plc, 338 Euston Road, London NW1 3BH by Martins the Printers, Berwick-upon-Tweed.

CONTEMPORARY SCOTTISH PLAYS
FOR HIGHER ENGLISH AND DRAMA

CONTENTS

CHAPTER ONE

INTRODUCTION

The aim of this collection is to provide high-quality drama and support material, which will help meet the needs of teachers delivering courses in English and Communication and Drama within the Higher Still framework, particularly since there are learning outcomes in both English and Drama that must be met through the study of Scottish texts. Liz Lochhead, Nicola McCartney and Sharman Macdonald have all been acclaimed for their powerful, contemporary drama. Their plays contain strong female characters and are set in a diverse range of times and places, bringing to our attention a fresh range of interesting characters in literature for the English curriculum. The three plays are sufficiently varied in complexity and theme, so as to offer a stimulating resource across a range of abilities and maturity. The collection should support students and teachers in a number of ways:

- ☐ by extending the range of Scottish plays available in print for study;

- ☐ by providing appropriate commentary on key aspects of the plays as background information for teachers;

- ☐ by offering clearly-structured, fully fleshed-out drama activities that will allow teachers to explore with students aspects of the plays in performance;

- ☐ by consolidating the development of students' skills and knowledge through the inclusion of specific oral, written and practical tasks;

- ☐ by highlighting how students can achieve particular learning outcomes for both the English and Communication and Drama Higher Still frameworks through the approaches outlined for each play.

The key innovative feature of the collection is the inclusion of a practical guide for teachers on how to organise and deliver lessons, in a way which helps to make the plays three-dimensional for students. The aim is not to 'give answers' but rather to enable students to engage actively with each text, and to develop their confidence and skill in analysing and responding to the writers' craft. Aspects of form, often a difficult area for students, are dealt with along with content. It is hoped that teachers will use the drama-based activities as the main focus for enabling students to engage with the text and not as an 'add-on' activity, thus recognising that learners acquire and process information in a number of ways: visually, aurally, through physical activity, in discussion or exchange with others and in solitary reflection. It's worth noting that the support notes, which are included within all the unit specifications for Higher Still English and Communication, make explicit reference to the need for a variety of approaches to teaching and learning.

For students attempting Access 3, in particular, the collaborative investigation of a text is highlighted as an important way to support learners.

For Drama students, the activities will be central to their preparation for the acting piece, which is one of the learning outcomes they need to achieve. For English and Communication students, the activities will help them focus on a particular aspect of the play and organise a coherent set of ideas around it. However, it is for teachers to make their own decisions about how they want to present each play to students. They could decide to adapt the activities used in one part of the play for another part, or they could identify a particular strand highlighted in the introduction to each play and trace its development through the text. Crucially, there should be space for students and teachers to make and share their own meanings from the texts.

CHAPTER TWO

GUIDELINES FOR TEACHERS

English and Communication

The texts and activities included are targeting two units in particular within the English and Communication framework, Literary Study and Specialist Study Literature. These units run at all levels in the framework, and one of the challenges for teachers is differentiating material to meet students' needs across the various levels. A closer look at the National Course Specifications reveals some particular issues in relation to assessment. For instance, the demands of the learning outcomes and performance criteria at the various levels in the English and Communication framework is, for the most part, split quite neatly into two groups: Higher and Intermediate 2 form one, and Intermediate 1 and Access 3 the other. In Literary Study and Specialist Study Literature the key difference between these two groups is the degree of *critical* analysis and evaluation that is required to achieve the learning outcome in both units. It is the development of the knowledge and skills required to successfully achieve these two challenging aspects of the performance criteria that this book specifically aims to address.

The demands at Higher and Intermediate 2 for the critical essay are considerable. Students are expected in their analysis to explain 'in some detail' at Intermediate 2, and 'accurately and in some detail' at Higher, ways in which aspects of structure, style and language contribute to meaning or effect impact. In their evaluation students must 'engage' or 'clearly engage' with the text(s), backing their evaluation up with evidence from the text. Even more, if students are to achieve A grades at either level, 'insight' or 'some insight' into the writer's use of literary technique is required, as well as the ability to 'establish and fully support' their evaluation of 'effectiveness' in their response to the text(s). Words like 'skilful', 'perceptive' and 'appreciative' feature enough in the performance criteria for teachers and students to realise that success will not be achieved easily. In particular, it is hoped that the drama activities presented in this book will support students in engaging with and subsequently evaluating the text. Students need to be able to use the skills and knowledge acquired in achieving the learning outcome for Literary Study in order to cope with Textual Analysis, which is now a compulsory part of the external assessment. Practice in this is offered at the end of the book.

Guidelines on good practice in the teaching of English have always emphasised the need for an integrated approach to the development of language. The activities that are included in this book not only address the requirements of the units already mentioned, but also provide opportunities for pupils to engage in aspects of Critical Listening and Group

Discussion. Since Oral/Aural Communication has become a compulsory and assessed strand of the Higher Still curriculum, it's vital that students are given as many structured opportunities as possible to, not only develop their own skills in these areas, but also to develop their awareness of the communication process. Many of the activities in this book will allow this to happen. Moreover, the play *Sea Urchins* has as a central issue the difficulties that arise through the characters' failure to communicate effectively. This can be used as a base on which general discussion on talking and listening can be built. Finally, teachers are always looking for meaningful contexts for encouraging students to write. The exploration of character and theme initiated by many of the drama activities have the potential to be developed into pieces of imaginative writing for the students' Personal Studies Folios.

Drama

The specific area of the Drama curriculum being targeted is the unit on Contemporary Scottish Theatre at Higher. It will be possible for students to fulfil the two learning outcomes required for this unit through the material in this book. The National Unit Specification support notes state that at least three post-1900 Scottish plays must be studied and considered within 'specified trends and issues: social, political and religious dimensions; use of history, nostalgia and popular tradition; issues of gender; and current productions and issues'. All three plays could readily be considered in relation to one or more of these trends or issues. Furthermore, each play, with its strong central female character(s), can be readily compared and discussed within these specified areas. With the range of activities on offer, students will be able to explore the plays from the perspective of an audience and an actor.

One of the performance criteria for the second outcome of this unit – perform an acting role from a contemporary Scottish play – states that students must be able to 'interpret the character convincingly, showing use of textual clues'. The range of activities mapped out over the three plays not only provides scope for students to choose a suitable performance piece, but also allows them to engage fully with the text. This should be helpful in enabling them to 'communicate effectively the overall portrayal of the character to the audience'.

Using the Guidelines for Students

English and Communication

The final section of this book addresses students rather than teachers. Specific tasks are set that reflect the kind of questions asked of texts in both English and Communication and the written component in Drama. Students are reminded of what they know already through their engagement with the text, and then given advice on what to include in their response in order to fulfil the learning outcome. Appropriate reference is made to the National Course Specifications in a user-friendly way. Students are directed to the text, activities, commentary and background information as required and key aspects relating to understanding, analysis, evaluation and expression are highlighted.

Teachers can (and probably will) choose to use this section as a focus for their teaching as part of a whole group lesson on writing a critical essay. However, able students could probably work independently. It could be that the strategies and structures offered provide a good 'halfway house' for internal assessment too. Ultimately, students will need to complete the learning outcome unaided but, for those who need it, a supported 'dry run' could be very useful in building their confidence and providing them with a systematic and organised approach to the task.

Drama

Drama students will find that the kind of support and guidance they need to prepare for their performance piece on a Scottish text is built in throughout the activities section of each play, where there are opportunities to explore in-depth the emotions and motivations of characters, and space to consider how they might respond to the actions or words of other characters and the events on stage. Like English and Communication students, they will become aware of particular themes and issues being worked through the texts.

It is through a written or taped assignment that students will demonstrate their knowledge and understanding of specified trends and issues in contemporary Scottish theatre. The advice and guidelines offered to English and Communication students on how to put together a critical essay will provide support for Drama students on how to put together their response. However, the performance criteria for this learning outcome require students to analyse *three* texts and discuss *two* specified trends or issues, so there is further guidance on how to compare texts and consider them within a particular theme.

The Plays within the Higher Still Framework

While it would be inappropriate to label the plays as 'Higher' or 'Intermediate', they were selected because they fit well in terms of complexity of form and content with the different levels within the Higher Still framework. *Medea* presents the greatest challenge for students because of its dramatic form and historical context, and so is probably best taught at Higher level. Students will need to know something of the background to the drama of ancient Greece, and this has been provided in the background information section and at appropriate points in the drama activities themselves.

Able students could look at other translations of Euripides' *Medea* as well as other drama of the period. An interesting Specialist Study in Literature might be pursued as a result.

The historical and cultural context of a text's production has been less of a focus for study in the English curriculum in schools and colleges, but not so in universities. Perhaps the opportunity to consider a text more fully within its context of production will appeal to students and open up possibilities for a more mature response in a critical essay. Certainly the written responses required by Drama students often focus on the historical, social, and/or cultural dimension in relation to a text's production. Liz Lochhead's *Medea (after Euripides)*, a contemporary Scottish version of a much older text, raises interesting questions about the play's production and reception.

The language of the play provides ample opportunity for in depth textual analysis for English and Communication students and the extended speeches of the leading characters will allow Drama students the scope to present an acting piece of suitable length and depth. The combination of clever language with a powerful theme and a strong central character will allow students to engage with the drama and so enable them to respond 'personally' to it. The highly-charged relationship between Jason and Medea and her final terrible revenge cannot fail to arouse the emotions of an audience.

Heritage, too, requires students to have some background knowledge but it's likely that they can bring some of their own knowledge to the circumstances of the drama. The political and religious tensions of Ulster have been well documented and most young people have some sense of the conflict in the Province. The play foregrounds the history of the troubles by setting the events of the play in the past and shifting the setting to Canada. Nicola McCartney's timeline of parallel historical events, included later, is illuminating because it not only succinctly connects the events of the play with 'real life' but also demonstrates the careful research that is required in order to produce a convincing drama.

Intermediate 2 students should connect readily with the characters and events of *Heritage*. Sarah McCrea and Michael Donaghue are attractive and appealing, and their love story can be readily linked to other contexts, for example *Romeo and Juliet*. In fact, *Heritage* has the potential to work, should circumstances demand it, with a bi-level group. There is sufficient complexity and theatricality for students to engage with the text at Higher level, and yet the play is accessible enough for students working at Intermediate 2. Again, there is scope to use *Heritage* as part of the Specialist Study in Literature, perhaps in comparison with *Bold Girls* by Rona Munro. Both plays deal with the same long-running conflict in different ways, yet there are connecting points between the two. The story of *Deirdre of the Sorrows*, which is central to the relationship between Michael and Sarah in *Heritage*, connects, too, with the 'mysterious' outsider, Deirdre, in *Bold Girls*. There are monologues by both Sarah and Deirdre, which work in similar ways to construct the drama in each play.

A major challenge for teachers is finding suitable literary texts for post-16 students who, in the past, would not have had the opportunity to study within the kind of framework offered by Higher Still. *Sea Urchins* has a number of strengths that make it highly appropriate for students working to achieve Intermediate 1 or, in some cases, Access 3. The learning outcome for Literary Study in English and Communication requires students to *respond* to features of a seen imaginative text, and in the Specialist Study in Literature they are asked to *review* their choice of text(s). While this does not make the same *critical* demand as the learning outcome at Intermediate 2 and Higher, students still need texts of substance that they enjoy and can engage with in order to produce a response that is sufficiently analytical in terms of the performance criteria for the learning outcome. So, although the demands are less, students must still be able to describe some of the more obvious ways in which aspects of structure, style and language contribute to meaning, effect and impact. Although students attempting Access 3 can respond in spoken as well as written form, they still need to perform within the understanding, analysis and evaluation framework outlined for the other levels which, of course, includes responding to aspects of form as well as content.

Sea Urchins contains two key aspects of form and content which can be identified and traced through the play in an obvious and systematic way. The use of popular music to create nostalgia and to highlight some of the tensions between characters is one, and the other is Sharman Macdonald's use of slashes (/) and asterisks (*) to indicate particular ways in which the dialogue is exchanged at various points in the play. Teachers can be confident that these aspects of the drama will be readily identifiable for students who need to present a written or verbal response to the text. For Drama students, there are interesting challenges presented by these two aspects of the text in terms of how the play might be performed.

Strategies for Study

Role on the Wall

Role on the wall (ROTW) is a strategy used in drama and is a highly-effective way to explore a character. It is an ideal exercise to allow insight into a character either for an acting piece or critical evaluation.

'Drama is practical, immediate and engages the emotions as well as the intellect. Drama brings a dimension of ACTION to the classroom through the imagined use of TIME – SPACE – PEOPLE.'
Jonothan Neelands

Because of its unique nature, ROTW allows the teacher and student to explore ideas relating to the character and the play. The student has the opportunity to recall information, call on personal knowledge, be creative and use imagination. As the three-dimensional picture emerges the student should feel ownership of the character, as they have pieced together an image that is both aesthetic and intellectual.

How to use Role on the Wall

To use ROTW draw a large outline of a person. It is best to use a large sheet of paper as the chalkboard is less permanent and more ideas can be added as the work progresses. This is best tackled as a whole group activity to allow suggestions to be made and discussion to come from the students before filling in the sheet.

- ☐ Use the space outside the figure first to think of words that describe the character. This space can also be used for words that are relevant but do not easily fit into the next step.

- ☐ When the discussion has gone as far as possible at this stage, move to the inside of the figure using words that describe feelings, thoughts and attitudes.

This exercise should develop a deeper understanding of the character and encourage imaginative thought and good use of initiative. It is also a less formal way to revise, encourage research and cement prior knowledge.

Role Play

Role play in this instance allows the participants to take on roles in the play to investigate an idea, develop a storyline or to explore a feeling. This activity can be done quite simply in the classroom. The script should be used as a starting point allowing participants the opportunity to use their own words to explore the topic.

How to use Role Play

- ☐ Discuss the extract from the play that is to be explored, outlining the place and time the conversation takes place.

- ☐ Ask the group to organise themselves into twos or threes.

- ☐ Ask each group member to choose a role from the given extract.

- ☐ On your signal they begin and on another signal they stop.

There is no need to see each improvised scene but it is important for the whole group to discuss what the role play has helped them find out.

Conscience Alley

Think of this as 'if walls could talk'. This is a very effective exercise and can be done quickly and easily. It allows instant 'gut' reactions to certain issues, feelings or situations.

How to use Conscience Alley

- ☐ As far as space will allow, ask the group to form two lines facing each other with enough space in between for a person to walk between the lines from the top to the bottom.

☐ Ask for a volunteer to play the part of the character that needs to be warned, helped or advised.

☐ As the person walks slowly between the lines, each side of the alley says a word that is pertinent to the situation.

This exercise can be repeated for many characters and can confirm a whole group feeling for a character or situation without asking the question: 'What do we think of …'
It also creates a unique atmosphere and again can instigate a very good and useful discussion, especially if someone has a different point of view.

Brainstorming

Brainstorming is not a new idea or particularly a drama-based activity, but it can be very useful to allow groups of participants to quickly formulate ideas.

How to use Brainstorming

☐ The best way to tackle this is to give a very short time limit to the group.

☐ Give out large sheets of paper and some pens; ask for one group member to report back to the whole group.

☐ Allow discussion and questions to each small group.

☐ Display the ideas to help with creative writing or character development.

Hot Seating

This strategy is more theatrical but again very effective in developing character, imagination or tackling revision in a more creative way.

How to use Hot Seating

☐ Discuss with the group the possibility of meeting a character from the play. How would they react to being face to face with someone they have only ever read about?

☐ Explain that this is possible. Choose a character. Ask the group to go into small groups and write down the kind of questions they would like answered.

☐ Using a group member, yourself or an outside agent (perhaps a fellow teacher, but they must be very familiar with the text). Introduce the character to the group and allow the question and answer session to take place.

☐ Once the questioning has finished, the character leaves the room or the teacher comes out of role. A full discussion should take place.

Diary Extract

This strategy is used in drama to determine a character's private thoughts and perhaps to embellish areas of the text that seem a little vague or to fill in time gaps.

How to use Diary Extracts

☐ At an appropriate point in the text ask the participants to imagine that they are one of the characters and to write an entry in their diary after a particular event, issue or scene.

☐ The entry in the diary can retell the story or the event but must also reflect the feelings, mood and opinion of the character.

☐ Ask individuals to read out their extract and discuss with the rest of the group.

Chapter Three

Medea by Liz Lochhead (after Euripides)

Background Information

Liz Lochhead's play, *Medea,* was commissioned by Graham McLaren, the artistic director of Theatre Babel, as one of a series of plays in his ambitious 'Greeks' project, which also includes *Oedipus* by David Greig and *Electra* by Tom McGrath. The aim was to transform great classical works into pieces that would not only engage a Scottish audience, but also relate to universal modern experience. *Medea* is a reworking of Euripides' original play of 431 BC, a tragedy, timeless and ancient, about a woman driven by desperation to kill her children. In her foreword to the Theatre Babel playscript, Liz Lochhead describes how she used Euripides' *Medea* as a 'complete structural template' but then 'let go' and incorporated her own elements, for example, Medea's meeting with the 'other woman', Glauke. However, perhaps the most significant shift in Liz Lochhead's version of the play is in the character of Medea herself. Unlike Euripides' Medea, her 'modern' Medea is not made supernatural at all; instead, she is all too human and so engages even more powerfully with a contemporary audience.

Euripides (474–406/7 BC) was an Athenian tragic poet who, unlike Aeschylus and Sophocles, was not actively involved in public life. Altogether he produced 92 plays, 17 of which were tragedies. Euripides' work differed from that of Aeschylus and Sophocles, carrying into a democratic age the traditions and outlook of an aristocratic society, in that his approach presented more of a challenge to established values and attitudes. Euripides, therefore, was a forerunner of the greater individualism of the next and following centuries. He was critical, sceptical and individualistic – in a sense, cosmopolitan. His drama deals less with the community than with the individual, less with the broad questions of religion and morality than with the emotions and passions – love, hate, revenge – and with specific social questions. In this aspect he looked forward to many of the issues and concerns of contemporary culture and society.

The Story

The Athenian audience who saw the first performance of Euripides' *Medea* would have been familiar with the whole story of the central characters so it is important for a modern audience to have at least some knowledge of the same story.

Medea is a sensational tragedy of love turned to hatred, incorporating the issue of miscegenation (the interbreeding of different races). To the Athenians, Medea was a princess of distant Colchis and a sorceress, a strange, barbaric figure from the mysterious East. The Athenians strongly believed that they were the champions of civilised life and so Jason's claim, when he defends his desertion of Medea for Glauke, that he has 'rescued' her from a foreign land and brought her back to a Greek house, would be received very positively. Medea fell in love with Jason when his search to find the Golden Fleece brought him with the Argonauts to the kingdom of her father on the eastern shores of the Black Sea. She helped him to regain the Golden Fleece and they escaped together – Medea murdered her brother and scattered his body into the sea in order to slow up her father and his fleet who were in pursuit. Later, they were married. Medea has also contrived the death of Jason's uncle, Pelius, in an endeavour to place her husband on the throne of his native land. The plan, however, fails. Jason, Medea and their two young sons (Liz Lochhead gives them a daughter too) have to flee into exile and there Jason deserts her, marrying the daughter of Kreon, monarch of Corinth.

On one hand, from a contemporary perspective, Jason is nothing but a self-seeking, self-deluding male, willing to accept the results of any crime committed on his behalf by his wife but absolutely incapable of accepting any responsibility. On the other, from the Athenian perspective, Jason is a man of respectable ambitions and Medea, the 'uncivilised foreigner', is the obstacle in his way to fulfilling them. Theirs is a physical, passionate love, but not a true marriage. Medea is the 'barbarian' who gives herself totally to the man she loves and, when the love fails, is consumed by hate. Tremble though she may at the thought of killing her children, this sacrifice, in her mind, must be made to expiate the treachery to which she has been exposed. In the end, in Euripides' original play, Medea flies from human sight in a magical chariot drawn by dragons.

Liz Lochhead's Medea

Euripides aroused great interest – and great opposition – in his time through his realism; his interest in psychology, particularly feminine psychology; and his unorthodoxy. His portraits of women in love and his argumentativeness speaks directly to the modern world. Like Liz Lochhead, he explores in his work the tensions, frustrations and challenges that women face when they assert their individual and sexual identity in a patriarchal world. Liz Lochhead's ability to rework and rearticulate fairy tale, myth and history with a feminist slant in plays such as *Dracula* and *Mary Queen of Scots Got Her Head Chopped Off* has resulted in powerful, new perspectives on familiar narratives. Likewise, *Medea* provides the perfect vehicle for Liz Lochhead's take on feminine psychology, in this case exploring the destructive power of the wronged woman.

Even the form of the original *Medea* fits well with some of the dramatic techniques that Liz Lochhead deploys so effectively in her own work. Euripides established a quite formal prologue, which summarised the action up to the point where the play begins. This was sometimes spoken by a god or a character in the play. In *Medea*, Euripides uses a chorus. In a similar way, Liz Lochhead uses a character to introduce the audience to the events leading up to the start of the play in *Mary Queen of Scots Got Her Head Chopped Off*. The satirical, witty and theatrical opening prologue of La Corbie, who acts as narrator in the play, not only fills the audience in on the background of the '*twa queens*', but also gives a whole set of representations of Scotland:

> '*National flower: the thistle.*
> *National pastime: nostalgia.*
> *National weather; smirr, haar, drizzle, snow.*'

The chorus played an important role in Greek drama. Although they stood aside from the main action of the play and commented on it, the drama was very much built from the interplay of chorus and characters. Euripides, however, was eager to make his characters more real and ordinary, and to use them for 'philosophising' on the events, which was to an extent out of keeping with the established dramatic structure of Greek theatre. His chorus was less closely connected to the plot and more like choral interludes in the ongoing action. He therefore provided brilliant and beautiful lyrics for the chorus to sing. In *Medea*, where his concern is the conjugal difficulties between Medea and Jason, the chorus operates as a kind of cynical commentary on the action rather than being directly involved in it. This is very much how Liz Lochhead uses the chorus in her *Medea,* as poetic commentators who use language cleverly:

> '*if women were once worms we've turned*
> *we won't be put down the way that once we were*
> *sling your old slanders of so called*
> *female faithlessness   sing us*
> *something new*'

Again, there are echoes of characters from Liz Lochhead's previous works. For example, of La Corbie in *Mary Queen of Scots Got Her Head Chopped Off* and also of Renfield in *Dracula*, who is frequently on stage providing a backdrop of perceptive 'mad man's' comments on the characters and action of the drama.

Liz Lochhead's translation dispenses with the awkward *deus ex machina* or divine commands of the gods which were an acceptable way of resolving the action of a play on the Greek stage. The supernatural element of Medea's character is removed and Liz Lochhead creates a fully modern version of *Medea* with which a modern audience can readily engage.

Use of language

From the opening prologue Liz Lochhead takes the Medea story and adds her own distinctive twist. The opening stage directions state that, not only do all the people of this country have Scots accents, their language use varies from situation to situation. Scots and Scots-English are interchangeable throughout the play, adding to the power and emotion of the central theme of the wronged woman who seeks revenge. However, there is no set pattern to the use of Scots – it is the language of the nurse and the bodyguard throughout the play but also erupts into the speech of the chorus at moments of high emotion:

> 'we weep for you too Medea
> mother of bairns
> murderer of bairns
> mother   murderer'

Note, too, how Liz Lochhead exploits the possibilities of language through alliteration and anathema in 'mother   murderer'.

Medea herself, the outsider, the exotic, speaks as an incomer – one who still sounds like a foreigner speaking 'very good' English. In this, Medea resembles Mary Queen of Scots from Liz Lochhead's earlier play with her hybrid Franco-Scots accent. Interestingly, Liz Lochhead has observed that on hearing the play in performance, it struck her that the conventional way of doing *Medea* in Scotland until very recently would have been to have Medea's own language Scots and the (to her) alien Corinthians she lived under, speaking as powerful 'civilised' Greeks, patrician English. This shift, as Liz Lochhead suggests, must speak of a genuine increased cultural confidence in Scotland.

The combination of poetic and everyday language, so typical of Liz Lochhead's style, is strong and direct in its message but clever and playful in its delivery. Word games and wordplay are woven throughout the text, adding a rich linguistic dimension to an already powerful narrative.

In this play, as with Mary Queen of Scots, a woman is in conflict with patriarchal rule and language is used to highlight this. The bodyguard reminds us in the opening scenes of male dominance and the power of kingship:

> 'get real old woman   what's the world about?
> Jason can do so Jason does
> Hello bride bye bye bairns'

The nurse and the bodyguard open the action, strongly Scots in their speech, discussing 'the spilte and wastit love' as Medea is cast off by Jason for a new young bride. The bodyguard is quick to remind us of the fixed hierarchy of the country they live in and their 'place' within it:

> 'girning on aboot the griefs of your betters?
> they wouldnae greet for you'

THE CHORUS

The words of the chorus as they address Medea and the audience switch in register and style. On the one hand they can be sneering commentators on Medea's plight, cynical, worldly wise, delivering in a 'switched on' knowing style:

> 'marriage over? shame   that's the end of it
> so get on with it'

And, as they point out, rather ironically:

> 'we were not born yesterday
> we are all survivors of the sex war'

On other occasions, when they sympathise with Medea, their language is strongly poetic:

> 'salt and bitter are those tears
> as the seas you sailed with him'

The chorus work superbly well, both as commentators on, and confidants of, Medea. Their language flows between intimate and formal, detached and involved. They both heighten and try to control Medea's emotional state and their linguistic style reflects this.

> 'Medea   you set sail from your father's place
> ... only to be dumped   dishonoured in a foreign land'

The juxtaposition of 'dumped' and 'dishonoured' is typical of the way language is used by the chorus, as is the switch to formal invocation for divine intervention when they realise Medea's determination to kill her children:

> 'Gods stop her   if Gods you are
> Mother Earth open up and swallow her now
> before she forever defiles you'

GLAUKE

Another unique addition to the drama by Liz Lochhead is the substitution of Medea's meeting with Aegius of Athens with the realisation of Glauke as the 'other woman', who is an active participant in the play. In the original she is simply referred to. This allows Medea the opportunity to speak directly to her rival and heightens the emotion of Glauke's death because Medea calculatedly kills someone whom she knows would look after her children:

> *'I'll be good to them   you may trust me*
> *for Jason's sake'*

The dialogue between first wife and soon-to-be second wife is charged and, particularly for a female audience, satisfying because the two women *and* the audience must hear both sides of the story. Medea draws on all her worldly wisdom and survival instincts in order to undermine and dismiss Glauke, while she in turn fights her corner and won't be put down. As the chorus remark:

> *'you are no feart   our Glauke*
> *but maybe you do not entirely grasp this situation?'*

There is also a self-conscious playing around by Liz Lochhead of her version of the drama during the interchange between Medea and Glauke. Theatricality is briefly unmasked when Glauke's attempt to demonstrate her understanding of Medea's position is met with the sarcastic reply:

> *'it is always useful*
> *to view one's situation from the outside*
> *see it from the point of view of the*
> *other players in the drama'*

JASON AND MEDEA

Of course, the most intense points in the play happen when Medea confronts Jason about his betrayal. She has already faced scathing comments from Kreon, Glauke's father, reinforcing traditional (and perhaps very Scottish) stereotypes of marital breakdown – the woman brought it on herself.

> *'malice is your middle name*
> *and your man threw you oot   who'd blame him'*

Jason's smooth-talking justification for his actions are nicely handled. On one hand, the situation of the play is ancient Greece where power struggles, political intrigue and, most importantly the maintainance of 'civilised', Hellenic culture, seem to merit drastic action and sacrifice, and on the other we have a man explaining his infidelity:

> *'it's not what you think!'*

Liz Lochhead adds humour to their interchanges through contemporary wordplay:

JASON

> *I could have crept back to you in secret   would have*
> *but you can't keep it zipped   you will talk treason*

MEDEA

> *I can't keep it zipped!*
>
> *who   what   could be worse than you?*

The closing scenes, where Jason is confronted by the death of his children at the hands of Medea, are deeply moving. As is so often the case, there are no winners in this situation despite Medea's claim that her pain is not as bad as Jason's:

> *'for I have your pain to comfort me'*

The parallel speech patterns in the final exchange between Jason and Medea emphasise their shared guilt and pain:

JASON

> *children   the mother you had*

MEDEA

> *children   the father you had*
>
> *end of story*

JASON

> *It's over   it's all over*

MEDEA

> *it will never be over   end of story*

As is fitting, the closing stage directions indicate that there will be a cacophony of voices talking over one another and bemoaning the events of the tragedy. 'If only ...' is a strong part of the closing message. There is a strong sense of divine intervention, the hand of fate shaping our destiny.

CHORUS

> *The Gods look down*
>
> *expect the unexpected*
>
> *what we wish for   work for   plan for   hope for*
>
> *think is bound to happen   won't*
>
> *what is fated   will*
>
> *end of story.*

Liz Lochhead brings seamlessly together Greek tragedy and the difficulties of contemporary male-female relationships.

The result is an intense play of sexual strife accentuated by racial disparities, boldly presented through its two central characters.

Medea

by *Liz Lochhead*
(after Euripides)

Medea

By Liz Lochhead

SETTING

The play centres around the main character, Medea, who has fled into exile in Corinth with her husband, Jason. Medea has just learned that he now intends to marry the daughter of Kreon, King of Corinth.

The chorus provide a commentary on the events of the play.

CHARACTERS

Medea	Princess of Colchis and wife of Jason.
Jason	exiled son of Aeson, King of Iocolus.
Three Children	of Medea and Jason.
Kreon	King of Corinth and father of Glauke.
Glauke	Jason's new bride-to-be.
Nurse	to Medea.
Manservant	
Guard	
Chorus of Women	

Act One

Scene One

A woman is talking to herself and us. This is the Nurse.

The people of this country all have Scots accents, their language varies from Scots to Scots-English – from time to time and from character to character – and particular emotional state of character.

Nurse	I wish to all the Gods it had never sailed the Argo had never set its proud prow atween the humped blue rocks of distant islands forced itsel through straits breisted waves to land on unlucky Kolchis why? why did the sun ever heat up the soil in which there split that seed that sproutit from sapling to a tall tree of girth enough to be felled to build its keel? why was it ever oared? why crewed wi heroes fit to filch the Golden Fleece? adventurers! my lady Medea would never then have sailed wi Jason

daft for him   doted!
would no have   for his sake
swicked Pelias' dochters into killing their faither
for Jason's sake she fled here to Corinth
wi Jason and their bairns   ingratiatin hersel
sookin in   a fawning exile   a foreigner
for his sake

now it all sours on her   see how he's turned
brave Jason's bedded a new bride   Glauke
dochter of Kreon the King   a princess of this land
and Medea left to rot
among the spylte and wastit love she's stuck wi
she's chucked out like
an old coat that nae langer fits him
nae wonder Medea winna be comforted   shivers
stinks of fear   canna eat
canna sleep   greets till she can greet nae mair
stares at the cauld grunn   greets again   greets sair
try soothing her   she's a stone
in kindness leave her be   she rolls in her rags
claws at hersel   keening
too late she screams remorse for a faither loast
a land abandoned   the betrayals
she made for Jason who faur waur betrays her noo
too late   too late she learns she should
have clung to what she had
the children – she looks on them with empty eyes
as if they're nothing to her
I'm feart for her   fear her
I shut my eyes and see Medea
creepan through the labyrinthine palace
follying her hatred like a thread
I dream of a dagger thrust in yon double bed
skewering the lovers thegither
I see the skailt blood of Kreon the king

she's capable of onything

A handsome young, strong Manservant enters with the Children.

Manservant well auld yin   my lady's lady
what are you daen dithering here
girning on aboot the griefs of your betters?
they wouldnae greet for you

Nurse here're these sweet wee children playing
no a care in aw the warld
what are grown up griefs to bairns?   play away
for your mither things could not be worse

Manservant	oh could they no? so much you know auld yin that's no what I heard I tell you
Nurse	what did you hear?
Manservant	I'm saying naething
Nurse	tell me what you heard
Manservant	to say naething is already to have said too much
Nurse	speak to me we're slaves baith in the same sair place in this catastrophe
Manservant	I know it and when I greet it will be for masel I heard talk they never saw me it was where the old men play at draughts and blether and mibbe blethers is aw it is I hope so word wis King Kreon and he's the boss means to banish these bairns and their mither
Nurse	no Jason he wouldna! their mother mibbe but no his best his maist beloved bairns
Manservant	things cheynge this new Jason the day does not give a tuppeny fuck for anybody in this hoose
Nurse	misery piled on misery and mair of it new agony afore the first has done its worst
Manservant	wheesht say naething if it is this black your mistress will ken aw aboot it soon enough
Nurse	bairns do you hear what a faither you have? I wish he were no I'll not say it I'll no wish my lord and master dead but by Gods the horror of how he treats those he should love!
Manservant	get real old woman what's the world about? Jason can do so Jason does hello bride bye bye bairns
Nurse	away in you go my bairnies watch them man keep them away from their mother her hurt eyes of hate what would she no do? harm all harm to your enemies Medea no those you love!

The first primal cry from Medea inside.

Nurse	there there wheesht my wee loves my bairnies
	your poor mither she's no right run
	keep away from her thon's no your mother
	the state she's in

The Manservant hurries them indoors.

From off Medea cries out in a voice that is not Scots but a foreigner speaking good English – an 'incomer voice'.

Medea	Why don't you bloody die you
	cursed litter of a cursed mother?
	I hate my life and all I've done in it
	I wish I'd never made you with your hated father
	let it all crash around us in the ruins it's in

Nurse	my marrow curdles to hear her curse what she most loves
	is it no true the grand and horrid
	passions of the high and mighty
	rule them more cruelly
	than they the rulers rule us humble folk?
	a quiet life we're thank Gods too dull
	to draw doon the vengeance of the
	ayeways angry Gods that look down and ayeways punish
	them who think theirsels somebody

Another – the second – primal cry from Medea inside.

Enter Chorus of women of all times, all ages, classes and professions. (The Nurse does not see, or react with, the Chorus, their initial communication is to each other and also in unison direct to audience.)

Chorus	That cry we heard it
	knew it in our bones it curdled our blood too

Medea cries from inside again – for the third time.

Chorus	we are sorry for your sorrow sister
	is that how they cry in Kolchis Medea?

Nurse	this house is a ruin ashes
	a cold hearth and the fire put out in it
	for ever
	he's lording it lolling in bed with his royal bit
	she lies in cold ashes inconsolable.

Medea calls out from inside.

Medea	I wish to all the Gods that I was dead and done with it

Chorus	oh daft to wish for death
	when it comes soon enough
	without you tempt it
	so your man fucks another? fuck him

loves her?   tough   love him do you?
you'll grow out of that

we were not born yesterday
we are all survivors of the sex war
married women   widows   divorced
mistresses   wives   no virgins here

marriage over?   shame   that's the end of it
so get on with it

Medea   justice   Gods
look down on me and see my pain
I killed my own brother for you Jason
now I'll see you dead and that damned royal poppet too

Chorus   bring her out and let us convince her
we're her friends   we can help her

Nurse   I'm in terror even to approach her
I know her
her cunning   her spells   her power
how far she'll go   and I'm feart o her
more even than I fear for her
she nurses her rage
like a lioness suckling her last living cub
claws at me   bull glares
would gore me   gash me
I'm anathema
that blank stare!

The Nurse goes inside.

There is silence from within. Chorus are listening, tense, for something that doesn't come. Very softly at first –

Chorus   that cry!
it was a cry we've heard
from the woman
opening the door to the telegraph boy in wartime

the cry from   the unquiet wife
opening the door
to the chequered hats of two policemen
late late on a foggy night

the cry from   the mother in the hospital corridor
when she sees the doctor's face

the cry from   the woman
whose lover's eyes have not quite lied
when she asked him
'tell me is there someone else?'

that cry
we have heard it
from our sisters   mothers   from ourselves
that cry
we did not know we knew how to cry out
could not help but cry
and we say

we are sorry for your sorrow   sister
is that how they cry in Kolchis   Medea?
rage yes rage at that traitor in your bed
salt and bitter are those tears
as the seas you sailed with him

Enter Medea – not a girl – but dignified, beautiful, calm and utterly reasonable. Somehow exotic.

Medea graciously approaches the Chorus.

Medea   ladies of all time   ladies of this place
and others   I'm here now
I know you've thought me strange 'standoffish' 'a snob'
you've said of me   not understanding my shyness
my coolness merely masked my terror of being snubbed
no one loves a foreigner
everyone despises anyone the least bit different
'see how she ties her scarf' 'that hair   outlandish'
you walked by my house with eyes averted
turned your nose up at my household's cooking smells
'why can't she be a bit more like us?'
say you Greeks   who bitch about other Greeks
for not being Greeks from Corinth!
it's true I've not been   a woman's woman
I can say
I was never a woman at all until I met my man!
maiden Medea   my father's daughter   was a creature
who did not know she was born   she knew such
sweet freedom!
if it is a struggle in a bed or behind a bush engenders us
then it's when we fall in love that genders us
Jason   I am a woman now!

right out of the blue
humiliation!   I was the last to know
the man who was more to me than my own life
is now the vilest man alive   my faithless husband

are we women not the most miserable
and mocked of all Gods' creatures?
our fathers scrimp and save
a dowry   a lavish wedding breakfast

to buy the man he sells us to
and then for better or worse   richer or poorer
in sickness or health   – your sickness his health –
this man lords it over us
our lives at the mercy of how his lordship feels
stuck with him and his every demand
we little women must look to him alone
for company   kindness   our meal ticket
our every trinket
the compensation?   they'll bear the arms!
oh yes   wartime
and they'll die for us!
well I'd three times sooner fight a war
than suffer childbirth once

if I can find some way of paying Jason back
and the man who gives his daughter to him too
promise
will you women keep my secret?

we women are too weak   they say   for war
wrong us in bed though   oh man
we'll have your guts for garters

Chorus   we promise you   we are women Medea
we know men   we know who's in the right
punish him for us Medea
but here's King Kreon   a man with his own agenda
what will happen now?

Enter Kreon with the modest personal retinue of a very very powerful man. His voice is strongly Scots. Like the Nurse, he is from this place. In common with all the other characters except Medea, he is blind and deaf to the Chorus.

Kreon   you   glowering hate face
husband dumped you   has he?
so you hate him   the world's no wide enough
to haud you baith?   you'll be happy
then to hear my decree   I banish you
take your bairns and away you go
right now   far from our borders
I make the laws   and execute them
only when you're gone   will I sleep easy

Medea   I am in the worst of the storm and battered by it
I'm all alone   it's all over for me
no harbour   no haven
not a cave to shelter in
and this I ask you
what have I done to deserve this?

Kreon	frankly I'm feart of you why no?
	feart you hurt my daughter why no?
	you're a clever quine and cunning
	malice is your middle name
	and your man threw you oot who'd blame him?
	I've heard you dared to threaten us
	no just the groom but the bride and me the king
	you'd do it too Medea
	I believe it so it's in self defence
	nothing personal I have to hunt you
	raither that than clap you like a pussycat the now
	then too late hear your tigress growl
Medea	I've heard this before
	I'm oppressed by my reputation
	the evil one the witch the clever woman
	don't educate your daughters Kreon!
	clever men are envied
	and despised the world has no use for them
	fools think them foolish
	the clever fear them
	put them down can't take the competition
	but a clever woman
	fie it is to fly in the face of nature
	an abomination
	fear me? I can't be very clever can I
	or I'd not be in this pretty situation?
	a man a king
	how could I why should I
	harm you who has so far done me no harm?
	you married your daughter to the man you chose
	no harm in that
	I can't fault you but my man married your daughter
	it's him I hate
	marry your daughter off and all the best
	good luck to her she's done nothing to me
	I hope they'll both be very happy
	all I ask is a quiet corner
	where I'll keep my head down I promise you
	bring up my children like a poor and honest widow
	saying nothing saying nothing
	you'll be my king I your most abject slave
	use me as you will understand?
	I'll do anything for you Kreon to show my gratitude –
Kreon	mild words but inside that seething cauldron eh?
	what's cooking

I was not born yesterday Medea
the more you sweettalk the less I trust
the man or woman who unleashes a tirade of hate
at least he's honest   you know where you are
but smiles   what's behind them?
get out   shut up
enough   get out   my mind's made up

Medea   I beg you by your daughters life –

Kreon   dinna waste your words

Medea   have you no pity?

Kreon   nane   just duty

Medea   oh Kolchis my home I cry for you

Kreon   get back there then why don't you?

Medea   Kolchis   father –

Kreon   – brother?
foul the nest there did you?   aye
I'd do the same to mine
if I did not drive you out   you murdering whore
like vermin from my doors

I love my bairn and next to her I love this place

Medea   love   I'd not wish love on anybody
not even on you my enemy

Kreon   you are a pain to me

Medea   I am   one pain from top to toe   I'm dying!

Kreon snaps his fingers and his men bristle, stand to attention.

Kreon   men!   your escort awaits you madam
up you get

Medea   I'm on my knees

Kreon   begging for bother and by Gods you'll get it

Medea   I'm going   I want to go   one favour though

Kreon   in the name of all the Gods what is it and then will you go?

Medea   one day   one day of peace and preparation
my children to take final leave of their father
they don't hate him
and I to make some desperate provision
where   how
to save my two sweet sons   my daughter

you are a father too   have pity on them
you are a man   you should protect the helpless
the weak   the women   children
you are a Greek   a man of reason
civilisation   shall it be said
barbarians treat women and children better?
you are a king   you have the power to show mercy

Kreon   I'm no a barbarian   I'm no a tyrant either
but by showing saftness
I've sometimes been the one to suffer for it in the past
so promise me Medea I'll no live to regret this
ach   you can have your day!

I say this though   and it's final
if the dawn comes up the morrow
and finds you or your brats still here within our borders
you're dead the lot of you
understood?

As Kreon exits with his retinue he talks aloud to himself.

Kreon   one day   that's no long enough
for any of the dirty tricks I'm feart o

Chorus   one day!   one useless day!
poor woman we feel for you
where can you turn
who'll take you in
contaminated as you are
with the worst luck that Gods could chuck at anyone
it's an overwhelming sea   you're in it up to here

Medea   evil is deep indeed
but I'm not drowning
while dire times are about to overtake the happy pair
and all their crawling kith and kin

unless it furthered my plans
do you think I'd have crawled to him   fawning?
that man
I sucked up   begged   touched him
Gods but my flesh did creep
I'd rather touched pitch or shit   I gagged but swallowed it
the fool   he's a dead man   could have thwarted me
but granted me my glory day
to make three cold corpses
of him the king   of the bride   and of the man I hate

my darlings   my familiars
so many ways of killing and which shall I choose?

I could set a fire beneath the honeymoon suite
and roast them like herrings
or slip silently through the palace
to where that bridal bed is made
and they'll have to lie on
with spilt guts where my sure dagger will spike them through
no   the female way is the best way
poison
the murderess' way and am not I the queen of it?
pretty poison   my certain expertise
never let it be said
the man was ever born who could do me down

Hecate   black goddess of midnight
help me now
and a black black wedding breakfast I'll cook up for them
women   useless are we?
good for nothing?
good for evil
and evil all the good I ever want to be good for again!

Chorus   water flows uphill   each stream's sucked up
backwards to its source
everything's upside down skew-whiff   insane
the way that men   we say the male sex only
can break their every sacred vow   and not fear
what nature'd do if she was a fraction as faithless
to Physics' laws   we say we'd see the world implode

if women were once worms we've turned
we won't be put down the way that once we were
sling your old slanders of so called
female faithlesssness   sing us
something new

Medea   you set sail from your father's place
mad for a man you didn't know   braved
voyage   rocks   storms   straits   sailors' eyes   us strangers
only to be dumped   dishonoured in a foreign land

Enter Jason. He goes firmly, directly, to Medea.

Chorus   his word is broken   all promises trashed
honour evaporated   another woman queens it in your double bed

Jason is a Greek too – but not from this place.

Jason   it is not what you think!
it's not the first time   you waste yourself
I've seen it often
the way you will let your tongue run away with you

when a low profile   meek words   acceptance of the status quo
would have been the way to keep your home
your words don't worry me Medea   sticks and stones
they're straw and chaff the worst of your curses
call me every vile thing that creeps I don't care
but Kreon is the King you rant at him
are you crazy?   count yourself lucky
exile's all the punishment so far proposed

I feel bad about it
although you've brought it on yourself Medea
and I won't stand by and see you starve
or the children go short or want for anything
call me every low thing that crawls   I'll still care for you

you make it hard for me   I've always done my best
to calm him down   persuade him you should stay
I could have crept back to you in secret   would have
but you can't keep it zipped   you will talk treason
court your own banishment

Medea   I can't keep it zipped!
who   what   could be worse than you?
I'd call you coward   you piece of vomit   man
who is no man at all except you're man enough to come here
amazing   shamelessness never fails to amaze
d'you think it brave?   how dare you
shit on those you say you love and then come visiting?
where in the depths
of your vile maleness do you get the nerve?
thanks for coming though
for I can ease my heart and watch you squirm

first things first   I saved your life
and everybody knows it   each Greek that sailed with you
the whole caboodle who crewed the valiant Argo
knows it   without my magic
you could not have yoked the fiery bulls
in the field of death   nor sown the dragons' teeth
except I killed the serpent whose loathsome coils
looped the Golden Fleece
and who was its guardian who never slept
I killed it   I made you Jason!
betrayed my own father   my royal line
ran mad for you   after you   to Iolcus   Pelias' place
more passion then than sense
I killed King Pelias to keep you secure
killed him by tricking his loving daughters
to unwitting patricide

horror and another royal house destroyed

so I did then   now   so!   do you
cheat on me   forsake me   bed a new bride

I gave you progeny
I'd have seen the force of a fresh liaison
were I barren but I bore you sons   you swore by Gods
who must be dead so simply you broke all faith with them
my hand that held yours   I should cut it off
my knees that parted to let you easy come between
defile me   I'm fouled by even memory of your foul touch

so Jason you love me and wish me well?   pray tell
friend   sweet husband   where am I to go?
to my father's house perhaps?   oh yes!
the father I betrayed to go with you
to Pelias' daughters?   they'd welcome me with open arms
that glad we did the old man in!
this is the state I'm in   my friends and family are history
they hate me now
I made enemies of everyone I ever loved
for you   hurt those I had no need to hurt
for you   and in return
you make me the happiest woman in Greece
envied by all   'what a husband   lucky woman
  you could
one hundred percent trust him   to betray you!'
and here's his wedding present to himself
rootless penury for his discarded beggar wife and brats
oh Gods   there're proofs to tell
true gold from fool's dross
why no hallmarks stamped on the hearts of men?

Chorus   a special anger   incurable
when lovely love is turned to hatred horrible

Jason   It seems that captain Jason must steer carefully
weather the tempest of your tirade
first   let's not exaggerate your role in my story
what you did for me Medea   you did it
in the first flush of lust for me let's face it
Aphrodite ought to get the credit
I was her darling   you were her mere instrument
a cunning woman   passion's puppet
wild to save my hide   well fine
I don't want to do you down   you brought it up
though   inflated it out of all proportion
excuse me   I'd say you got more than gave quite frankly
dragged from the backwoods to civilisation

from brutish pigswill chaos to sweet law and reason
to this place where   Gods help them   they've made
  much of you
your cunning   your so sexy skills
if you were stuck in the sticks would they be sung about?
fame matters   oh it does   to you and me Medea
embrace it
it's our fate to be sung about not sing!

so much for all that
my marriage with the princess   it's not what you think
politics not passion   what I feel for her is nothing
to the sweet hot love that once I felt for you!

calm down   it's a good thing potentially   listen
we're on the run   blown in from Iolcos
all of us in every kind of deep shit till I land lucky
on the safe shores of marriage with the daughter of the main man
we're laughing!
what's eating you's the sex thing   it's not
that I've gone off you and fancy fresh young flesh to fuck
that's crude   I'd not have thought you'd have gone
for such mean and clichéd thoughts Medea
I thought we knew each other better than that
and I don't want more kids   our brood
aren't they enough for both of us?   but
I'll not be nothing   nor will our boys be beggars
if they have new royal brothers in one united first family
it's for the best   don't you get it?

cunts for brains!   that's women   they're all the same
happy in the sack and all the world's a bed of clover
if that goes sour they go spare
and hate you   sex!
I wish there was another way to get us sons
without women the world would be a lovely place

Chorus   well said Jason   your arguments are clever
we understand you do your wife a favour
by dumping her?   we beg to differ

Medea   maybe there's something wrong with me
I'm not like other people
I don't call them clever words that can't
cloak evil in a plausible coat   wrap up this crap
in fancy phrases but one thing gives the lie to it

you did it behind my back

Jason   and if I'd told you?
listen to the unreasonable rage of you!

Medea   what it is is this   a senior statesman
with a foreign wife   a savage   I'm an embarrassment to you

Jason   it's not what you think!
it's not for sex   it's not for snobbery
will you take a telling?   my royal wedding
but for bossclass brothers for our boys
to best protect them

Medea   protection?   poisoned prosperity?
I want no part of it

Jason   you'll see   eventually   you'll change your tune

Medea   you're wrong   but   torture and torment me
you're safe   I'm exiled abandoned and alone

Jason   you brought that on yourself

Medea   so I did!   I took another woman and abandoned you!

Jason   you cursed the royal family

Medea   and yours Jason

Jason   we are going round in circles   this gets us nowhere
if you love our boys leave them here Medea
you've fucked it up for you
your own big mouth got you exiled
still I'll do everything to help I can
cash   letters   I'll bust a gut to find
someone kind enough to take you in

Medea   screw your favours Jason   your foul friends
are no friends of mine

Jason   Gods are you watching?
I've done everything I could   for you   the kids
but you fling it all back in my face
you're a madwoman   it'll be the worse for you

Medea   go on   you're hot for her   go mount the cow
no malingering   get married man
your honeymoon will end in bitter tears

Exit Jason.

Chorus   desire   excess
and what desire is not excessive?
gets us into such trouble   does us in
drives us wild   makes us gluttons for punishment
oh Gods save us from that hotshot Cupid
and his brutal bullseyes

desire   excess
yes   better avoid it like the plague
or we've not the sense we were born with

no tangles in snarled sheets
no white nights in beds we should not be lying in
the best hope for us?
celibacy
or the next best thing   the cosy old
comfy married bed that's full of snores not battles

Gods save us from your miserable fate!
those of us who have been there before
are glad we are not there now

Gods send a miserable fate
to the one who locks away his heart
against the one he ought to love!

the things he said to you!
punish Jason for all of us Medea!

Medea   maybe Jason is not worth it
this pain   this pain
it paralyses me
you women are filled with ire   on my behalf   I feel
emptied

Jason is right   my children would be better off
if I leave them here with their father
who loves them   he loves them
loves them and can offer them

everything
so much   so much
I love my children
can I leave them?

can I convince myself to
play the part of one of you   until I learn it?
can I get philosophy?   sigh and say
'it happens'   'I am not the first and I won't be the last'
'in one hundred years it will be all the same'?

can I wear the mask of moderation?
can I?
as if when Cupid   Aphrodite's child
sweet Eros   drove the shaft of his arrow into my heart
as deep as the feathers   he
never
struck me   with love for Jason I'm stuck with for ever?

Enter Glauke – a very pretty, very young girl. Alone.

Chorus   we are amazed   how dare she?
here's the princess   proud Glauke
do you know this place?
this person you dare to approach?   we're quaking!
you are no feart   our Glauke
but maybe you do not entirely grasp this situation?

Glauke   Medea   my lady
I think it's daft we should fight like this
over a man   I am Glauke –

Medea   I've heard of you   well   my girlie Glauke
what should we fight about instead?

Glauke   they say you are a witch   but I don't believe it

Medea   believe it   you bit of thistledown
one breath and I could blow
an allergen   an irritant   like you away

Glauke   I don't think so   I'm no some lightweight
bit of fluff   he loves me   I did not plan it
I never wanted my happiness should hurt another woman
do you know how much it hurts me
my happiness should hurt another woman?
but if a man no longer loved me   wanted freedom
he could have it
I'd be too proud to try and keep him
I don't hate you

Medea   do you expect me to say the same?

Glauke   that would not be reasonable
I can understand it if
at this moment   you think you hate me
Medea

I know what you and Jason have been to each other
in the past   these things are not easy
even though for you and Jason
everything has long been over
in the   man and wife sense of things
still you are your children's mother and father

Medea   thank you for these homilies

Glauke   you're welcome

Medea   it is always   useful
to view one's situation from the outside
see it from the point of view of the
other players in the drama

Glauke	I think so otherwise we are at the mercy of our passions
Medea	and Gods save us from such a fate! the horror of being a prisoner inside our own vile consciousness unable to feel any pain but our own pain torn internally by the snarling warring imperatives of our passions when a little empathy imagination walking the odd mile in the other person's shoes would put everything into perspective
Glauke	I think you mock me I may not be as clever as you but I'm not stupid.
Medea	you mock me you may not be as clever as I but I no longer have my husband I made that man
Glauke	the past the past what's done is over! you live inside your own self only you live in the past
Chorus	maybe someday if she lives so long she will suffer but the girl Glauke is in love and happy now!
Medea	I made that man and now a fool of a slip of a girl is to feast on what is left of him? so 'everything has long been over for Jason and I in the man and wife sense of things'? you believed that? the oldest lie in the book we fuck all the time
Glauke	your womb is a dried up pod rattling with shrivelled old seeds you cannot give him any more babies and my sweet firstborn already is kicking in mine
Medea	indeed I tell you take it as a friendly warning in the man and wife sense of things between Jason and I things have not yet begun

Glauke   I did not come here to quarrel
            I am a civilised person   a Greek
            these things happen   we must
            for the sake of the children if for no one else
            make the best of things

            I am to marry a man who is a father already
            and who loves his children
            I want him to be happy
            Jason's wishes for the children's future are that they should stay with us
            I'll be good to them   you may trust me
            for Jason's sake

Chorus   maybe someday if she lives so long she will suffer
            but the girl Glauke is in love and happy now!

Glauke   think about this   calmly   when I'm gone
            Jason would love to see his three oldest children
            at our wedding
            if you ever loved him   you will send them

Glauke exits on swift light feet. Medea paces silently, seething.

Chorus   we think you show forbearance indeed Medea
            the best that can be said in mitigation of the young
            is that they are not yet old
            her unkindness to you is unforgiveable
            but maybe understandable?
            we disliked her too
            young beautiful women
            in the wrong but righteous about it   are very hard to take

            nevertheless she sounded sincere
            about loving the children   even if it is for Jason's sake?
            we were shocked at first   the mothers among us
            when you said you'd leave them here with Jason
            then we had to see it made good sense
            you said yourself so much   so much
            you love your children
            you must leave them?

Medea   hell will certainly have frozen over first!
            her own words
            have sealed her fate for ever
            her father's doom   and her husband's too
            want my children at her wedding does she?
            she shall have them
            here's my hellish plan   I'm proud of it
            listen   ladies   it is lovely!
            I'll send the granny or the grunt
            to get Jason again   I'll beg   grovel a bit

soft words   remorse I could have doubted him
the dad he is is the best dad
the new bride *so* sweet   I'm reconciled
I'll let the children stay

as if I could ever leave them
here   ringed around by my enemies
and taught to hate me!   never!
but they're my booby trap   oh my beauties
we'll do her in!
they'll take her my wedding gifts
a silken robe   a golden crown
that will brand her skull like redhot iron
and soon as the pretty flimsies touch her flesh she dies
the abortion in her womb
aborted like all her tomorrows   extinguished utterly
I'll snuff her out
and all who touch her die as well
so toxic will be her corpse   oh yes

then   I can't say it   do it then
I'll kill the children   must
to save them
shall I let my sweet boys become cruel men like their father?
shall I let my daughter grow up to womanhood
and this world's mercy?   never!
I'll kill you first   my darlings
then when I've done for Jason utterly   I'll die happy

Chorus   Medea   we are your friends   we want to help you
don't do it!   life   death   Gods' law
you cannot!

Medea   you could not   I must

how else will hard hearted Jason
learn his crying lesson?

Chorus   tears for yourself   the bitterest taste you'll swallow –

Medea   let's get a move on   ladies
less talk   more action
nurse!

Nurse enters.

Medea   nurse   send the man to run for Jason

Nurse bobs a curtsey of obedience and goes back inside.

Chorus   you are not our kind   but
every animal would die for its young

Medea   stop this!
what greater power than the love of a mother for her children?
every animal would die for its young
is that not nature's way Medea?
the mother sheep offers her own white throat
to the wolf and saves her lambs
cornered   the savage she-wolf
sacrifices herself for her helpless cubs
even the mild bird surprised in the nest
can be a winged and whirling devil
with a slashing beak

The Manservant exits from the house, bows to Medea and hurries off for Jason as ordered, even more urgently –

Chorus   a mother should die for her young   Medea
not be her children's murderess

hell itself will reject you
there is no reparation
you can never be purified of this crime   for humankind
it is our horror of horrors   how can you?
your sons you suckled at your breast
looked in their eyes and smiled on them
now you'd look them in the eyes
and slash them to their knees?
your daughter whose hair you brush and plait

who kisses your face and makes you laugh
when she lisps the
wrong words of the Kolchis song you taught her
oh will you wrap her own bright braid
around her throat and break her neck?

with the hardest of hearts   with the hardest of hands

still you cannot do this

Enter Jason. He keeps his distance from Medea.

Jason   here I am
for all your hatred I'm still here
what new malison?
or have you   it's too much to hope for!
come to your senses?

Medea   Jason I swallow my pride here
and   you know me   I don't find that easy
I beg you to forgive me   my foul temper
hurts me as much as it hurts you   believe me
but turn the other cheek   can't you?
for the sake of the sweet love we had in the past?

it's over   I know that now   I'm reconciled to it
I've been a fool   why rant and rave
at what cannot be helped?
you did not fall in love with a younger woman
I know that now   the politics!
it was beyond me at first I don't mind admitting it
too emotional to be rational like you always said!
forgive me!   but of course I see now
it's for the best   for all of us
the future of our sons and daughter is what matters now
and that's always been your first thought
forgive me   they must have royal brothers
I see that's why you're marrying

I wish you well   my old darling

we women have such petty natures sometimes!
good you're big enough to rise above
the dog eat dog   snarl for snarl
vicious circle I indulged in earlier
all I want to say is   I was wrong

The Nurse comes out of the house with the Children.

Medea   children!   don't shrink from us
we both love you
come kiss your daddy   see like I do

Medea kisses Jason.

Jason and the Children embrace. An aside from Medea.

Medea   Gods the hell of it   the horror of knowing what I know
hiding what I must hide
the dagger agony to see them hug him
when never in this world
will they stretch out their sweet warm arms to me again
as long as they live   as long as any of us shall live
my heart breaks   I can't   I must

look dear hearts! my quarrel with your dad is done
grown up anger!
your innocent eyes will not see
such a shameful scene again
my cheeks are wet with happy tears

Chorus   we're crying too   we wish to all the Gods
there was not worse   we fear there's worse
to come

Jason   there's my old own sweet girl I recognise
no more of that bitter harridan

not that I blame you altogether
it was a shock   I'm sure   and only natural
for a passionate woman to get a bit upset
it took a wee while   but you
understand!   that's excellent!

boys! and daddy's own wee princess   are you listening?
your father's been giving it a lot of thought
your future

Jason takes his older Son and rumples his hair smiling at the other two, including them.

Jason   one day   with your brother and sister
                 you'll be one of the toffs in Corinth
                 the ruling classes   leaders
                 or a leader's wife   first lady!
                 why not ?   no hopes are too high
                 nothing's too good for Jason's children
                 and all you have to do to make your daddy happy
                 is grow up good and strong
                 eat   work   and   play
                 play the game   play hard   play fair
                 fear nothing   your daddy   and the Gods   will
                 always be there for you   to protect you

                 now Medea   what's the matter?
                 more tears!   why?   nothing
                 in these bland words that should upset you

Medea   nothing   I was thinking of our children

Jason   well   be assured I'll take good care of them

Medea   I know you will   my tears are
                 just   a mother's
                 they need their father's hand   that's true
                 but I'm their mother
                 and when you wished them grown and powerful
                 it hurt that's all   for I won't see it
                 banished as I'll be   I'm not arguing
                 I understand
                 in my absence Glauke   will accept them
                 my lovely children   who'd not love them?
                 ask   your bride
                 to ask her father to let the children stay

Jason   she's a gentle girl   is Glauke
                 I know they'll learn to love her

Medea   and she them!   I will help them   gifts!
                 fetch them nurse

The Nurse hesitates, then –

Nurse   madam

Nurse exits.

Medea   no wedding without presents
     I've a pretty pair to send her
     in the children's name a shawl
     of the finest silk a golden crown

Nurse re-enters with gifts, walking carefully.
A box, and on top of it, a crown on a cushion.

Medea   boys take this box and carefully
     keep it closed what is inside it must not crush
     you hear me! and darling girl
     her bridesmaid this crown
     on its floral cushion but hear me do not touch!
     or you will dull its lovely shine

Medea turns to Jason.

Medea   my darling girl to your new darling girl
     your lucky one with
     the best man in all the world to bed her Glauke
     and we'll decorate and crown her
     wrap her for you like a present
     Glauke in cloth of gold and with a golden crown

The Children, heads held high, begin to exit slowly with the presents proud and pleased.

Jason   stop children! this is too much Medea
     we can't accept I won't take them
     Glauke has everything she needs it would be greedy
     she's not short of frocks
     the palace groans under the weight of gold and silks already

     save these for yourself

Medea   even Gods and millionaires like gifts
     gold brings luck and I want your bride to have it
     I know they'll learn to love her
     she will love them too

Jason   take the presents children
     it would be a shame to disappoint them
     they'll enjoy their small role in our ceremony
     darlings deliver these petty tokens
     then come back and tell your mama
     that what she hoped would happen
     happened and Glauke smiled on you

Exit the Children in a solemn procession with Jason.

Chorus   that's it!
no hope for these bairns now
the road they walk on's to their death
not long!

Medea   she'll grasp the gold tiara – tara!
her own hands will crown her golden head
with her own bright death

it shines!
that robe of cloth of gold
and from its gleaming folds there rises   perfume   amber
put it on!
she will   she'll shawl herself for a wedding
with her only marriage partner   death

Chorus   miserable Jason
you did for her
you did for
your own bairns too

we weep for you too Medea
mother of bairns
murderer of bairns
mother   murderer
what an end to a domestic commonplace!
the adulterous husband in the other woman's bed

The Children and the Manservant come back on. Nurse hurries the children inside, soon re-enters, listening.

Manservant   madam the bairns are reprieved
they're safe   no banishment
I waited at the palace   watched
when my lord Jason and the bairns came back
we were over the moon
word wis among us slaves   the quarrel's over
he was smiling   the   bride   thon Glauke
oor mistress in place of you   she
smiled too   picked up your wee lass
and sat her on her lap
hauding the bairn's wee hand against her belly
whisperin that she'd feel her baby brother kick
kissed her
then set her down again

Medea   tell me from the beginning

Manservant   first thing
the children went up to her   saluted   curtseyed
the princess bowed and solemnly she

took your bonny presents
from your three bairns' hands
madam   why turn away so pale?
you're pleased are you no
to ken the bairns are spared?

Medea lets out a cry.

Manservant   what's wrang?

Medea lets out another even louder cry, falls to her knees.

Manservant   did I speak out o turn?
I shouldna have tellt you about Glauke and your lassie
mind I never said your lassie liked it!
but it's good news shairly?

Medea   you said what you saw   my sweet and faithful servant
you are not to blame

Manservant   don't greet   my lady
I hate to see a bonny woman greet
others   madam   afore you
have been pairted from their bairns
what we canna cheynge we hae to thole

Medea   'thole it' I shall!
sweet servant I'll obey you   nurse! away
go inside and get food ready for the children

The Nurse exits. Medea moves closer.

Medea   are you my faithful servant?

Manservant   my lady Medea knows I am

Medea   and a man to trust?

Manservant   tomorrow I go   with you into exile
you will find me   faithful   discreet   any service
I can render you
would be the pleasure   madam
no jist the duty   of a servant of a lady
as gentle and as beautiful as you
Medea   my good and lovely lady

Medea   there is   a certain small thing
no I cannot ask you –

Manservant   ask   anything!

Medea   go back to the palace   no   it's no job for a man!
the wedding   can you come back and tell me
what the bride was wearing?

Manservant   madam I'm no much of a man for describing frocks

Medea   I would be very grateful   in your debt indeed
            truly I am sure you'll do it very well

Manservant bows and goes.

The Children enter, playing. Medea, alone with them, looks upon her Children.

Medea   children come and kiss your mama
            you'll never know how much your mother loves you
            children I am to say goodbye to you
            the only things I have left to love in this life!
            I thought my heart was dead   but I still love you
            goodbye before I see you grown
            before I dress you for your weddings
            or make your marriage beds

            I chose this way but by the Gods it's sore
            was it for this I suckled you and weaned you
            laboured long to give you life
            and the hopes I had
            that you'd take care of me when I was old
            and when I died would close my eyes
            and clothe me for my coffin and a decent burial
            the natural cycle of things   sweet thought
            no hope   my beauties

            I can't do it   I've lost my nerve
            it's not right   their shining faces
            it won't happen!
            I'll take them now and run

            what is wrong with me?   my enemies
            off scot free and laughing at me?
            come on   woman   do it   dare
            are you so weak that motherlove can turn you?

            shall I let my darlings
            be toyed with by fate
            fall into the savage hands of my enemies
            run and they'll catch us   inevitable
            inevitable I   save them first.
            the bride is crowned now   dressed
            for her wedding and her bridegroom death
            she's on her way   I know it
            I'm on my way too   it's a cruel road
            and crueller still the road I send my darlings on.

            my lovely boys   look at you
            straight limbs   growing up strong
            like your mother wants you to

> give me your hands   your sweet lips!
> such eyes!   be happy wherever you go
>
> a hug   let mama hold you
> the soft skin   sweet breath of children!
> go inside   go inside
> your mama's coming soon
> to put you to your beds

The Smaller Boy and the Girl go inside. The Bigger Boy hesitates as if anxious to comfort his mother, offer to be a big boy. She smiles on him, touches his head to reassure him and he goes inside. She turns again unable to go in.

Medea   what I am going to do   it is the worst
              I know it   I must do it   I will do it.

Chorus   happy the woman who has no children
              happy   that woman
              she cannot then bear the pain of losing them
              suppose you've raised them
              they've survived   they thrive
              they're up and perfect and you're proud of them
              still the Gods can snatch them
              death   disease   or war
              can decimate our hopes
              deaths of our children
              this is the one pain the Gods should not ask us to survive

Medea   friends it's time   waiting's over
              here he comes   quite out of breath
              my good and faithful servant

Manservant comes running back on in terror, gasping.

Manservant run   run   you bitch of hell
              you really did it and you've done for us as well
              a ship   a chariot   go

The Nurse enters, waits, afraid, still, by the door.

Medea   what happened?

Manservant they're dead   as well you know
              the princess   and Kreon the king her faither tae
              deid   your poisons   bitch

Medea   I never heard you speak a finer word
              as the royal correspondent
              you're the man for me

Manservant you're mad   you really did it
              by the Gods   you are gled you did it!

He staggers away from her in horror. She comes up close, as if coming on to him, as if she's hypnotising him.

Medea   calm down   catch your breath   my man
don't rush it   I want the whole story
sing up   spit it out
was it really such a horrible agonising way to go?
don't spare me one of the delightful details
the worse it was the better

Manservant   the ceremony was done
Kreon kissed his daughter
shook the hand of her new husband
and took his leave
mindan the company how   in the great hall
there wad be feasting later
in the meantime there was dancing
whistling and cheering   applause from us servants
when the happy couple took the floor thegether

then did the bride's eye no alight
on the crown your lassie'd brocht her?
nothing for it but she left her husband's side
laughing   ran and took it up
set it   gold on gold   on tap of her hair
when she pulled oot that soft silk shawl
there was a sigh went up at its shimmer
and she slipped into it
smoothing it over her breasts and shooders
Jason whistled   she shimmied to the mirror
and stopped   stilled by her own
silvered beauty in the glass
stared smiling   totally taen on wi hersel
as why should she no be?

then – something hellish – before our eyes
her face cheynged colour   she swayed   reeled
across the floor   her legs buckling under her
only just made it to a chair
one of her servin lassies thought she was
only carrying on   that it was an joke
she whooped   then she saw
that her majesty was foaming at the mouth and
her eyes turned all milky and opaque flickering
wi the pupils rolled back   and the colour she was
which was the colour of clay   of death
but she was gasping
ripping scarves of breath from the air
drawing them into her lungs
drowning   the servin lass cheynged her tune then

the shriek she let out   Gods   it made
all our blood run cold
stuck there as we were like stookies
wi the horror of it   then it was all running feet
everywhere and the palace rang with shouts as they
tore the place apart looking for her faither

Jason just stood there   the look on his face
one I hope never to see on another human face again

for the length of time it takes a good runner
to lap the racetrack she was slumped unconscious
then she found her voice   her eyes bulged
she began to scream and scream
for a twofold agony began to attack her
on her head that golden circlet
became a filigree of flame melting and dripping
liquid fire   and the silky shawl
the other present from the children
began to shrivel   suck   and paste itself
to her skin   smothering her   strangling
branding her soft flesh
as if she was fire itsel   she leapt
rolling in agony   trying to put herself out
no one but her father would have known her
blebbed and burning as she was
her melting flesh falling off her bones like
tallow from a flamboy or   fat from a lamb on a spit
bubbling and bursting like
resin drops on a burning pine
till at last her horrid corpse
was blackened   silent   and still

we shrank back   we were terrified
there was none of us would touch it
we'd seen   we knew

till Kreon came   poor man
ran in   cried out   fell on the corpse
cradling it   sobbing
'Gods let me die with you!' he cried
'the parent should not outlive the child'
and he wept till his auld eyes could weep nae mair
and he was all gret oot
but when he went to staun up
here did the corpse no stick to him
as ivy clings to laurel   and it was
a dance macabre right enough
as the auld fellow tried to struggle free

and the deid weight of the deid daughter
pu'ed him to his knees again   the sair fecht of it
tearing his auld flesh from his aged bones
till at last he snuffed it   croaked
and there they lie
father on top of daughter   corpse on corpse
in a horrid parody of an unnatural embrace

the Gods are good
somebody was listening when he cried 'I want to die'
it could be said he   right royal   got his wish

and that's that
no surprise to you   Medea
by the Gods I'm feart frae you
mair feart even than I am feart o Jason
and the soldiers he'll bring with him
to torch this place

The Manservant runs to the frozen-in-fear Nurse and shakes her.

Manservant they'll kill us
I don't think we have snowball in hell's chance
but we maun
run auld yin   run

Nurse   I canna

The Manservant – getting nowhere – flees in terror.

Chorus   Jason has suffered most horribly the day
as he well deserved to   truly
but that poor silly bairn   the bride
born to the bad fate of being Kreon's daughter
that sent you Jason   death   for a bridegroom
and your honeymoon destination   hell

Medea   friends   nothing for it now
there is one way   and quickly
delay would be fatal   savage revenge comes running
another's hand   not a mother's loving hand
would kill my children

ring your heart in steel
raise your hand   that sword   do it!
flesh of my own flesh   this bitter place
where I must kill to prove my love

Medea goes inside to do it.

Chorus   Gods stop her   if Gods you are!
Mother Earth open up and swallow her now

before she forever defiles you
with the spilt blood of her own children
the eye of the Sun that is too bright to look upon
look down   stop her in her tracks
burn her to a cinder
let the light reject her utterly   but stop her

pointless   the pain of giving birth to them?
useless   your love of them?

it was for them   to get your bairns
you braved those narrow straits
between those jagged bruise coloured rocks
sailed close to death   and no for Jason

your raging heart!
remember the price the Gods exact
for the stain of spilt kin blood

you're stone   you're iron
your heart is nothing human
sex   makes birth   makes death
but here is a broken circle
here is nothing natural

Jason – distraught – enters

Jason   where is she?
                   that   monster is she in there?
                   or did she run   no hiding place
                   no hole in the earth   nowhere can she escape
                   the royal vengeance that hunts her down
                   I'm here to get my children   before some one
                   kills them for their mother's crime!

Jason enters the house. A silence.

Chorus   Jason   you poor man
                   sorrow   you don't know
                   you don't yet know the half of it

That cry from Jason.

Jason re-enters, a broken and emptied out man. Medea re-enters calm and cold.

Jason   my children

Medea   you don't feel it yet   when you're old you will

Jason   my boys   my darling girl
                   you killed them

Medea   to kill you Jason   while you are still alive

Jason	you have put yourself beyond all pity
	I wish you dead but to touch you
	even with my sword's tip would disgust me

Medea   nothing you do to me can touch me now
we're out of reach   beyond you

Jason   let me bury my children

Medea   they are not dead to me

Jason   out of their bright wounds their avenging furies swarm!
justice   blood for blood

Medea   flesh of my flesh   revenge

Jason   I must have been mad   was mad for you
I did not know you
I know you now!

Medea   tigress?   fury?   harpy?   witch?   she wolf?
monster?   yes I am!
for I have torn out your heart and devoured it.

Jason   your pain is just as bad as mine

Medea   wrong   for I have your pain to comfort me

Jason   children   the mother you had

Medea   children   the father you had
end of story

Jason   it's over   it's all over

Medea   it will never be over   end of story

Jason   I wish I had never held you
a beautiful monster in my arms
I wish I had never turned to you in the night
never felt my seed spurt to your foul womb
never let you give birth
to this

The Nurse starts muttering very softly her lines from the beginning of the play. A pared down but completely recognisable to the audience version.

At the correct points for them to finish in sync with the end of the Nurse's speech – timing is here suggested by single (Jason) or double (Chorus) slashes but will need adjustment, experimentation (and could well contain silences and gaps that will be filled in by either or both the other speakers' key lines or single words ringing out clearer among the cacophony) – Jason, marked (/) (and beginning with 'I wish to all the gods / they had never been born / for this') then a line or so later the Chorus, marked (///) (and beginning with 'the gods look down', omitting their last line 'end of story').

Thus both Jason and the Chorus join in with respectively their last words of the play (Jason) or a premonition of their last speech to come (Chorus).

So that this Nurse's speech is vocally the forefront of a trio, and the cacophony ends with her penultimate line ('Medea would never then have sailed wi Jason') and her last line rings out clear in a silence.

Nurse	I wish to all the Gods it had never sailed the Argo
	had never set its proud prow atween the humped blue rocks
	forced itsel through straits
	to land on unlucky Kolchis why?
	why (/) did the sun ever heat up the soil
	in which there split that seed
	that sproutit from sapling to a tall tree of girth enough
	to be felled to build its keel? (//) why was it ever oared?
	why crewed wi heroes fit to filch the Golden Fleece?
	my lady Medea would never then have sailed wi Jason
	daft for him doted! fated damned.

If there is a coda for the music it is now. Then in the clean silence the Chorus clearly and simply repeat their last speech with – this time – the last line.

Chorus	the Gods look down
	expect the unexpected
	what we wish for work for plan for hope for
	think is bound to happen won't
	what is fated will
	end of story.

Black.

End.

Activities

Character Study – pages 21–22
Role on the Wall

It may seem quite early in the play to start a ROTW but in this case we have a reasonable amount of information on both Jason and Medea.

Split the class into two and ask one group to create a 'picture' of Jason, the other Medea.
Bring the groups together and have one person from each group report back.
Use this as a basis for a discussion on how the group thinks the characters will react and develop.

If you can display these in the classroom, participants can add to or strike off words as the play unfolds. It should also serve as a marker to show the many different moods and sides of Medea.

Exploring the Chorus – page 25
Brainstorming

The use of the chorus in this particular version of Medea is a very interesting one. In Greek times the body of people involved in the chorus was mainly used to tell the story; the sheer volume of the voices would be able to reach the farthest spot in the theatre. It was sometimes used to act as the conscience of some of the characters.

In groups, ask the students to brainstorm the type of people that they think are in this particular chorus and why.
Detailed discussion should be encouraged as to the reason for the choices.
The script does give one or two suggestions, this could be a starting point.

Note:
It is interesting to note that in the plays, Medea *and* Hippolytus, *it is thought that Euripides may have found the Chorus an encumbrance because both plays deal with individual's emotions and not huge public events.*

Counselling Glauke – page 37
Conscience Alley

Medea and Glauke have just met. Medea is feigning understanding of the situation. As soon as Glauke leaves she is planning to murder her at the wedding.
The subject of this conscience alley is Glauke. How would we advise, warn or counsel her? The group may also want Jason or Medea to walk down the alley so that they can offer opinions or advice.

Developing the Story – page 49
Hot Seat

The bodyguard has returned after witnessing the death of Glauke and Kreon. Hot seat the bodyguard and Jason.

Medea's Story – page 51
Hot Seat

Hot seat Medea as a form of revision. To change the focus slightly the activity could take place in a court of law or a psychiatrist's office, or any other relevant location.

Time is a Great Healer?
Hot Seat

Ask groups of twos to take on the roles of Jason and Medea having a conversation two years later. Ask the groups to decide where this conversation would take place.

Suggestions may include: the palace; prison; hell.

This activity would primarily serve as revision.

Character Studies

It is presumed that you, the student, will have already read the play and therefore have a good understanding of the storyline and the characters involved.
To further assist in the acting pieces and to serve as a starting point, there is a brief character outline below of four of the main characters: Medea, Jason, Glauke and Kreon.

When beginning to learn a role for performance the actor has to do a lot of work in order to understand the character; learning lines is only one part of it. Actors must get to know the character they are playing. Below is a list of helpful areas.

- ☐ What is the relationship between the role you have chosen and the other characters in the play?

- ☐ What kind of person is your character?

- ☐ What moods does your character have?

- ☐ What is his/her past history?

- ☐ What is his/her state of mind?

- ☐ Can you relate to any of the feelings or emotions shown by your character?

You can find out a lot of the information above by reading the play and making notes as you go along.

Below is a *starting point* for your own character study:

Liz Lochhead said that *Medea* is "*a tragedy, absolutely timeless and ancient, about a woman driven by female desperation … to killing her children*".

The quote above underpins the whole essence of Medea. She is a strong woman physically and mentally but has weaknesses. Her main weakness in a sense is her inability to put the past behind her and move on from her own desire for revenge.

Medea is a complex character to play with many sides to her personality. She must be seen to change in whatever situation comes to her. She should not be portrayed as a caricature. She also has the ability to make the audience feel sorry for her and at times be on her side until, of course, her hatred becomes overbearing and we see the madness ensue.

She is a powerful force to reckon with and Glauke coming to her should be seen as an act of bravery and/or stupidity.

Liz Lochhead says that the story is 'timeless and ancient'; in other words, this type of scenario has been happening for a long time and will continue to do so. At some point in our lives we all experience the feeling of rejection in some form or other. The majority of us handle it in a very different way from Medea … thank goodness!

Medea

Medea is the strongest character on stage and her part is written in such a way that an audience cannot fail to recognise her as the main character (apart from the fact that her name is in the title). She therefore is introduced by another character for us and we are allowed to create a mental picture of her before we see her.

The nurse is the first character we meet. She relates the story so far and talks about Medea, letting the audience see the importance of this character and the treachery that is about to unfold.

> 'I wish to all the Gods it had never sailed   the Argo'

The nurse is like a narrator; she introduces the main character to us and also keeps us up to date with the story, wishing the Argo had not sailed and Jason not been on it, and that her lady had not gotten into this unholy mess.

She tells us how Medea has 'murdered' in order to be with Jason, how they fled to Corinth with their three children and how she has had to ingratiate herself and 'sook in' to make herself less of a foreigner and, now, how none of this matters as she has lost her husband to another woman. Medea is deeply hurt by all of this as we realise; she has nowhere to turn and no one to turn to. The nurse paints a vivid picture of Medea crying for a father she has lost and how she looks at her children 'with empty eyes'.

At the end of her soliloquy she leaves us with a chilling thought concerning Medea:

> 'She's capable of anything'

Medea's entrance is extremely dramatic – we hear her long before we see her. We realise the nurse's story is true. Her voice echoes out telling of how she hates her children and their father.

She is a woman scorned, hurt, humiliated and, above all, abandoned. After all she has done for her husband and their children. She has stopped at nothing to save Jason.

The hatred of her children is a classic scenario of a deeply disturbed woman who cannot even look at the children she has conceived with this man, who has deceived her and ridiculed her publicly.

'I hate my life and all I've done with it'

We begin to think that she only hates her life because of her present situation, not because she has murdered and lied, but because the plan has not worked in her favour.

The different aspects of Medea's character are outlined below.

Depressed

'I wish to all the Gods that I was dead and done with it'   (page 22)

She cannot live with the deep hurt she feels.

Obsessive

She is unable to present a reasonable face to those around her because all she can speak of is her situation, how she has been wronged and how she seeks revenge *(page 24)*.

Clever and convincing

She appeals to the King and uses his male chauvinism for her own gain *(page 25–28)*.

> *'one day   one day of peace and preparation*
> *my children to take leave of their father*
> *they don't hate him*
> *and I to make some desperate provision*
> *where   how*
> *to save my two sweet sons   my daughter*
> *you are a father too   have pity on them*
> *you are a man you should protect the helpless*
> *the weak   the women   children'*

She then instantly changes and mocks him for allowing her her day of glory to kill the King, Jason and his bride, Glauke.

In her encounter with Glauke towards the end of the play she cleverly sows a small seed in the princess's head. She tells her that she and Jason are still enjoying a physical relationship. Glauke, however – at this time being so in love – does not take the bait, but one feels she may remember this later in her relationship with Jason.

Determined

The chorus try to guide her away from such murderous thoughts but she wants nothing but to have her 'glory day' *(page 38)*.

Angry

'I can't keep it zipped!'

We see this in her speech with Jason; she has a very typical argument with a man that she once loved and probably still does, hence her anger. She is capable of hurting but we see that Jason is very blinkered in his attitude *(page 30)*.

Loving

She does love her children and for a time we feel she will 'do the right thing' by them and move on, but her seething need for revenge will not falter.

Astute

Jason tries to tell her that he is marrying Glauke not for love but as a career move to make a better life for her and the children. She easily sees through this *(page 35–37)*.

Cruel

She makes her own children accomplices in the murder of the King and Glauke when she sends them with the gifts to the wedding. Her past life proves her cruelty *(page 42–43)*.

Ruthless

We think that she is going to relent and save her children, but she has by this time so convinced herself that it is her duty to seek revenge, she kills them to torture her husband as she feels he has done to her *(page 45–49)*.

Mad

Jason   'my boys   my darling girl
          you killed them'

Medea   'to kill you Jason   while you are still alive'

She has killed her own children to prove her love. She feels that her children are still with her and that they will never be dead to her *(page 50)*.

Other words to describe Medea are: cold, calculating, pathetic and heartless.

Jason

Jason is what, in modern terms, we would call a user, a social climber, and a man who will immediately change to suit whatever situation he finds himself in. He will always be on the winning team.

To play Jason you would have to show a certain amount of arrogance and selfishness. Perhaps his only saving grace is that he loves his children and can see that Medea is unstable. We are unsure if he knew this earlier in their relationship but he chooses to ignore it and uses this to his advantage.

In the final scene he is distraught. He cannot believe what he sees: not only has his ex-wife killed his new wife and her father, the King, but she has also killed their children to make a point about her feelings on the matter. She repulses him *(page 51)*:

> 'I wish you dead   but to touch you
> even with my sword's tip would disgust me'

Glauke

Glauke is reasonably innocent in all of this. She is the pawn being used by the King and Jason to gain what they want. She has fallen in love with a man who is clearly a social climber and who will stop at nothing to get what he wants, as long as he doesn't get his hands dirty in the process.

Glauke knows that Jason is someone else's husband but has chosen to believe whatever Jason has told her in his attempt to get her to fall for him. Glauke thinks that she can make Jason happy even though a previous wife could not.

In her conversation with Medea we discover that she is pregnant – a sure way to get her man *(page 35–37)*:

> 'and my first born
> already   is kicking in mine '

She also has a nasty streak which we see when she tries to intimidate Medea by divulging conversations she has had with Jason about his ex-wife. She doesn't succeed in her ploy but does sufficiently annoy Medea enough for her to hatch a plot there and then to kill Jason, Glauke and Kreon.

Kreon

Kreon appears to be a weak man. He is afraid of Medea and tells her so *(page 26)*:

> 'frankly I'm feart of you   why no?
> feart you hurt my daughter   why no?
> you're a clever quine and cunning
> malice is your middle name '

He loves his daughter and is frightened of what Medea will do. He knows her history but it appears that his source of reference is Jason. His weakness is that he doesn't see Medea's strength and gives her a day to get herself together; he does not expect her to be able to muster any kind of damage in that time.

CHAPTER FOUR

HERITAGE
BY NICOLA MCCARTNEY

Background Information

Heritage is set in Canada and the action spans a period of six years from spring 1914 to spring 1920. The play is extremely well researched and, although the action centres round the young Sarah, 20 when she retells the tale of her relationship with Michael, Nicola McCartney also interweaves details of the political struggle in Ireland and the Great War in Europe during that troubled period in history.

Nicola McCartney effectively uses historical and geographical distance to explore contemporary unrest in Northern Ireland and also, very powerfully, incorporates stories from the Ulster cycle of old Irish tales into the text. The main focus is on one of the most famous tales of the cycle, *Deirdre of the Sorrows*. Michael, with his Catholic background and Republican sympathies, still strong despite the fact that he is third-generation Canadian, retells the tale, in episodes, to Sarah. With her 'Orange' connections and scripture-quoting mother, Sarah has a very different perspective on Ireland, the country she has recently left. The young couple, literally from opposite sides of the river that separates their families' farms, come together against a backdrop of mutual exploration of their respective cultures and attitudes.

The story of *Deirdre of the Sorrows* is an anchor point for the two main characters. The tragedy of Michael's death in the opening scene mirrors the tragedy of the death of Naiose, the young warrior and Deirdre's lover. As the play progresses, and the relationship between Sarah and Michael develops, so the events of the tale unfold. Eventually, they can tell the story to each other and it becomes central to holding them together as outside pressures attempt to force them apart. Sarah, rather than Michael, becomes the sole teller of the tale as she loses him to the rhetoric, and eventually the violence, of Nationalism.

What Nicola McCartney succeeds in doing is layering the play with meaning. She not only connects contemporary Northern Ireland with its past by incorporating the language and rhythm of the old tales, but also creates a rich linguistic and lyrical dimension to the text. The central love affair of the play speaks directly to a young, contemporary audience. Sarah and Michael's relationship has all the drama and heightened tension of 'star-crossed' lovers located in an interesting historical and cultural setting.

Timetable of events around the World and in *Heritage*

	1912	1913	1914	1915	1916	1917
World		USA: Woodrow Wilson becomes President	June – assassination of Duke Franz Ferdinand, in Sarajevo August – World War I begins Oct/Nov – Battle of Ypres Pope Pius X dies, succeeded by Benedict XV	April/May – Ypres, poison gas fire	Battle of Verdun July – Battle of the Somme	USA enters World War I Battle of Vimy Ridge – Canadian soldiers are heavily involved Russian Revolution – death of Tsar Nicholas II
UK			Declaration of war on Germany	Coalition Ministry	Lloyd George becomes Prime Minister	
Ireland	Ulster Covenant signed in Belfast Home Rule Bill passed Gaelic League has 13 branches throughout Ireland and ½ million people learning Irish	UVF (Ulster Volunteer Force) start gun-running at Larne in anticipation of resistance to home rule			Easter Rising – leaders executed and become 'holy martyrs'	Irish Convention comes together but is a failure Attempt to force conscription onto Irish met with strong opposition
Canada		Apex of the wheat boom Threatening economic depression takes hold	Population at 8 million Influx of immigrants sparks vehement Protestant nativism Depression – high unemployment and low wheat prices	Coming out of depression – wheat prices soar, but so does cost of living	Conscription crisis Transcontinental railways in ruin	August – Military Service Act – conscription introduced to feed forces on Western Front Farm workers are exempt from conscription
Heritage	McCrea's move to Ontario, Canada Peggy dies aged 2 years		March/April – Sarah meets Mike September – Sarah leaves school, her 14th birthday	Summer – McCrea's build the barn	November – John McCrea leaves home for the War Trip to Regina	

1918	1919	1920	1921	1922
Great flu epidemic begins and in 12 months kills 40 000 people worldwide November – Battle of Mons – Canadian soldiers are heavily involved World War I ends	Woodrow Wilson wins Nobel Peace Prize USA: De Valera goes on campaign and speaks to big crowds of supporters, but falls out with Republican leaders like Cohalan	December – De Valera's visit to USA ends	USA: Warren G Harding becomes President	
Emancipation of women – votes for women over 30 years	Treaty of Versailles			
Sinn Fein now main Nationalist Party December – at general election, Sinn Fein wins all but 4 seats outside Ulster Breakdown of law and order – guerrilla war and bloodshed Prior to election, Sinn Fein activists comb country for supporters 'stand by men of 1916' slogan	'Troubles' begin – IRA (Irish Republican Army) attacks RIC (Royal Irish Constabulary) and Black & Tans – War of Independence 21 January – 1st Dail Eireann May – murder of Jack Milling RM at home September – soldiers shot on Methodist Church parade at Fermoy, killing one.	December – Britain attempts to provide a solution to the 'Troubles' July – Oliver Plunkett made a 'Blessed' RC martyr Attacks on Catholics in North, burning homes. Riots and sectarian violence is widespread 21 November – Bloody Sunday in Croke Park	Partition of Ireland – Anglo-Irish Treaty June – Appeal by King for a truce as violence continues and escalates	March – Irish Free State created Civil War begins
General election – vote-rigging and disenfranchisement of 'enemy aliens' Women given the vote Major railways put under public ownership Schools reform practically wipe out Roman Catholic and French-speaking schools from the Prairies	May – Winnepeg general strike Wheat prices begin to decline	Aruthur Meighen succeeds Borden as Prime Minister Wheat prices hit lowest prices – depression	Brief depression 1921–22 William Lyon MacKenzie becomes Prime Minister of a Liberal Government	
Christmas – John McCrea returns from the War	June – Bad frost causes John McCrea to lose crops Emer dies of influenza	Mike dies whilst trying to burn down the barn		

The power and theatricality of the play is immediately established in the opening scenes. The dream sequence, which reveals the final tragedy of Michael's death, uses dance, a drum and flute, the instruments of traditional Irish music, as well as the marching bands of the Orange Order, to establish the passion of the drama. The drums are heard again later in the play, as the Orange bands of the Protestant community practise and march, and in the repeated 'boom boom' of Sarah's later speeches when she addresses the audience directly, telling more stories of conflict as her brother joins the British Army and goes to war in Europe.

As Sarah moves into the light on a darkened stage, her opening speech establishes her as a storyteller, someone filled with poetry and emotion.

> 'Nearly day.
> Sun bleeds morning
> Over pigs and sheep and hens and goats
> Over the land of Shining Waters
> Over Canada'.

The beauty and harshness of the landscape and the mixture of heavy work and opportunity that faces the settlers are brought to the fore. Michael is presented to the audience very much through Sarah's eyes and the complex set of interconnections between characters, time, place, community and culture are cleverly established in the closing lines of scene two, where Sarah and Michael jointly recite the opening of 'their story', the story of *Deirdre of the Sorrows*.

The shift to Michael telling the story himself highlights his desire to connect with his past. The tale he is telling outlines the to-ing and fro-ing of people between Ireland and Scotland and, of course, from both countries to further shores. His and Sarah's families are just two of the many who have sought a 'better' life. What the first encounter between Sarah and Michael reveals is how religious, cultural and economic divisions in Ireland have not only created conflict, but also established a very different sense of history between Catholics and Protestants.

MICHAEL

> *I will tell you a story as I have been told it. One night, Conor mac Nessa, King of Ulster, and his knights —*

SARAH

> *Ulster's not a kingdom.*

MICHAEL

> *It used to be.*

SARAH

> *When?*

MICHAEL

> *A long time ago. Shall I tell you or not?*

The differences between the two households are quickly established. Ruth, Sarah's mother, is first encountered reciting scriptures and her voice is skilfully worked into a dialogue with Michael as he tells the tale of Deirdre, a story that Ruth, unlike Sarah, doesn't want to hear. Hugh, Sarah's father is hardworking and ambitious, keen to prove himself a success. While he can establish a neighbourly and cooperative working relationship with Peter Donaghue, Michael's father, he will not tolerate the developing romance between Sarah and Michael. The dominant female figure in the Donaghue household is Emer, Michael's grandmother. She provides for Michael the link to the past history and hardship of Catholic Ireland. She speaks Gaelic with him, something that his liberal-minded father will not do, and it is Emer who sees the worth in Sarah despite, like Ruth, warning her off a relationship with Michael.

As well as the central narrative of Sarah and Michael, there is a complex mix of sub plots, stories from the past and family histories which develop alongside and interconnect with it. For example, Emer recounts the tragedy of the Potato Famine, which drove her family from Ireland, in a style reminiscent of Sarah's storytelling:

> *'It came so sudden*
> *Morning*
> *Mist rises up out of the Lough'*

So style, as well as substance, begins to link Sarah with Ireland's past. However, Peter issues a warning to Sarah to be careful of history,

> *'history's more dangerous a friend than an enemy.'*

Peter Donaghue is more tolerant than most, yet his traumatic marriage has left him with a live and let live approach. Tolerant but passive, he is unwilling to become actively involved in change; it is this lack of involvement that does not challenge Michael's determined shift towards Republicanism. Michael absorbs a rhetoric whose slavish following will play a key role in his violent death.

As the title suggests, then, heritage is the central concern of the play. It is what maintains divided communities and destroys lives. Even though Hugh states that:

> *'we're Scots Irish Canadian British subjects, Sarah.'*

suggesting a hybrid identity, created from many sources. The reality of the situation is that most characters operate within the limitations of their particular upbringing rather than embracing the possibilities of multiculturalism. As Sarah's key speech declares:

> 'Heritage
> A brand burned in deep
> Through skin of centuries.
> Scarring forever
> The soul
> The land
> The memory.
> The future.'

As the real 'rebel' in the play, Sarah is continually challenging the constrictions of her heritage. She will not accept the constraints forced upon her, even if it means a savage beating from her father, at the behest of her mother. Sarah's final speech of the closing scene is suitably enigmatic as she comes to terms with her future without Michael. It lacks the poetry, but not the emotion, of the opening scene in its nearly monosyllabic delivery:

> 'Home
> Not home
> Not beautiful
> No more'

The very open final lines, lack closure and suggest, if anything, possibilities. Sarah must leave behind the old 'certainties' and any bitterness if she is to make a new future.

> 'Six road ends
> Which
> Nearly day'

Heritage

by Nicola McCartney

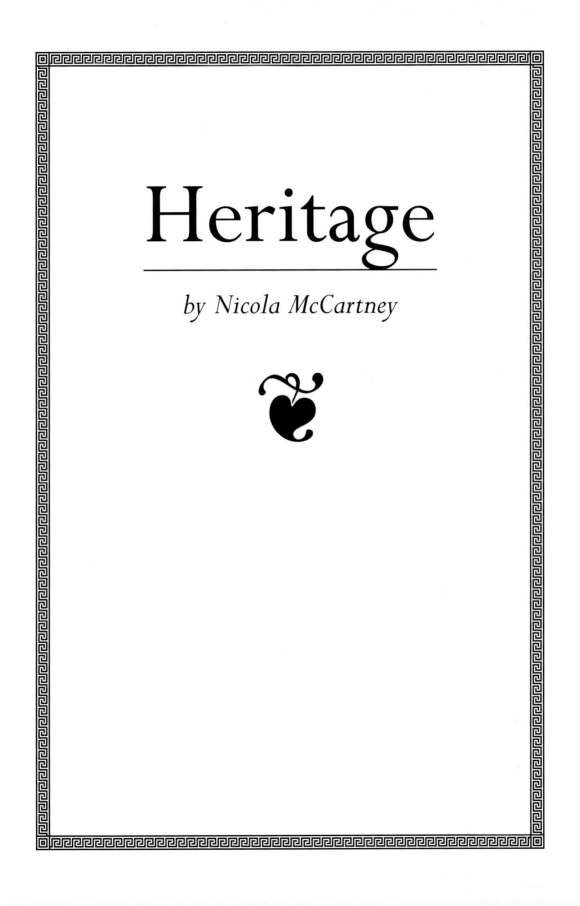

Heritage

By Nicola McCartney

SETTING

Farmlands surrounding the fictional township of Stanley, west of Yorkton, Saskatchewan, Canada.
The action spans a period of six years from Spring 1914 to Spring 1920.

CHARACTERS

Sarah 20 years, at the time of the telling of the story. We see her retrospectively as a young girl aged about 14 and upwards.

Michael Her lover. About a year older than Sarah. A third generation Canadian of Irish Catholic descent.

Hugh McCrea Sarah's father. An Orangeman and a farmer. Early forties.

Ruth McCrea Sarah's mother – also around forty.

Peter Donaghue Michael's father. Around fifty. A farmer. Born in Canada.

Emer Donaghue Michael's grandmother. Irish and still retains the accent – about eighty.

Act One

Scene One

A dream: the stage is lit by fire. A boy dances slowly at first to the beat of a drum. The dance grows more frenzied as the beat quickens and a flute comes in. The sound of people shouting and running in alarm.

Fire consumes the boy dancer.

A scream.

Blackout.

Silence.

The sound of a woman weeping.

Scene Two

Sarah drifts ghost-like into the light. Her clothes are spattered with an ashen dust and her face and hands are dirty with the same.

Sarah Nearly day.
Sun bleeds morning
Over pigs and sheep and hens and goats
Over the land of Shining Waters
Over Canada
Where we have come
To reap the Wheat Boom

I will tell you the story

In the wheat country
Winter comes hard
And Spring comes harder,
Walking along river valley
To home
Pulling top coat chill proof tight
It is bitter
No shelter
Trees felled mercilessly
But still more forest than I remember from home
Ice twists on strange boughs of
Kentucky coffee
Tulip Tree
Sassafras
Sycamore
Spruce
Jack pine
Red pine
White pine
Black walnut
Blue Ash
Balsam Fir
Basswood
Chinquapin Oak
Sugar maple
Left in the rush of clearance
Sharp bite of the axe
Signal of settlement
Boots heavy sludge through
Heavy clay soil
Each step a job of work
Panting
To the top of the rise
Breathless

Below me
Vastness of the plain
Dotted with matchbox houses
Fields sleepin under white snow meltin
Spattered little brown patches where the plough went in late
Criss-cross sewn together with snake-rail fences
Muddy grey below stretches wide under muddy grey above
Forever

Spring time 1914. Michael appears. He is carving out of a block of wood – a boat.

Sarah I will tell you the story
By the big river
I met him
My boy
Mine
All mine
Top of the tallest tree and jump off boy
Fight boys twice his age and still win boy
Boy acted like he could take on the world
With one arm tied behind his back and still win.
Fearless, they called him.
Not cruel.
Never.
No sir, not he.
I will tell you the story
Listen
I will tell the story to you
As I have been told it.
I met him by the big river,
In early Springtime
When the freeze of Winter was beginning to thaw
When the days were on the turn
And they said that war was coming

One day when she was out roaming
The hills and fields round about
Deirdre spied the young warrior

Sarah & Michael [*joining in*] "Take me away from this place," Said Deirdre. "For you know that Conor the king Has sworn to take me as his bride. I have no desire to spend the rest of my days Wedded to an old man."

Scene Three

The same: by the stream.

Michael "It is my *geis*, my solemn word of honour to rescue you." said Naiose. With the help of my brothers, the sons of Usnach, I have got a boat. But we must go quickly. We will leave this place tonight, my love and never return." So, in the middle of the night they fled and set sail off the northern coast. And Naiose wept as he left, for it was the land of his father. Across the sea they sailed to Scotland. There the Scottish king welcomed the warrior . . .

Sarah Hey boy! What are you doin?

Michael Nothing.

Sarah I heard you talkin to yourself.

Michael Not me.

Sarah Only idiots and mad people talk to themselves. What were you sayin?

Michael	Nothing.
Sarah	What's that in your hand?
Michael	Nothing.
Sarah	You are one big Nothin! Let me see!
Michael	It's a boat.
Sarah	It's more the shape of a coffin than a boat. I bet it sinks like a stone. This is our land. You have no right to be playin in it.
Michael	This land belongs to the Carew's who have gone up to Vancouver. It's not sold yet.
Sarah	It's as good as. My father has gone to the land agent today to bid for it.
Michael	So has mine.
Sarah	My father has one hundred acres this side of the water.
Michael	My father has two hundred on this side.
Sarah	Get out of our river!
Michael	No one owns the water – except God. This is no river anyways. It's a stream.
Sarah	It's a river. See, it reaches all the way into the distance.
Michael	It doesn't matter how long it is, but how wide. This cannot be a river because I can jump its width.
Sarah	Go on then, jump.
Michael	No.
Sarah	Do it or I say that you're a liar.
Michael	I am no liar!
Sarah	Well, I say you are one and I say that this here is a river.
Michael	It is a stream.
Sarah	If you can't jump it then you're a liar and must tell me the story.
Michael	What story?
Sarah	The one you were telling to yourself just now.
Michael	And if I can jump?
Sarah	Then you're not a liar.
Michael	But what do I get?
Sarah	Your good name back.
Michael	My name is good anyway. I want something else.

Sarah	What?
Michael	A kiss.
Sarah	Get away! I will give you no such thing.
Michael	Run home to your mama little cry-baby!
Sarah	I'm no cry-baby!
Michael	Well, I say you are one. And a scaredy too.
Sarah	And sure what's there to be scared of? . . . Only if you jump the river.

Michael attempts the jump and falls in the stream.

Sarah	Trying to walk on water now?
Michael	Will you give me a hand?

She helps him.

Michael	You're right, it must be a river. Now we're on the same side.
Sarah	Let go of my hand . . .
Michael	I'll wait for my kiss then?
Sarah	A kiss is a thing you'll never have from me. A cuff on the lug, maybe!
Michael	So you fight, girl?
Sarah	Better than you!

She takes a swing at him.

Michael	That's fancy footwork. I don't blame you for mistaking this here for a river. I thought so too when I was a child.
Sarah	I am thirteen years old and five months.
Michael	Near as old as the century. That must make you very wise indeed!
Sarah	Wise enough not to fall in a river –
Michael	Just to fall on your ass in the dirt instead. I'm Michael Donaghue of Quebec, now of Stanley Township, Saskatchewan.
Sarah	Well, I can't say I'm pleased to meet you, Michael Donaghue.
Michael	What do they call you?
Sarah	Sarah McCrea of County Antrim, Ireland, now of Saskatchewan.
Michael	You're John McCrea's younger sister.
Sarah	How do you know my brother?
Michael	I fought him once.

Sarah	What for?
Michael	He called me a Papist bastard.
Sarah	Are you?
Michael	I'm a Papist; but no bastard.
Sarah	Who won?
Michael	He did. He broke my nose.
Sarah	Good!
Michael	But I cut his lip. So, Sarah McCrea of County Antrim, now of Saskatchewan what drove you here?
Sarah	What?
Michael	How come you to Saskatchewan?
Sarah	All's I know is my father says he's seen an advertisement offerin settlin on farms and the next thing I know we're on a steamship out of Belfast.
Michael	My grandmother came out of Derry on a sailing ship.
Sarah	We sailed on the Cunard line – passenger class. It took us near two weeks.
Michael	My grandmother says the ocean is very wide, bigger even than Lake Ontario.
Sarah	Much much bigger!
Michael	Maybe the ocean gets smaller as you get bigger – just like the river.
Sarah	I think the ocean will always be very big, for my mother says that you can only cross it the once and then it's for a lifetime.
Michael	Is Ireland very green?
Sarah	In summer it is. Why do you not go to the school?
Michael	I'm too old.
Sarah	The Martins are Catholics and they go.
Michael	I didn't want to go and my father said I didn't have to if I didn't want.
Sarah	I wish my father'd say that.
Michael	What is Derry like?
Sarah	I don't know. It's on the other side of the country, as far away as we are from Regina maybe. Isn't that funny? Here I am in Canada but I've never been to Londonderry. I've been to Belfast though.
Michael	I know nothing of Belfast except through the newspapers.
Sarah	I was only there the once on the way to the ship. My Uncle William drove us there in the carriage. We came in from the north of the city, down from the mountains

and there it was all spread out in front of us – the Lough, linen mills and factories and a new city hall just built all in white marble. I thought it was the biggest grandest place there was on earth until we passed through Toronto.

Michael	I will go to Ireland one day.
Sarah	Sure what would you want to go there for?
Michael	To see where I come from.
Sarah	Canada is a far better country than Ireland.
Michael	Do you think?
Sarah	Yes, I do.
Michael	Why's that?
Sarah	Because lots of reasons. Because you can grow peaches here. Tell me the story now.
Michael	Why do you want to hear it?
Sarah	I like stories.
Michael	I will tell you the story as I have been told it. One night, Conor mac Nessa, King of Ulster, and his knights –
Sarah	Ulster's not a kingdom.
Michael	It used to be.
Sarah	When?
Michael	A long time ago. Shall I tell you or not?
Sarah	Go on and tell it.
Michael	Without interruption? Okay . . . One night, Conor mac Nessa, King of Ulster, and his knights were feasting at the house of his chief poet, Felimidh. They ate and drank their fill and the great hall was full of the sounds of merrymaking. Felimidh's wife, dutifully prepared the feast and played the hostess the whole night long, even though she was heavily pregnant. At last, filled with good food and ale, the guests began to fall asleep. Quietly Felimidh's wife made her way through the sleeping company to her own chamber, for the day had been a great strain for her . . .

Ruth appears.

Ruth	"I will incline mine ear to a parable: I will open my dark saying upon the harp . . ."
Michael	And great pain warned her that her child would soon be born.
Ruth	Wherefore should I fear in the days of evil, when the iniquity at my heels shall compass me about?

Michael	But passing through the great hall, the child in her womb gave out a cry . . .
Ruth	They that trust in their wealth . . .
Michael	A shriek so loud that it roused the sleeping courtiers . . .
Ruth	. . . And boasts themselves in the multitude of their riches . . .
Michael	. . . Who seized their arms and rushed to see what it was that had made such a terrible sound . . .

Scene Four

Night: The same day.
The McCrea farmstead. Sarah and Ruth in the kitchen place. Ruth reads from a big, old family bible.

| Ruth | . . . None of them can by any means redeem his brother, nor give to God a ransom for him: for the redemption of their soul is precious, and it ceaseth forever – that he should continue to live eternally and not see the Pit. For he sees that wise men die . . ." What's that? |

Sarah runs to look out of the window.

Sarah	It's not them.
Ruth	Yorkton's not so far away that it should take them this long.
Sarah	I wonder if they've stopped off at the Milling's?
Ruth	Why would they do that?
Sarah	Maybe I should go over and see.
Ruth	Maybe you should be in your bed. "For he seeth that wise men die; likewise the fool and the senseless person perish, and leave their wealth to others. Their inner thought is that their houses will continue forever, and their dwelling places to all generations . . ." I worry for them, out and about this country so late and the roads in such a state.
Sarah	Maybe they were ambushed?
Ruth	What?
Sarah	By Indians.
Ruth	Oh for pity's sake.
Sarah	Mary Trimble was attacked by Indians.
Ruth	No she wasn't. The Indians are all on reservations now.
Sarah	Well, six of them come . . .
Ruth	Came. Six of them came . . .
Sarah	Yes, while her father was away over to Yorkton to get the doctor for her mother

who was sick in bed and near dyin.

Ruth   I don't want to hear about it.

Sarah   Mary and her two sisters had to hide under the bed while her brother stood guard with her father's hunting rifle. They thought they would all have their throats cut.

Ruth   Sarah –

Sarah   One of them was all painted and he came right up to the window and pressed his face against it with his eyes staring all wide and bloodthirsty – just like that.

Ruth   Get away out of it! I let you sit up with me for company and this is what you do!

Sarah picks up the bible

Sarah   I was only sayin. Shall I read on?

Ruth   Put it away.

Sarah   How old is this?

Ruth   You know how old it is.

Sarah   Your mother's mother's.

Ruth   It's raining now. The roads'll all be washed away.

Sarah [*reading inscription*] "Ruth Milling m. Hugh Henry McCrea, Nov. 1898". This isn't your writing.

Ruth   It's my mother's.

Sarah   John Hugh, Sarah Elizabeth . . .

Ruth   She wrote in all your names too. She had a beautiful hand.

Hugh enters.

Hugh   By jings, I'm knackered this night.

Ruth   Hugh! Where've you been 'til this hour?

Hugh   The roads is all churned up with the thaw. 'Twas heavy going for the oul' mare.

Ruth   I told you not to be going away up there in this weather!

Hugh   Were you worryin about me, my darlin'?

He embraces her

Ruth   Get away o' this you old goat! And take your boots off.

Hugh [*to Sarah*] Yes, ma'am. And how's my other girl?

Sarah   I was watchin out for you.

Hugh   I'm glad you was for I've plenty news to tell ye. Oh, yes indeed I have.

Sarah   Tell me!

Hugh	The wee boys all in bed?
Ruth	Long ago. Which is where this one's goin now.
Sarah	Ach, Mammy!
Hugh	Sure, let her sit up a while and have a yarn.
Ruth	Never let it be said I was the one that spoilt her. Where's John?
Hugh	He's takin the order back over to Samuel's.
Ruth	At this hour? Could he not have left it 'til the morning?
Hugh	I think he's got sweet on young Miss Rebecca Milling.
Ruth	He's only a boy.
Hugh	Fifteen years makes him near a man. He'd some sort of present he wished to deliver to the young lady. He wouldnae tell me what.
Ruth	Wasting money he's no call wasting . . .
Hugh	He washed before he went out this mornin and I could hae sworn all these years he was afraid o' water!
Sarah	John's got a sweetheart!
Ruth	Don't be teasing him now.
Hugh	Why would she be teasin him when she's got an admirer herself young Master Robert Milling.
Sarah	I can't marry him. He's my Mammy's cousin.
Hugh	Who's talkin of marryin?
Ruth	He's fine looking.
Sarah	He's too old.
Ruth	He's not nineteen yet.
Sarah	And he smells like a chimney with all that tobacco he smokes.
Ruth	I never knew he smoked tobacco.
Sarah	Sometimes he chews it up and spits it out.
Hugh	Jays, that's desperate.
Ruth	Hugh!
Hugh	A vile habit.
Sarah	I don't want him.
Hugh	Good on yeh.
Ruth	She might be glad of somebody to take her, for she'll make no housewife.

Sarah	Are you hungry, Daddy?
Hugh	Starvin! My stomach feels like my throat's been cut.
Ruth	Well, if you would come in for your meal at the proper time, and not leave it spoiling . . .
Hugh	And if I come in at the proper time you'd be complainin about the work I hadnae done.
Ruth	Wash your hands! *[to Sarah]* Be careful with that plate, don't drop it!
Sarah	I won't.
Hugh	Would you look at that! Ham.
Ruth	You've seen ham before.
Hugh	I'm only sayin we're a damn sight better off . . .
Ruth	Hugh! Mind your talk. *[to Sarah.]* Don't let me hear you repeatin that.
Hugh	. . . better off where we are than where we were. *[to Sarah.]* Here, this is for you?
Ruth	Not more of those books.
Hugh	Books is a good present.
Sarah	Western Girl's Companion.
Ruth	Filling her head with a load of old nonsense.
Hugh	It's just stories.
Ruth	She's bad enough as it is. She had you and our John attacked by Indians tonight.
Hugh	No Indians is goin to attack me, don't you worry.
Sarah	Thank you, Daddy.
Hugh	You can read to us out of that later.
Sarah	How was Yorkton?
Hugh	Big and busy.
Ruth	Did you get the cloth I asked for?
Hugh	Aye.
Ruth	And the lamp oil?
Hugh	I got all on your list. Give yourself peace missus.
Ruth	What's all this cuddling and getting on? Have you been at the drink?
Hugh	I had a wee nip to celebrate.
Ruth	Celebrate what?

Hugh	Wait and hear. Sarah, where's my pen and writin paper?
Sarah	Are we to write to Uncle William, Daddy?
Hugh	We are. For we have news to tell and you shall write it, Sarah.
Ruth	What's happened?
Hugh	Wait and hear . . . *[to Sarah]* Set down the date first.
Sarah	May 14th, 1914 . . .
Hugh	Dearest brother William . . . It has been twelve months since I writ my last letter to ye. I send these few lines . . . There's a start. Let me look. Aye, that's good. That's very good now. *[to Ruth.]* The chile has a fair hand.
Ruth	Aye, she can write well, but she's slow with her other learning.
Sarah	I do my best.
Ruth	Aye, at sitting daydreaming! I wonder you've hands left on ye at all with the number of slaps they've had for wandering attention.
Hugh	Who's been baitin my chile?
Sarah	That schoolteacher, Mr Rutherford did the day.
Hugh	For why?
Ruth	I lost my place at the readin.
Hugh	I thought you liked readin?
Sarah	I do.
Ruth	Dreaming!
Sarah	I wasn't dreamin, I was thinkin.
Hugh	Isn't that desperate? Thinkin's what school's for, is it not? Well, you tell Rutherford the next time he comes at you with that stick your oul' da'll be down to the schoolhouse to knock him onto his Scotch ar–
Ruth	Hugh!
Hugh	I was goin to say 'back'.
Ruth	You'll do no such thing. *[to Sarah]* And better still the next time I hear you've had correction, I'll give you the same again when you get home, do you hear me?
Hugh	Give the chile peace, missus. She'll be outa school in six months and not need much figurin or letterin to keep a house.
Sarah	What will I write to Uncle William, Daddy?
Hugh	Now, let's see. *[Thinking]* I suppose we must tell him about the hoose . . . The new hoose is bilded last summer, a wooden frame hoose of two storeys. Ruth has it all fitted out lovely.

Ruth	Tell him I still favour the old-fashioned stone cottage above timber. I fear of fire in these houses.
Hugh	I tell you what, I'll build ye a double-fronted hoose, a stoan hoose like the Milling's one day, missus. Would that please you?
Ruth	It would.
Hugh	Then I'll do it. And it will be twice as big and as tall as the Milling hoose and oor farm will be three times as big as their farm, and Hugh McCrea will be four times as rich!
Ruth	It's you she gets the dreaming from indeed.
Hugh	Is it now? *[to Sarah.]* Set this down . . . Brother, I come back from the agent in Yorkton today havin bought another thirty acres of good land.
Sarah	You got it!
Hugh	I did so.
Ruth	You did what?
Hugh	I've bought part of the Carew place. That makes one hunder'd and ninety acres of good fertil' soil. I had to bid against our neighbour Donaghue.
Sarah	He's a Catholic, isn't he?
Hugh	He is. *[to Ruth.]* What's that face for? You're not anger'd?
Ruth	You would talk it over with a child before your wife?
Hugh	I wanted to surprise you with it, Ruth.
Ruth	How much did you pay for it?
Hugh	Only eighteen dollars an acre.
Ruth	Five hundred and forty dollars!
Hugh	It's good pasture land. The best for grazin cettel with the stream thereby.
Ruth	We've only two milk cows, for pity's sake.
Hugh	At the minute, aye. But I reckon to buy another head and a bull with this year's harvest money.
Ruth	If you can get a price for the wheat. How're you to afford it?
Hugh	I went to see Hector Smyth at the bank.
Ruth	Lord!
Hugh	He's one of the Brethren and he'll give me a good rate.
Ruth	We're mortgaged up to our necks and still you're taking on more debt.
Hugh	That's my affair. Never worry, missus.

Ruth	How can you tell me not to worry, Hugh McCrea, when you go off and do such things without asking me first?
Hugh	And since when did a man have to seek permission from his wife to wipe his nose, eh?
Ruth	He does when he's about to take the family into wreck and ruin!
Sarah	Ma–
Ruth	Keep your nose out!
Hugh	Wreck and ruin?
Sarah	Mammy–

Ruth [*to Sarah*] Go to bed!

Hugh [*to Sarah*] Stay where you are! [*to Ruth*] Wreck and ruin! Jays, missus, can you never be happy but you allus have to see the dark side of a thing?! Look at these hands. Look! These are the hands that signed the deed to this land. These are the hands that did the plantin and the bildin. These are the hands that the money passes into and out of again.

Pause

Ruth	Go to bed, Sarah.
Hugh	I would have her sit up and finish the letter.

Pause.

Hugh [*continuing the letter*] God, Willy, I never knew I was alive until I got out of Ireland and woke up. What a country this British North America is! Good land with the finest soil and all your own to do with as you see fit with no older brother Henry at your back givin orders and no landlord to come and claim his share of your toil at the month's end. There's been a small depression here of late but it has not hit us too hard for we haven't got enough yet to lose. It was a right thing I done in coming here. If I'd stayed at home as you are doing, I would still be in rags working in the dirt and the mud with nothing to show for it. If only you would pluck up the courage and come too I wonder would you send me seeds of Balm of Gilead and also some of the lily I have it in mind to sow a flower garden out in front of the house, a memory walk so that Ruth can have all the colours and scents of home about her. Send any other seeds you might think of for such seeds is dear here. You will wrap them in a piece of oiled paper then fold your letter up and then paste them in the crease and stick it down twice to hide them well. We will walk on the Twelfth this year again. Young John will play the flute he is comin on well at it the Orange Order is strong out here. Tell Reverend Acheson that on account of his letter and the certificate of transfer he give me, the Brethren here have been very good 'til us. I hear talk that the Ulster Volunteers has landed rifles at Larne this month it is a sorry business bloodshed but better that than Home Rule. Remember me to the Brethren. Write soon and send us news of home,

Sarah	Will you mention Peggy, Daddy?

Hugh	Surely, we must mention her . . . As I am sure you heard from Lizzie Milling, our youngest child, Margaret, died from the pneumonia, aged two years before Christmas last. The winters is very severe here. Remember us also to brother Henry and the family.
Ruth	Don't sign my name to it if you're writing to that one.
Hugh	Would you rather be back in Ireland, Sarah?
Sarah	I like it here.
Hugh	Good girl! Let's see now. *[reads over the letter.]* That's fine! Look at that Ruth, isn't that fine now? *[to Sarah]* Ah, you're a clever one. I must sign my name now. *[writes].* Yours with affectation/–
Sarah	–/Affection, Daddy.
Hugh	Aye. Your brother, Hugh . . . That's good. *[to Sarah]* Now write on the envelope to Master William McCrea, McCreas Farm, Ballinderry Road, near Ballymoney, County Antrim, Ireland.

Scene Five

Late September 1914. Sarah, walking through the pasture. Michael enters.

Michael	Heah!

He throws her a stick.

Sarah	Who goes there?
Michael	I am Naiose, Red Hand Knight of Ulster.
Sarah	You cannot step upon this shore.
Michael	Me and my bride seek refuge here with the Scottish King.
Sarah	Stay and prove yourself.

They 'sword-fight'.

Sarah	You waited.
Michael	I had nearly given you up. What kept you?
Sarah	Oul' Rutherford made me stay behind.
Michael	On your last day? What for?
Sarah	Knockin over a pile of books.
Michael	Clumsy!
Sarah	Got you!
Michael	Mercy!
Sarah	Die!

Michael	It's not in the story that you kill me.
Sarah	I will spare you and your bride. Stay here and live as my brother.
Michael	In return for this I hereby pledge my allegiance and skills as a warrior to your service. Say, who has offended the honour of our Protector?
Sarah	Mister Rutherford.
Michael	Death to Mister Rutherford!

They flay away at an imaginary Mister Rutherford.

Sarah	No more Mister Rutherford!
Michael	What did you learn?
Sarah	Countries and their capitals. I got them all right and oul' Rutherford said "it's a wonder Miss McCrea. For though you have now reached the age of fourteen I had doubts that you could count to that number. I am glad to discover that on your very last day of education you have learned at least something."
Michael	I'll test you.
Sarah	I'm done with school.
Michael	Turkey?
Sarah	That's a hard one!
Michael	Istanbul. Great Britain?
Sarah	Too easy.
Michael	Canada?
Sarah	I'm not stupid!
Michael	France?
Sarah	Paris.
Michael	Italy?
Sarah	Rome. Harder.
Michael	Egypt?
Sarah	I don't know that one.
Michael	It's Cairo, stupid.
Sarah	I'm not stupid! Another!
Michael	Bosnia?
Sarah	Sarajevo where the Duke was shot and the War started.
Michael	Very good. The master was right – you're not as stupid as you look.

Sarah	Mr Rutherford said that it is Canada's duty to give whatever help she can to the efforts of the Allies on the Western Front.
Michael	Russia?
Sarah	You can volunteer.
Michael	I don't want to,
Sarah	Why not? You're old enough. Our John will go as soon as he is sixteen.
Michael	Of course he will. He'd enjoy killing people.
Sarah	That's a terrible thing to say.
Michael	Running Huns through the ribs with his bayonet.
Sarah	He's braver than you.
Michael	I won't fight. For it is not our war.
Sarah	It's a threat to the British Empire.
Michael	And this is Canada. *[He hands her a gift: A handkerchief.]* Happy birthday!
Sarah	You have no call giving me presents.
Michael	D'you like it?
Sarah	It's pretty. Did you sew it yourself?
Michael	I found it. In my grandmother's linen chest.
Sarah	Will she not miss it?
Michael	It belonged to my mother, I think. See the little flowers?
Sarah	Lilies. Thank you.
Michael	It's okay.

She kisses him.

Michael	I am Conor mac Nessa, King of Ulster. Where is Felimidh, my chief bard?
Sarah	Here I am, sire!
Michael	You have pleased us, Felimidh, with this feast and revels. We will retire now to our chamber for the night.
Sarah	I will be Felimidh's wife. The feast is over and she is very tired . . .
Michael	Passing through the great hall . . .
Sarah	What's her name?
Michael	She doesn't have one.
Sarah	She must have a name.

Michael	She is called Felimidh's wife.
Sarah	That's not a proper name.
Michael	Alright, Ethne . . . passing through the great hall the child in her womb . . .
Sarah	Ethne's womb.
Michael	. . . gave out a cry, a shriek so loud that it roused the sleeping warriors who seized their arms. Felimidh feared the men at arms. *[He plays Felimidh.]* "it was the scream of my wife's unborn child that has wakened you," he said. *[He plays the warrior again.]* "Call your wife before us," said the chief warrior. Trembling with fear . . .
Sarah	This is my part.
Michael	She was so frightened she could only answer
Sarah	No mother knows what sleeps in her womb
Michael	That's right! But, later that night she gave birth to a child – a girl child with shining eyes and fair hair. Cathbad the druid prophesied over her. "You, O Deirdre of the Sorrows . . ."
Sarah	You can't be all the parts.
Michael	You are Felimidh's wife. That is the only girl in this bit of the story.
Sarah	I want to be the Druid.
Michael	You don't know how to be a Druid. You don't know what a Druid is.
Sarah	I do too! It's a sort of magician.
Michael	No a Druid is a "seer".
Sarah	Like a fortune teller or a tinker?
Michael	Sort of, but grander.
Sarah	That's easy.
Michael	Okay, you be Cathbad . . . The druid took the baby gently in his arms and prophesied over her.
Sarah	What do I say?
Michael	How can you be the Cathbad if you don't know the words?
Sarah	Because you will tell me. Come on!
Michael	You, O Deirdre of the Sorrows.
Sarah	You, O Deirdre of the Sorrows.
Michael	Will grow up into a beautiful young woman.
Sarah	Will grow up into a beautiful young woman.
Michael	Vivid as a flame.

Sarah	Vivid as a flame.
Michael	With lips as red as berries and hair as gold as corn.
Sarah	With lips as red as berries and hair as gold as corn.
Michael	So beautiful that you will bring great sorrow to the province of Ulster.
Sarah	So beautiful that you will bring great sorrow to the province of Ulster.

Peter enters unseen and listens to them.

Michael	Violent deeds will be done because of your beauty
Sarah	Violent deeds will be done because of your beauty.
Michael	And you will bring death to the king's son.
Sarah	And you will bring death to the king's son . . . How was that? Did I make a good Druid?
Michael	You were okay. A bit too fairground perhaps. The warriors, alarmed by such a dread prophecy immediately demanded the child's death that Ulster would be spared this fate.
Sarah	But then Conor the King spoke forth.
Peter *[joining in]*	"I decree that the child be sent far away from Emain Macha to be reared by a nurse until marriageable age. Then I will take her as my queen" he declared. And he sent her out of harm's way to a lonely place to be raised by a nurse, the poet Levercham, who taught her many things, and a poor herdsman was her foster father.
Sarah	It's a good story.
Peter	It is.
Sarah	I had never heard it before Mike told it to me.
Peter	I'm sure you hadn't. *[To Michael.]* Where've you been? You've been gone since dinner. You know there's baling to be done yet.
Michael	I lost track of time.
Peter	It's nearly supper. Who's your friend?
Sarah	Sarah McCrea.
Michael	Sarah, this is my father, Peter Donaghue.
Sarah	Hello.
Peter	Pleased to meet you, Miss McCrea. So you're the one my son neglects his work for. He's been keeping you a secret.
Sarah	Are you ashamed of me?
Michael	No.

Sarah	I'm sorry to keep him from his work. He came to meet me after school but I was late.
Peter	It's not your fault that he's work shy.
Sarah	I just finished at the school today, you see.
Michael	It's her birthday.
Sarah	I wanted Mike to come celebrate with me.
Peter	Well, I hope you take to whatever occupation you choose better than my son has took to farming.
Michael	I'm sorry about the baling.
Peter	No matter. Plenty more work tomorrow. Come on! We must get home. I'd rather go fight in the trenches any day than face your grandmother when late for supper.
Michael	Can Sarah come to supper with us?
Peter	I expect she has a home of her own to go to.

Scene Six

Later: the Donaghue house.

Emer	It came on so sudden.
	Morning
	Mist rises up out of the Lough
	Hovers over
	So quiet
	You can hear a woman whispering a mile off
	Day before, potatoes good
	Now leaves all black
	Crumble into ashes
	Palm stains dark
	Air hanging heavy
	Smell of sickness
	Smell of
	Death
	Fields
	Weeping-wailing
	Women and children.
	My daddy
	Poor cottier
	Lost foot on the land.
	The British!
	Not even a crust of bread to chew upon
	They give us
	Ship off cattle and grain we've raised
	To serve up on English dinner tables
	While our children

> Perish.
> Protestant Ministers
> They dishing out bowls of free soup
> But you must recant
> Must throw away soul.
> So we live on
> Grass seaweed and shellfish

Michael [joining with her] "Grass, seaweed and shellfish."

Emer That was the beginning of the great disease that destroyed Ireland, Mihal.

Sarah What's recant?

Michael To turncoat on our Catholic faith.

Emer That's right, son.

Michael They say some people ate human corpses.

Sarah They ate the dead people?

Peter God in heaven!

Emer I never saw that now. But they say some turned cannibal. No one can know how we suffered. I pray to God that you nor yours may ever know.

Peter Mike, you were walking the top fifty acres this morning?

Michael Yes.

Sarah [to Emer] And then you came to Canada?

Emer For £5.00 passage each we sailed on the ship Superior out of Derry on 13 July 1849.

Peter [to Michael] Notice any damage?

Michael No.

Peter [to Michael] Are you sure?

Michael [to Peter] Sure, I'm sure.

Emer We sailed into Quebec City on 4 November. I was eleven years old.

Sarah That's the age I was when we came here. We sailed on the Cunard line.

Emer Coffin ships they called them. But all my family survived it.

Peter Good. So, one hundred and ten acres at forty bushels an acre . . . That makes . . .

Emer Peadar! We're talking.

Peter Excuse me. Carry on.

Emer My father really wanted to go to Philadelphia.

Peter	Four four 'o' at ninety three cents a bushel . . .
Sarah	Why?
Peter	The great Republic.
Emer	But it was too expensive.
Peter	Makes two thousand seven hundred and twenty eight dollars with tax and a bit more off. That's good isn't it?
Michael	Very good.
Peter	Miles better than last year. How's your father's harvest, Sarah?
Sarah	Not as big as that I think.
Emer	Ah, we should've gone to America at last.
Peter	Liberty and justice for all! Except liberty for a Catholic man to vote for his own government.
Emer	Thousands were driven out because of the Great Hunger.
Peter	They were leaving in their droves long before that, mother. Opportunity forced them out long before a bit of potato blight.
Emer	You remember all this, Mihal. It is where you come from.
Peter	He was born in Canada. He was raised in Canada. He will work to pay his taxes to the Canadian government. He is Canadian.
Emer	Cuimhnigh ar sin, a mhicil.[1]
Michael	Cuimhneoidh mé, a mhamó.[2]
Peter	Don't start on that.
Michael	Tell about the uprising.
Emer	The Young Irelanders?
Michael	This is a good one.
Peter	Oh yes! Tell us about the Young Irelanders. That was a great glorious uprising, Sarah. Somebody's gun went off by mistake and another Paddy lost his shovel in a County Tipperary cabbage patch!
Emer	Your father was in the Movement.
Peter	The sins of my father are not mine to be judged for.
Emer	Holy God! Your father was no sinner. There was never a finer –
Peter	Here we go.

[1]You remember all this, Michael.
[2]I will, Grandma.

Emer	Never a finer man than him. I'll not sit here and listen to this you, you – traitor!
Peter	Then go to bed.
Michael	Dad, let it go.
Peter	No.
Emer	No respect. He has none!
Peter	I have respect for facts and truth,
Emer	We should've stayed in Quebec beside our friends.
Peter	On the good British land granted you by the good British government. You and my father were happy to take that, weren't you? Be careful of history, Sarah.
Emer	Bringing us out here to be surrounded by Puritans!
Peter	History's more dangerous a friend than an enemy.
Emer	You always were a lover of the British!
Peter	Don't begin on that now.
Emer	Oh it's "don't begin on that" now I'm speaking of things he doesn't want to hear. Ti raibh aon mhaitheas léi, ar chor ar bith, maitheas ar bith.[3]
Peter	Nothing but a load of lies and bitterness.
Emer	Ní féidir faic a insint duitse.[4]
Michael	Céard faoi a bhfuil tu ag caint?[5]
Emer	Is cuma, a mhic.[6]
Peter	We have company.
Michael	Ta tu ag caint faoi mo mhathair, nach bhfuilir?[7]
Peter	She hardly knew your mother.
Michael	Ba mbaith liom fios a bheith agam.[8]
Emer	Bhí sí posta cheanna.[9]
Peter	She was a widower!
Michael	An raibh?[10]

[3]She was no good at all.
[4]You couldn't tell him anything.
[5]What are you talking about?
[6]No matter, son.
[7]You're talking about my mother aren't you?
[8]I want to know.
[9]She was married before.
[10]Was she?

Emer	Niorbh fhéidir caint leis, thug me rabhadh dho Thug a athair rabhadh dhó.[11]
Peter	Michael, it's time for Sarah to be going home.
Michael	It's not late yet.
Peter	I think it is.
Michael	Céard atá i gceist agat? Abair liom, a Mhamo![12]
Emer	Iarr ar d'athair.[13]
Michael	Ni insionn sé faic domsa.[14]
Peter	In English! The pair of you! *[to Michael.]* There's nothing I haven't told you.
Emer	Where is she now, eh?
Peter	Wherever she is she's getting peace and rest.
Emer	Better than she deserves.
Michael	Céard atá i gceist agat?[15]
Peter	Will you stop!
Sarah	I'd best go, Mike.
Peter	I'm sorry, Sarah. Michael will take you home in the wagon.
Michael	I want to know what she means.
Peter	She's confused.
Emer	My mind's as sharp as razor –
Peter	You're tongue is. *[to Michael]* Take your friend home. It's late.
Sarah	Thank you for supper.
Emer	No trouble.
Sarah	Can I come again?
Emer	B'fhearr e mura dtiocfadh se' anseo aris coiche.[16]
Michael	Cén fath?[17]
Emer	Bí curamach a mchicil, Maidir le ceard atá a dhéanamh agat.[18]

[11]There was no talking to him either; but I warned him. His father warned him.
[12]What do you mean? Tell me, Grandma.
[13]Ask your father.
[14]He never tells me anything.
[15]What do you mean?
[16]It's better she doesn't come here again.
[17]Why?
[18]Be careful of what you are doing, Michael.

Peter   Sarah is always welcome here.

Sarah   Thank you. Goodnight.

Michael   I want to know what she means.

Peter   Another time. Goodnight. *[to Mike.]* Don't be late home. You'll have to rise early to make up the work from today.

Michael   Okay! Okay! Slán, a mhamó.[19]

Emer   Slán a mhic.[20]

Sarah and Michael exit.

Emer   A Dhía dhilis![21] Goin the same way. Just like you, every bit of him.

Scene Seven

Summer 1915. The Twelfth of July.

Sarah   Dub a dum dubaduba dum
Dub a dum dubaduba dum
Big Lambeg beats
Boom boom
Boom boom
One head made of ass's skin could shatter a window.
And boom and boom and boom boom boom
Shudders and shakes you to the liver
High "G" on the "D" flute
Thrill of pain it gives you in the heart
Brother John marching, puffing, whistling
Isn't he doin well?
Go on John!
It is old but it is beautiful
And it's colours they are fine . . .
Banners unfurl beneath trees green.
Sons of William, orange
Loyal Sons of Canada, gold
Fluttering by
Dub a dum dubaduba dum
Boom boom
Dub a dum dubaduba dum
Boom boom
For heh~ho
The lily-O!
The royal orange lily-O!
King Billy on a white charger leading

[19]Goodbye, Grandma.
[20]Goodbye, son.
[21]My G~od!

Sunday Best parade
Sashes all fire colour
Marching
Past women in hats
And girls in frocks
And wee boys in long trousers
Waving
And singing our songs
Man with lance
Man with Bible, our Bible
Man with white gloves and a big sword
With ting and toot and crash and boom We'll guard old Derry's walls . . .
Marching
To the Field.

Our field
Of cake and ginger beer
And lemonade
And aniseed drops
And candy sticks
And kick the can
And hide and seek
And swing on a rope
And red, white and blue.
Our day out
Of tea and sandwiches
And cold meats and currant buns
And summer salad
And little nips of whiskey while the women's backs are turned
And Let us pray
Our Father Which Art in Heaven
And The Lord's My Shepherd
And God bless Sir Edward Carson
And "God Save Our Gracious King!"
And Ireland shall never submit to Home Rule
And Ulster will fight and Ulster will be Right
And God Bless our forces on the Western Front
And Keep the Empire Protestant.
Oh God our help in ages past
Our hope in years to come
Our day.

Scene Eight

Later, the same night. The McCrea farmstead. The kitchen place. Ruth and Sarah, sewing.

Hugh [*raising his glass*] To the glorious and immortal memory of King William of Orange who saved Ireland from Popes and Popery and brass money and wooden shoes. And to any man who denies this toast, may he be rammed slammed and jammed into the Great Gun of Athlone and fired into the Pope's belly and the Pope into the Devil's belly and the devil into hell and the door locked and the key thrown away forever!

He drains his glass.

Ruth	Will you mind your talk! *[to Sarah.]* Have you not that finished yet?
Sarah	It's near done
Ruth	Can you manage?
Sarah	It's only a few old socks, ma.
Ruth	Let me see . . . What's this?
Sarah	What's wrong with it?
Ruth	Will you look at that!
Hugh	Don't ask me now. Nothin at all to do with me.
Ruth	How many times do I have to tell you – small stitches, even stitches.
Hugh	Sure big or small makes no difference as long as it all holds together.
Ruth	You want holes in your clothes do you? *[to Sarah.]* Give it to me.
Sarah	I can fix it.
Ruth	Just let it be.
Sarah	I'll start over.
Ruth	Leave it alone I tell you. Leave it alone. It's a disgrace you are to me a disgrace.
Hugh	Who d'ye think was asking after you today at the Field, Sarah?
Sarah	I don't know.
Hugh	Robert Milling.
Ruth	What was he asking you for? He saw me himself.
Hugh	He was asking me if ye was walkin out with anyone? I said no. That's right isn't it?
Sarah	It is.
Ruth	Of course it is.
Hugh	Then he asked me if he could coort ye.
Sarah	And what'd you say?
Hugh	I told him ye were too young yet. "Come back when she's forty," says I. "That'll be time enough for her to be thinkin of coortin."
Ruth	Well you needn't think that you'll sit here until your forty. No help to met at all. *[to Hugh.]* No more now.

Hugh	Missus, I'm on my holidays.
Ruth	You've had enough to down the fish.
Hugh	Ach, there's one or two of them no' dead yet.
Sarah	It was a big parade today, Daddy.
Hugh	It was.
Ruth	Our John did well.
Hugh	He did; though I think he hit a few wrong notes in "Lily Balero". Jays my ears was ringin.
Ruth	He did not!
Hugh	I'm tellin ye. Aye, it was a grand day.
Hugh	D'ye know, Samuel was tellin me even some of the Red Indians has formed their own lodges now.
Sarah	How can they? They're infidels.
Hugh	Ah, well, y'see it's all come about through confusion. The first big red chief who had the idea, he thought a lodge meant a teepee.
Sarah	How do you join the Orange, Daddy?
Ruth	Don't be stupid! You know women cannot join.
Sarah	Why not?
Ruth	Because it's only for the men.
Hugh	In case we have to fight.
Sarah	For what?
Hugh	For the Empire.
Sarah	I don't see the need for it.
Hugh	There's need for loyalty everywhere in the Empire, Sarah.
Ruth	Who's been filling your head with talk like that?
Hugh	With the war on and the Home Rulers trying to break up the Union.
Sarah	It's my own opinion.
Hugh	She's havin opinions now!
Ruth	That's what comes from too much talk!
Hugh	Well, here's an opinion for you! This is British North America. We're no republic here yet.
Sarah	I'm sorry.

Hugh   It hurts me to hear you speak like that . . . Come here and tell us one of yer stories.

Sarah   Which one shall I tell you?

Hugh   Any one you like.

Sarah   I've a new one. It's about Ulster. I hadn't heard it until I came here, isn't that strange?

Hugh   It is. Go on.

Sarah   It happened many years ago. One stormy night, after a fierce battle, Conor the King was feasting at the house of his poet, Felimidh. A child was born to Felimidh's wife.

Ruth   What story's this?

Sarah   The story of Deirdre of the Sorrows. Do you know it?

Ruth   I do not? Where did you hear that?

Sarah   At school once.

Ruth   I don't think so.

Sarah   It's about Ulster.

Ruth   I don't want to hear it.

Sarah   Why not, ma?

Ruth   Because it's not in our heritage, Sarah.

Sarah   But we're Irish.

Ruth   Our ancestors were Scottish. We're Irish but British too.

Sarah   And now we're livin in Canada, so what does that make us?

Hugh   We're Scots Irish Canadian British subjects, Sarah. That's what we are.

Scene Nine

Sarah   Heritage
A brand burned in deep
Through skin of centuries.
Scarring forever
The soul
The land
The memory
The future.
Carried across deathbeds
Across oceans
To far away land.
Running deep into the soil

Blood in the veins
And fire in the blood
What fire!
Sixty thousand miles from here
Big guns go
Boom Boom
Boom Boom
At Ypres
Canadians
French
British
Irish
All
Defending the Empire
Boom Boom
Sixty thousand miles away
They harvesting and reaping
And counting the dead
Sixty thousand miles from
Planting and harvesting and profit.

Scene Ten

Late summer 1915. The McCrea farmstead. They are building a barn. Sarah remains on stage throughout. Hugh enters.

Sarah   Ten cows now
Twenty sheep
And one hundred and ninety acres
Planted
Corn, oats
And wheat
Farm laid out neat now in strict rectangle
Wooden frame house at the one end
Stable here
Outhouses on this side
Here
Orchard that will grow apples, plums, cherries
And peaches.
There
Vegetable garden
Leeks, beets, carrots, potatoes, cabbages
Grapes, melons, squash
In front
Orange lilies in the memory walk
Sown from crease of the letter seeds
From home.
And now
The barn

Hugh	Here we go! One, two, three – lift!
Sarah	Progress.
Hugh	I need two more men on the back wall. Two I said – you and you. Come on, let's go!
Sarah	Men from Italy Doukhobours and Ruthenians Irish men Orange men To build the new barn Log on log Plank on plank Up and up Tower of Babel
Hugh	You! Get me two ropes!
Sarah	Ready for Harvest Ready to hold the wheat of Boom Boom Wheat Boom
Hugh	No. Ropes, man. Ropes! Does anybody here speak English?
Sarah	Tap tap tap Whistle of saw through wood Rhythm of the future
Hugh	No, no, no. Jays! Does anybody speak English here? All hands to the pump! Sarah! You know how to drive a nail home, don't you?
Sarah	Yes, Daddy.
Hugh	Well, get to it! John, reach me my claw hammer. Hurry up! I'm tellin ye, no one's raised a barn so quick as this.
Sarah	My nail goes in Bang South wall Facing America

Ruth enters.

Ruth	Sarah!
Hugh	She's helpin me.
Ruth	Indeed she's not. *[to Sarah.]* I thought I asked you to lift beets for the dinner.
Sarah	I'll do it now.
Ruth	Hurry up! There's eight hungry men to cook for.

Hugh	D'ye know what I'll do when I have finished the barn? I will dig out foundations for the stoan hoose. Would that please ye?
Ruth	If we could afford to pay for it.
Hugh	We'll pay for it twice over with the way things is going. Wheat prices is over one dollar a bushel. I reckon on near to thirty bushels an acre. That makes near –
Ruth	A thousand dollars.
Hugh	Aye, wi' taxes and all considered. That'll pay the note on the land and a bit besides.
Sarah	There's somebody coming up the road!
Hugh	Who is it?
Sarah	Mister Donaghue! And Michael!
Ruth	What're they doing here?
Hugh	Now! We have to be neighbourly. Donaghue's a polite, quiet sort of fella. The Cathelickes here is of a differ'nt nature to the Irish ones.
Ruth	They're just as sleekit here as anywhere. The only thing as bad as a Cathelicke is a Yankee in my book.

Peter and Michael enter.

Hugh	Good day.
Peter	Good day to you. Are you well?
Hugh	Couldn't be better. Yerself?
Peter	Well enough. It's a scorcher.
Hugh	'Tis that.
Hugh	You remember my wife, Ruth?
Peter	Missus McCrea.
Ruth	Mister Donaghue. How is Missus Donaghue?
Peter	Oh, fighting fit.
Ruth	Give her my regards, won't you.
Peter	She'll be pleased to receive them. This is my son, Michael.
Michael	Hello, sir. Missus.
Hugh	We know him.
Ruth	Sarah, away and get those beets for me.
Sarah	Yes, Ma.

Ruth	Now!
Peter	Hard to work in this.
Ruth	The heat would kill you so it would.
Peter	Looks like it's going to be a skyscraper.
Hugh	Biggest I know of in the township.
Peter	You must be expecting a good harvest?
Hugh	I've busted my back getting every acre I can broke and planted. I have hope.
Peter	Yes, it's a fine place you have here.
Hugh	Three years of hard work.
Peter	Have you enough men?
Hugh	There's myself and young John, Lightbody and Trimble there from the lodge.
Peter	I know them.
Hugh	And a couple o' Russian fellas. The two Italians is bloody useless. *[to an Italian offstage]* Not that way! Turn it round! God's sake!
Peter	If you need any more pairs of hands, Mike and myself are willing. Aren't we, Mike? Mike?!
Michael	What?
Peter	I said we're willing to help?
Michael	Sure.
Hugh	That's very decent of ye.
Peter	Ah, well. We're all in the same boat out here, aren't we?
Hugh	We are indeed.
Ruth	I must away in and get the dinner on.
Hugh	Will ye stay wi' us and have a bite?
Peter	If we're welcome.
Ruth	Of course you're welcome. Sarah!
Sarah	I'm doing it.

Ruth exits.

Peter	Where shall we start?
Hugh	Well, I could use another big man like yourself on the back wall and the boy here can help our young John with the door frame.
Peter	You're the boss man. Got enough tools?

Hugh	Another hammer wouldn't go amiss.
Peter	There's one in the wagon. *[to Michael.]* Well, go on. Go and help John.

Michael exits.

Hugh	I think they've had disagreements.
Peter	That one disagrees with everybody – even himself.
Sarah	Tap tap tap Noon day sun Overhead High One wall raised Another Begins I Fingers scrabble through Dirt Pulling Up from earth

Michael enters.

Michael	Your brother's driving me crazy!
Sarah	What's he doin?
Michael	He keeps whispering at me.
Sarah	What's he whispering?
Michael	Papist! Papist!
Sarah	Is that all? He's only teasing you.
Michael	He's a fool. Twice he's belched in my face.
Sarah	Don't let him away with it.
Michael	I'm on his territory.
Sarah	I'll get him for you later if you like. I always get him back when he's sleepin.
Michael	I can defend myself. If I could just take a swing at him I'd crack that idiot grin of his.
Sarah	Then do it and stop talking about it.
Michael	Come away!
Sarah	I have to do this.
Michael	Come on! Up to the stream. We'll go swimming.
Sarah	It's all dried up.
Michael	Come for a walk then.

Sarah	I have to do this.
Michael	I can't work in this heat.
Sarah	D'you want to land me in trouble?
Michael	Don't talk to me if you don't want to.
Sarah	I want to.
Michael	Why is your barn so big?
Sarah	Because my father wants it to be.
Michael	It's four times the size of your house.
Sarah	He's goin to build a bigger house. Out of stone.
Michael	Why?
Sarah	I don't know why.
Michael	No one builds their houses out of stone here.
Sarah	It's what she wants. And what she wants she gets.

> Tap tap tap
> Build it up higher
> To the roof
> Passing hand to hand

Peter and Hugh examining the building. Hugh drinks from a mug of water.

Peter	It's a piece of work.
Hugh	We'll have it filled to the brim in no time at all.
Peter	The door frame's crooked.
Hugh	What?!
Peter	That join there. That upright is cut at a steeper angle than the crosspiece. The edges don't sit smooth together.
Hugh	I wouldn't have noticed that.
Peter	Until you tried to hang the doors. The whole frame would twist and leave a gap open for the wind to come and blow away your wheat.
Hugh	Honest to God . . . Young ones allus do everythin in a hurry. John!
Peter	No use asking them to do it. May as well do it ourselves and do it proper.
Hugh	Aye.
Peter	The heat is surely blazing.
Hugh	Here.

He hands Peter the mug. They share the water.

Hugh	It's very good of you to help us out like this. You're a good wood worker.
Peter	It was my trade before farming – one of them, anyway.
Hugh	How many trades have you had?
Peter	Carpenter, cooper, railroad digger. And prospector.
Hugh	You were at Dawson City?
Peter	Not for long.
Hugh	I wish I'd been here to see that. Did you find anythin?
Peter	Not much gold. I was too late. I got a wife, though.
Hugh	I've allus been a farmer. And my father and his father was too. I don't know nothin else.
Peter	My father had a small holding in Quebec.
Hugh	You give it up?
Peter	I'd had enough of the place. It didn't exactly bless me with fortune.
Hugh	It's good to have a man of your experience around. I appreciate it. If there's anythin' I can do for ye all's ye have to do is ask.
Peter	Thanks. I'll keep it in mind.
Sarah	Broil Bake Boil Midday heat Sit men Table round Women Dance attendance on Bow heads Father says
Hugh	Let each man give his own thanks to his own God whatsoever that may be.
Sarah	Then Feed them Fill them all up With meat and potatoes Spread before them Best china Clink

Outside the house

Ruth	Sit down, Missus Donaghue and catch your breath.

Emer	Thank you.
Ruth	How did you get away over here?
Emer	I walked.
Ruth	You must be done out.
Emer	Not at all.
Ruth	Why don't you step into the house?
Emer	I'll sit here.
Ruth	You'd be better off in the shade.
Emer	I will not go in. Thank you.
Ruth	Will you take a cup of tea?
Emer	I have no thirst for tea. How is Sarah?
Sarah	I'm helpin too.
Emer	Good for you. The men shouldn't be allowed to think they do all the work.
Ruth	Can I not get you even a wee drink of water?
Emer	Alright, I'll take a cup of water.
Ruth	Right you be, Sarah.

Sarah exits.

Ruth	So . . . How are you keeping, Missus Donaghue?
Emer	Well enough.
Ruth	Your son and grandson have been very good to us today.
Emer	It's a modest wee house isn't it?
Ruth	It does us.
Emer	I lived in a shanty much the same myself when first married.
Ruth	My husband is talking of a new house.
Emer	Men are always starting on one thing before another is finished.

Peter enters.

Peter	What're you doing here?
Emer	I brung you this. A bit of bread and cheese and a sup of milk to keep you going.
Peter	We've already eaten mother.
Ruth	Beef and potatoes.
Peter	Missus McCrea gave us a good dinner.

Ruth	Surely you didn't think I'd let them starve Missus Donaghue?
Emer	Take it – in case the boy gets hungry later.
Peter	You'll kill yourself, walking out in this heat.
Emer	I'll walk where I want to walk, when I want to walk it.
Peter	So you will. I'll not be concerned for you more.
Emer	Nothing to be concerned about.
Peter	How will you get home?
Emer	I will sit here and wait 'til you are done.
Peter	We'll be at it a while yet.
Sarah	Rafter by rafter Roof goes up Bang bang Goes the hammer Each nail A hope A reason To stay Sun begins to settle Meeting land
Hugh	It is finished!
Sarah	My father says And starts his climb Sure-footed on Shaky ladder To the top The very top Of the barn
Hugh	Hullo, Sarah!
Sarah	Hello!
Hugh	What a view!
Sarah	What can you see?
Hugh	The whole world! I believe I can see the whole world – all the way back to Antrim. *[he waves.]* Afternoon, brother Henry. How ye doin'? I'm glad to hear it. Me? Oh I'm just dandy now. Can't complain. The farm? As well as can be expected for a man only here three years. Four times the size of your holding. And my barn's ten times the size of your'n!
Ruth	Get down from there before you fall and kill yourself you old fool.

Hugh	What do you think, wife?
Ruth	That you'll fall and kill yourself.
Hugh	The barn?! The barn?!
Ruth	It's good as any I've seen.
Hugh	Better I think.
Emer	It's still only firewood, not a treasure house yet.
Peter	Mother!
Ruth	Are you thirsty?
Hugh	I could drink a river.
Ruth	Lemonade's all I have.
Hugh	That'll do.
Ruth	Come down and get it then. There's refreshment here for you and the men. Sarah will pour it out for you. *[She hands jug to Sarah].* Don't spill it. There's just enough.
Sarah	Yes, Ma.
Ruth	Bring it back when you are done. I must get in out of this heat.

Ruth exits.

Michael	Look at you, a proper little Felimidh's wife. Dance with me.
Sarah	Michael mind!
Michael	Dance! Dance!

Sarah lets the jug fall.

Sarah	Oh God! Oh my God! It's broke.
Michael	It's only an old jug.
Sarah	Did anybody see?
Michael	I don't know.
Sarah	So stupid! What am I goin to do?
Michael	You can make more lemonade.
Sarah	No! Quick! Pick the pieces up.
Michael	Sarah, it's only a jug.

Ruth enters.

Sarah	I'm sorry.
Ruth	I told you to be careful.

Sarah	I know my Granny gave it to you.
Michael	It was my fault, Missus McCrea . . .
Sarah	It just fell outa my hand.
Michael	I was messing about and I bumped into her . . .
Sarah	I'm sorry, Ma.
Michael	I'll pay for it.

Ruth *[to Michael]* Have you no work to do?

Michael exits.

Sarah	I'm really, really sorry.
Ruth	All right, don't make a song and dance out of it.
Sarah	Maybe Granny will send you a new one if you ask her.
Ruth	I carried it with me the whole way here.
Sarah	Maybe we can get some of that glue and stick it back together again.
Ruth	It won't be fixed now.
Sarah	I can try.
Ruth	No. It's broken. Let it be

Scene Eleven

Sarah   Spring
Year of Our Lord
Nineteen hundred and sixteen
Arctic blast cold chill from the north
The ploughing begins
And
Father scatters seeds
In the pasture
Good grass sown from the seeds of home
And it grows.

Letter from home tells
More warriors in battle
Red Hand
Defending Ulster
Green Hand
Defending Ireland
Rise up
All
Defending
Heritage.

Scene Twelve

June 1916. Michael in the pasture. Michael reads from a copy of an Irish newspaper, The Worker's Republic. Sarah enters.

Sarah	Hey boy! What you doin?
Michael	I thought you were my father.
Sarah	Skivin are you?
Michael	Taking a break.
Sarah	I went up to the house to look for you. Your Granny says to give you this.

She gives him a bottle corked sloppily with paper.

Michael	Thanks.
Sarah	What're you doing out digging on a Sunday?
Michael	Peter says we're behind on the sowing.
Sarah	Remember the Sabbath day to sanctify it
Michael	Honour thy father and thy mother that thy days may be long upon the land which the Lord thy God giveth thee. I know my commandments as well as you.
Sarah	You might make a priest but you'll never make a farmer.
Michael	Good! If I have to stay here the rest of my life I'll go mad.
Sarah	Where else would you go?
Michael	Toronto or maybe St John. They're building three factories a day in the East.
Sarah	You can go only if you promise to take me with you.
Michael	It is my *geis.*
Sarah	For I have no desire to marry Robert Milling and spend the rest of my years wedded to my first cousin.
Michael	I hate him.
Sarah	You hardly even know him! He's asked my da to start courting me as soon as I'm sixteen.
Michael	What do you say?
Sarah	I say no.
Michael	He's a good catch. He's gonna be a lawyer. You could live in a big house in the city, have fancy clothes and a motor car.
Sarah	I don't want a motor car.
Michael	Don't have one then.

Sarah	And I don't want Robert Milling.
Michael	Then don't have him either.
Sarah	What're you reading?
Michael	Nothing?

She examines the newspaper.

Sarah [reads]	We must accustom ourselves to the notion of arms to the use of arms . . . Bloodshed is a cleansing and sanctifying thing, and the nation which regards it as the final horror has lost its manhood. There are many things more horrible than bloodshed and slavery is one of them.
Michael	Isn't it marvellous?
Sarah	Isn't it marvellous? No. It's a load of horse manure if ever I heard one.
Michael	You can't say that!
Sarah	Why not? I'll say it again if you like.
Michael	Sarah –
Sarah	Patrick Pearse is talkin a load of old horse man–
Michael	Give it back!
Sarah	No!
Michael	It's my newspaper.
Sarah	It should be torn up in squares for the outhouse!
Michael	Now!
Sarah	Come and get it.
Michael	You're being a child, Sarah!
Sarah	Oh, who's the big man now? Have it back – I don't want it.
Michael	Thank you.
Sarah	Thank you
Michael	Stop it!
Sarah	Stop it!
Michael	This is about freedom. You wouldn't understand.
Sarah	Then don't talk to me anymore.
Michael	I'm an Irishman.
Sarah	You're as Irish as the grass in the big pasture – the seed may have come from Ireland but the soil it grows in and the rain that waters it is Canadian.

Michael	I know more of Irish history than you do.
Sarah	I was born there.
Michael	I speak Irish.
Sarah	I was born there.
Michael	You don't have to be born in a country to belong to it.
Sarah	Your father says you're a Canadian and he should know.
Michael	The year before I was born Luke Dillon, the Fenian, tried to blow up the Welland Canal to stop –
Sarah	– Canada sending troops to the Boer War. You're not going to blow up any canals, Michael?!
Michael	Each generation for the past three hundred years has risen up to free our land of the British. It's tradition.
Sarah	It's murder. Another commandment broken.
Michael	Your lot started it all bringing guns in and killing Catholics in their beds at night.
Sarah	My lot?!
Michael	I'm sorry . . .
Sarah	Leave me alone.
Michael	Come on.
Sarah	Get away from me you, you – Fenian! . . .
Michael	It's only play
Sarah	You can't call it play when you get so worked up about it.
Michael	Deirdre was raised as Conor commanded. Every day she grew more beautiful. Her lips were red as berries and her hair as gold as corn as Cathbad has foretold . . .
Sarah	I'm not an idiot!

He moves towards her.

Michael	One day when it was snowing and cold as cold, Deirdre was watching her foster father preparing a young calf for the table. As he flayed the skin from its carcass, blood flowed out across the frozen snow and a raven circled overhead, ready to drink from the stream . . .
Sarah	If only I could meet a man like that, said Deirdre, with hair raven black and skin as white as snow and cheeks as red as blood.
Michael	"Luck is yours, Deirdre," replied Levercham. "For not far from here, at Emain Macha, there is such a man. His name is Naiose, a young warrior in the service of the king."

| Sarah | If that is true then I cannot rest until I have seen him. |

Scene Thirteen

November 1916. Donaghue farmstead. Emer sits alone, sewing.

Emer	Mihal's not here. He's gone to a meeting of the parish men with his father.
Sarah	Can I wait for him?
Emer	Step in and keep the cold out.
Sarah	I brought you this. It's Butter Pound.
Emer	Thank you. We are not big cake eaters in this house. I'm surprised your mother let you out a night like this.
Sarah	I'm on my way back from an errand to the Trimbles.
Emer	She doesn't know that you have come here?
Sarah	No.
Emer	Sit by the fire to warm yourself.
Sarah	Thank you.
Emer	You shouldn't walk the roads in such snow.
Sarah	I told Mike I would come . . . He said he'd teach me the set dancing.
Emer	What would you be wanting to learn all that for?
Sarah	He thinks I should know it. What do you make?
Emer	Nothing in particular. I sew for it's own sake.
Sarah	It's beautiful.
Emer	It's a pretty pattern.
Sarah	I'm a terrible needle-worker. My mother says I've a hand like a foot.
Emer	It's the eye that's important. As long as you can see you can sew.
Sarah	I must be blind then too.
Emer	Here.
Sarah	I'll ruin it.
Emer	No matter, it's only cotton. It can be ripped out and started over.
Sarah	What do I do?
Emer	Hold the needle like so.
Sarah	It's not the proper way.

Emer	There is no proper way, only what's comfortable. Is that better? Follow this line here. That's it. Now turn the stitch like so . . . A little too big. See. Like this.
Sarah	I'm no good at all.
Emer	All it takes is a bit of practice. Keep on with it. How is your mother?
Sarah	Well, thank you, though she always gets sick for home coming into the winter.
Emer	I've been here near seventy years and I still sicken for it.
Sarah	Why did you not go back?
Emer	I met my husband, a good Irishman, and he wanted to stay. We cleared our land, had our children. There was nothing to go back for.
Sarah	Except to see it again.
Emer	Here, give me your hand – the one on which you will wear your weddin ring . . . We used to do this when I was a girl. It tells your fortune. Now, I take the needle and rub it three times like this. Put your hand out flat, palm first.
Sarah	It circles.
Emer	That means you will have a boy. And again.
Sarah	Another boy.
Emer	Two sons is a good start. It swings. That's a girl. It's good to have one girl. No. No more. Ah well, two boys and a girl's not bad at all.

Michael and Peter enter.

Sarah	Good evening.
Peter	What are you doin out on a night like this?
Sarah	I came to have my dancing lesson.
Michael	I'm sorry we're late.
Peter	Dancing is it?
Michael	I'm gonna teach Sarah the set dancing.
Emer	I don't see what she needs to know all that for.
Peter	No better way to keep warm. *[to Sarah]* Have you been made welcome?
Emer	Of course she has! Do you think me unmannerly? I will make the tea.
Sarah	I brought you a cake.
Michael	Thank you. May I eat it now? I'm starving.
Emer	There's plenty here for you to eat.
Sarah	Your granny was tellin my fortune with the sewing needle. I'll have two boys and a girl she says.

Michael	They will be well-provided for with a lawyer for a father.
Sarah	Stop teasin me you!
Emer	What was the news?
Michael	Conscription! All the talk is of conscription. If it comes to it I'll not go.
Peter	Easy. They haven't done it yet. All's speculation, but you should have heard them flapping and quacking away like ducks as usual.
Michael	Better to be flapping now than shot in the head later.
Peter	Better a clear and reasoned head, Michael. *[to Sarah.]* What d'you think?
Sarah	Of conscription?
Peter	That's what I asked you.
Sarah	They need soldiers.
Peter	Would you go?
Sarah	I can't.
Michael	Dad –
Peter	Imagine.
Sarah	I wouldn't.
Peter	Why not?
Sarah	I don't understand it all, but –
Peter	Good answer.

Michael *[to Sarah]* Give me your coat.

Peter	We'd better clear the floor if we're to have dancing.
Emer	I don't see the call for all this fuss.
Peter	If he's to teach her, then he must teach her properly.
Michael	Right. I'll show you. Pretend we're standing in a circle. You're opposite me like this. Now I'll show you the basic steps. And one and two and three and cut and back and back and one two three four. See? Now you dance to me.

Sarah tries.

Michael	No come down on your heel at the last, like this.
Sarah	I can't.
Michael	It's easy once you practice. I'll do it with you.

He guides Sarah in the dance.

Peter	And one and two and three and cut . . . That's it!

Michael	We'll try again.
Emer	I'll show her. It's better a woman shows a woman how to do a woman's steps.
Michael	No. *[to Sarah.]* That's it.
Peter	Well done.
Michael	That's only the first part. Now, I dance round you like this . . . Now you dance round me.
Sarah	How am I doing?
Peter	You've got the spirit of it.
Michael	Now grab hold of my hands.
Emer	What're you doing, Mihal?
Michael	And we swing like this.
Emer	Be careful.

Michael begins turning Sarah round and round.

Peter	Give them space.

The dance quickens pace.

Michael	What d'you think? Am I a good teacher?
Sarah	You are.
Peter	It was fine. Wasn't it, mother?
Emer	Those weren't the right steps.
Peter	It's only a start. Only a start.

Blackout.

Act Two

Scene One
November 1916

Sarah	First nip of winter in the air
	Down to the city
	We go
	To bring in the supplies
	To take John
	To War.
	Quietly under darkness
	We creep
	Out of the house
	Children curled up in arms

And into the wagon
Horses clip clop
On heavy earth
Passing by
Sod huts of the Doukhobours
Passing through
At six road ends
Township of Stanley
Lot 42
Grist mill
Saw mill
Merchant shop
John Leaming from England
Two churches
Anglican
Presbyterian
Schoolhouse
Orange Hall
Passing through.
Passing along
Long deserted roads that will soon be
Flowing rivers of mud
Driving rain and sleet
Then frozen under snow.
Knife wind cuts through
On the plains
Stretching out on all sides
Ocean of land.
Morning wakes up
Before us lies
City on the horizon
Queen of the Plains
Regina
Capital of our province.
Slowly we haul into
Huge and heaving
Mess
Of mills
Factories
Shop fronts
Just opening up.
Big engine
Belching steam
Green carriages
New and shiny
Not to carry our cheap cheap wheat
But our men
On the platform

Tears
Embraces
Farewells
Engine blasts
One two
One two
And he is gone
My brother John
Not yet seventeen years
Off to fight
The enemy
Sixty thousands miles away.

Scene Two

November 1916. Regina. General store. Ruth and Sarah are sorting through materials. A sign reads: "No Ruthenians employed here."

Sarah	He'll be all right, Ma.
Ruth	D'you think so?
Sarah	Look how happy he was getting the train – he was dead proud of hisself.
Ruth	Pride'll be no shield to him. I wonder at you father letting him go like that.
Sarah	Mammy, he wanted to go.
Ruth	Thousands of them dead already.
Sarah	Our John'll not let anybody kill him. He told me he was coming back with a German's helmet as a souvenir.
Ruth	Have you all the bags?
Sarah	Aye.
Ruth	Shoes . . . Shirts . . .
Sarah	What's that sign mean?
Ruth	It's to discourage the immigrants seeking work. How many boxes of that liquorice did you lift?
Sarah	Two.
Ruth	I said three. We'll have to go back to the confectioners . . .
Sarah	Why don't they want them?
Ruth	Because there's too many of them and they've no English. Now, material for the winter dresses.
Sarah	How much do we need?
Ruth	Now, let's see you and I are of a size. I'd say that's twenty yards. Mind now, we only have fifteen dollars to spend.

Sarah	But my daddy gave you near sixty dollars.
Ruth	Shh! D'ye want everybody to hear?

They begin to sort through lengths of material.

Sarah	How about this one?
Ruth	Too gaudy. Something simpler I think.
Sarah	This one?

Emer enters.

Ruth	Too expensive. This one here is good, but not so warm. Oh, well we'll just have to wear extra layers. If only you were able to help me, but you're like a spider weaving its web with a needle in your hand!

Sarah *[to Emer]* Hello.

Emer	Hello, Sarah.
Ruth	Missus Donaghue.
Emer	Missus McCrea. I see we all have the same idea today.
Ruth	It's that time of year.
Emer	Now that is a pretty sort of fabric.
Ruth	I was just saying that.
Emer	Poor quality though. But sure when you haven't much you must make it go further.
Ruth	Isn't that so. Sarah, we'll take the velveteen.
Sarah	I thought it was too expensive.
Ruth	Not at all. It'll be far warmer to wear. This one's more a Spring fabric – I told you that. We'll take that one.
Emer	'Tis a lovely job of work, dress-making. I had no daughters to sew pretty dresses for. No granddaughters neither, only big strappin boys in our stock. Y'have no sons yourself?
Ruth	Four as you know. The oldest, John, is just left for the War.
Emer	That must distress you sorely.
Ruth	He goes to do his duty. So we must be proud of him. I wonder at your grandson's not going.
Emer	I do not. Why would he be fighting for the British?
Ruth	I think we come from different stock.
Emer	I'm sure we do. Now this here is a fine material. Good heavy winter cloth. Only two

dollars a yard. I think I shall have myself ten yards of it. Good day to you, Missus McCrea.

Ruth   Good day.

Emer   Good day, Sarah. I'll be seeing you again soon, no doubt. Your daughter and my grandson, Mihal are friendly, y'know.

Ruth   They're acquainted I believe.

Emer   Oh, not just acquainted, but thick, very thick. We can't keep them apart. Good day again.

Emer exits.

Ruth   You go up to that woman's house?

Sarah   I've been there.

Ruth   Often?

Sarah   Several times.

Ruth   What would your father say if he knew?

Sarah   Where's the harm in it?

Ruth   Harm?! Making love to a Catholic.

Sarah   I'm making love to nobody.

Ruth   Your father a leading member of the Order.

Sarah   I know that.

Ruth   With a Catholic for a son-in-law. What are you thinking of?!

Sarah   Mother, people'll hear you.

Ruth   Don't tell me to be quiet!

Sarah   I didn't.

Ruth   This would never happen at home. Your grandfather wouldn't let the like of this go on, I'm telling you.

Sarah   Are we takin this material or that one?

Ruth   You would know all about it he your grandfather was here.

Sarah   For God's sake, Ma!

Ruth   You thank heaven we are in a public place . . . Never swear at me!

Sarah   All right.

Ruth   And never ever go there again, d'you hear me? There's an end to it.

Scene Three

Spring 1918.

Sarah   Spring
        Nineteen hundred and eighteen
        Awakens us
        Out of frozen sleep
        America turns its hand
        To a different plough
        War Machine
        To dig it up
        Plough it up
        Churn it up
        Europe
        More guns
        More mines
        More dead
        All along the Western Front
        Boom Boom
        Boom Boom

Scene Four

June 1918. The boundary between the Donaghue and McCrea farmsteads.

Peter   It was a hard frost last night.

Hugh   Very hard for June.

Peter   You're planted early.

Hugh   At Easter.

Peter   I wait until these few trees are in full leaf. The spring warmth is deceptive.

Hugh   There's some damage done, I think.

Peter   It usually comes about now. Think you've got a good crop and then it's gone.

Hugh   The weather here is surely differ'nt to home.

Peter   May I take a look?

Peter examines a head of grain.

Peter   Red Fife?

Hugh   I suppose you've planted Marquis?

Peter   It withstands the frost better. Gives a larger yield.

Hugh   Everybody's all Marquis wheat these days.

Peter   It's hard to keep up.

Hugh	Oh, I keep up all right. I bought me a new plough and two more horses there a month or so back.
Peter	On loan?
Hugh	Aye, but I have doubled my acreage this year.
Peter	I got a new seeder.
Hugh	On loan?
Peter	No, bought it outright. The head's glassy that's a tell-tale sign, and see, there's the white ring circling the stalk.
Hugh	It's ruined then?
Peter	Maybe. Maybe not.
Hugh	We'll pay the note back. We will. If wheat prices just holds at the two dollars.
Peter	You must strip the heads and quick about it.
Hugh	Where do I cut?
Peter	At the first joint below the head, like this. See? I'll give you a hand.
Hugh	You can spare the time?
Peter	I won't finish this today. I seem to have lost my helper, again.
Hugh	It's hard when they don't take after you.
Peter	They must go their own way. You're short-handed yourself.
Hugh	I hired me a few men. One from the Ukraine and a Doukhobour boy. I get twice as much work done myself in a day than the two of them together.
Peter	They will not play the servant here.
Hugh	Bolsheviks – all of them! And argue over pay terrible. I miss my John. But we will have him back for harvest if God spares him.
Peter	You'd word from him, I hear.
Hugh	Yesterday.
Peter	Good news that he is safe.
Hugh	We thought we had lost him he was wounded at Vimy.
Peter	That's honorable.
Hugh	Aye. He is a brave lad. How is it that your boy doesn't go?
Peter	He doesn't want to.
Hugh	He's one of the few young lads his age about here not volunteered yet. Does he sicken or something?

Peter   No. He just has his own mind.

Hugh   His own?

Sarah and Michael in the pasture.

Michael   Naiose and his brothers undertook brave missions for the Scottish King.

Sarah   Deirdre kept a veil over her face at all times, lest the King see how beautiful she was.

Michael   And the king wondered what lay behind the veil.

Sarah   One morning, before the day had woken up, the King's steward stole into the brothers' encampment. Coming upon the lovers asleep in an embrace,

Michael   His eyes fell upon the face of Deidre. And he wept, so beautiful was she.

Sarah   Returning swiftly to the King, he said,

Michael   Sire this morning I saw the most beautiful woman in the world. She lies beside Naiose. Let's kill him as he sleeps and take her for your own.

Sarah   No, said the King. I will win her love a different way. Each day, the King sent his steward secretly to Deirdre.

Michael   Most beautiful lady, the King of Scotland loves you. He asks you to leave this warrior and come to be his wife.

Sarah   I will not go, she said, for I am promised to another.

Michael   But the King would not take no for an answer. Each day he sent the steward to woo her.

Sarah   And each night, when Naiose returned Deirdre told him everything.

Michael   Close your eyes.

Sarah   Why?

Michael   Just do it.

Sarah   What is it?

He puts a strawberry up to her lips.

Sarah   Strawberries!

Michael   I grew them myself.

Sarah   I thought the frost had killed them all.

Michael   Not these ones. Are they sweet?

Sarah   No, but not bitter neither. Sort of in between. Taste.

Peter and Hugh hacking at the wheat.

Peter   How much is rotted?

Hugh	About half.
Peter	I'm sorry.
Hugh	Those boys over in Winnipeg have it all sown up.
Peter	We must stick together. I wonder that you don't join the League of Farmers.
Hugh	We never had such things in Antrim. Sure we had meetings, but not organised demonstrations.
Peter	And that's why you're farming wheat in Canada now instead of flax back home.
Hugh	It smacks of socialism to me.
Peter	What else are we to do? This government's sympathy lies, not in people but in profit.
Hugh	We must all get behind the war effort, that's what I told our John.
Peter	If the new settlers want to go, let them go. They are still wedded to the old country. We Canadians have other business.
Hugh	You don't back the war?
Peter	Oh, it's not the war that bothers me. Let them fight it – it's a just enough war. It's this Conscription business I don't like.
Hugh	You Catholics is all opposed to it.
Peter	Nothing to do with being Catholic. Canada's a nation on her own, free to fight her own wars, not the rest of the world's.
Hugh	That's Fenian talk where I come from.
Peter	Where you come from maybe. Here, it's just progress.

Sarah and Michael in the pasture.

Michael	The King began to grow impatient.
Sarah	He set traps for Naiose and his brothers.
Michael	He ambushed them.
Sarah	He sent them alone into battle against hundreds of enemies.
Michael	But each time the brothers survived.
Sarah	One day the King's steward came to Deirdre and said
Michael	You must leave Naiose and come willingly to the King as his bride or be taken away by force and your lover and his brothers slain.
Sarah	I will not go with you, she said. Do you know what would go beautiful with these just now?
Michael	What?

Sarah	Silverwoods ice cream. You ever had it?
Michael	Not Silverwoods.
Sarah	When we first came into Toronto we ate Silverwoods ice cream.
Michael	When Naiose returned that night she told him of the King of Scotland's treachery.
Sarah	We must leave Scotland.
Michael	So away they fled, fugitives adrift on the sea once more . . . I've never been to Toronto.
Sarah	Never?
Michael	Not even once. Furthest I've been, excepting where I was born, is Winnipeg.
Sarah	Look at me! I'm covered!
Michael	Lips as red as berries you have.
Sarah	Little seeds pop pop popping.

Sweet like sugar cane.
Sugar sweet little strawberry kiss.
Flutter belly like jumping off
High tree into stream.
Hands grapple my hands.
Arms holding him
Fingertips firm pressing into my shoulder
Hands on my hands, my legs
Hands up and under my skirt to my
Belly
So close
Skin on skin
His touch
Feather soft
Oh he is beautiful!
Scent of his hair all meadow perfume.
Eyelash tickle on my cheek
This is not a bad thing.
I bury myself
I rise and fall on him
Like the big ship on the ocean.
Bad.
No.
Not bad.
Not me.
Never.
Between my legs he rests.
And his hair is soft as hay.
Like good hay sown from the grass seed
Sent in the crease of the letter from home.

No, not home.
This is home.

Scene Five

June 1918. The McCrea farmstead.

Ruth   What's lost?

Hugh   Near all except forty acres.

Ruth   What's to be done?

Hugh   The oats will be alright. We'll have to make oor money out of those. The bildin of the new hoose will hae tae wait a while. *[to Sarah]* Ye've been goin up to the Donaghue house.

Sarah   So I have.

Hugh   Often?

Sarah   Only once or twice.

Ruth   Didn't I tell you not to go up there?

Sarah   You did.

Ruth   I warned you.

Hugh   Hush, Ruth. *[to Sarah.]* I don't like it that you see Michael Donaghue so much.

Sarah   I don't see him often.

Ruth   Yes you do.

Sarah   He's a neighbour.

Hugh   No one's tellin you not to be neighbourly. Just break the habit of seeing him alone.

Sarah   Why?

Ruth   Sarah!

Hugh   No, it's a straightforward question. *[to Sarah]* I dunnae like his father's politics.

Sarah   His father never talks about Ireland.

Hugh   Whatever he thinks of Ireland is his own concern.

Sarah   Then what is it?

Hugh   They're Republicans through and through.

Sarah   They're Canadians.

Hugh   That's the same thing in my book.

Sarah   No it's not.

Hugh	Are you contradictin me? I'll have nae truck with Republicans.
Sarah	All I'm sayin is, da, this here's a new country. You're always tellin us that.
Hugh	There's some things that shouldnae be forgot.
Sarah	More things that shouldnae be remembered.
Hugh	Where does she get these notions from?
Ruth	Where do you think?
Sarah	I get them from myself. It's my own opinion.
Hugh	Opinions is it now?

Ruth *[to Hugh]* You've brought it on yourself.

Hugh	Well, here's an opinion for ye: it turns me to think o'you wi' him.
Sarah	He's my friend.
Ruth	I hope friends is all it is.
Hugh	Ruth . . .
Ruth	Well, is it?
Sarah	Friends is all.
Ruth	I've never made friends of a Cathelicke in my life. Their bigotry is too much.
Sarah	Michael's people are good, kind people, ma.
Hugh	Better see him nae more in future.
Sarah	I can't just stop speaking to him, Daddy.
Ruth	You do as you're told to do.
Sarah	He's my friend.
Hugh	Alright, you've done nae wrong. He's on'y your friend and that was fine while youse were children but youse're near grown now. Things is differ'nt when you're grown.
Sarah	I don't see how.
Hugh	Because people is all differ'nt. D'ye understand?
Sarah	I understand.
Hugh	There now. You willnae see him again sure ye won't?
Sarah	No.
Hugh	D'ye promise me? . . . See him again I'll be hard on you. D'ye hear?
Sarah	I hear.

Hugh	And if he comes here to see you . . . Come on! There are plenty more young men to take your fancy, eh? There's young Robert Milling, soon to be a lawyer like his father and his grandfather before him. He still pays you attention.
Sarah	I thought it was unnatural to marry a cousin.
Ruth	It could be worse.

Scene Six

November 1918

Sarah	Fall
	Leaves
	On gold fields
	War
	No more
	Germany
	Turkey
	Austria
	All fall down
	Bow
	To righteous
	Empire
	No more
	Boom Boom
	Armistice
	End
	Half come home
	Of those who went
	And some of they
	Are only half
	Of what they were.
	Brother John returns
	But not to harvest.
	Hollow as reed
	Pale as milk
	All a-tremble
	Screaming
	Terror
	Sweat lashing
	She rock-a-byeing him in her arms
	Sayin
Ruth	There, there my son. You're alright now. You're home.

Scene Seven

November 1918. The pasture.

Sarah	He saw men lyin dead.
Michael	And killed too.
Sarah	I expect so. He won't say more about it.
Michael	Things can start moving in Ireland again. There will be elections for the new parliament next month. We will be a Republic before Christmas.
Sarah	Don't talk to me about that!
Michael	It's important.
Sarah	It's all anyone can speak of now – you, my father.
Michael	Where'd you say you'd gone?
Sarah	Into Stanley, to Leaming's for cotton.
Michael	That's not a good lie.
Sarah	They'd never think that I'd lie to them, so one lie's as good as another.
Michael	I don't like sneaking about like a criminal.
Sarah	Then don't come and meet me anymore.
Michael	Take your hair down . . . I like the look of it that way. It's a woman's hair.
Sarah	Look above. What a sight!
Michael	Sharp-shins going south. All the way down to Florida.
Sarah	There's thousands of them.
Michael	They're flying high.
Sarah	Means a hard winter.
Michael	Wouldn't you just love to be away up there with them?
Sarah	Why don't we go?
Michael	Where?
Sarah	Toronto, like you said.
Michael	I'd go to the United States or British Columbia. There's farms to be had up there.
Sarah	Think again, you're no farmer –
Michael	Toronto it is then.
Sarah	When'll we go?
Michael	In the Springtime, after the planting.

Sarah	Why not today?
Michael	Today it is then.
Sarah	What'll we do there?
Michael	Go to Silverwoods dairy.
Sarah	We could get married.
Michael	What do you mean?
Sarah	What I said.
Michael	We can't do that.
Sarah	Who says?
Michael	The Pope.
Sarah	Why not?
Michael	If we don't pray in the same church together we can't marry.
Sarah	I think we've done worse than pray together, Mike.
Michael	I know that.
Sarah	So I'm to give you this all for nothing?
Michael	It's not for nothing I hope.
Sarah	You tell me. All's I know is I've given you all of me. Do you love me?
Michael	Sarah?!
Sarah	Tell me.
Michael	Yes.
Sarah	What's the matter? I can say it. I love Michael Donaghue! I'd tell anybody.
Michael	Taím i ngrá leat.
Sarah	In English.
Michael	I love you. Now you say it in Irish.
Sarah	Tam i ngrá leat.
Michael	That's terrible!
Sarah	Then to hell with the Pope!
Michael	Shhh! Don't say that, Sarah.
Sarah	Why not? He can't hear me.
Michael	You're a rebel, d'you know that? You're a hardened revolutionary, Sarah McCrea.

Scene Eight

The McCrea farmstead. The kitchen place.

Hugh	So you're returned.
Sarah	I have.
Hugh	Where'd ye go?
Sarah	Out walking across the fields
Hugh	On your own?
Sarah	You know I wasn't. She saw me.
Ruth	Who do you call "she"?
Hugh	Ah, Sarah. Sarah, what did I tell ye?
Ruth	Remember what ye said, Hugh.
Hugh	What possessed ye after all we talked about?
Ruth	Hugh?
Hugh	I know what I said. *[to Sarah]* What did I say til ye?
Sarah	That I was to walk out with Michael Donaghue no more.
Hugh	But you did so.
Sarah	I did.
Hugh	Sarah . . .
Ruth	Headstrong she is.
Hugh	Alright, alright. I'm tryin to talk til her!
Ruth	Talk til her! How many times have you talked til her?
Hugh	Will ye leave it in my hands.
Ruth	She cannae carry on like this. You the one said it. Soft!
Hugh	Soft, am I now?
Ruth	No weak. D'ye hear me? Weak. You backed up arguing with your father about your share of the land being willed away to Henry.
Hugh	Don't start on that again, missus. My father was dyin –
Ruth	No matter! You backed up and let the land go making yourself no better than a hired hand . . .
Hugh	Christ, ye have to back years –
Ruth	Don't curse!

Hugh	Ye always have to go back years! Every bloody difference we have . . .
Ruth	Bringin us away across here to this place to make a somethin out of nothin.
Hugh	To make us a fortune!
Ruth	To live in a sod hut, break our backs and lose a child and not a word have I ever spoken –
Hugh	You say plenty. In words and in looks, always downin me.
Ruth	I only ever worked to raise you up.
Hugh	Shut your mouth now!
Ruth	I tell you this and I tell you no more: you give into this one here the night and ye'll surely have a Fenian for a son-in-law. I will not stand by and see our blood mixed in with that. Now either you do what you said you would or I'll do it myself.

Pause.

Hugh undoes the belt from around his waist.

Hugh	Come here to me, you.
Sarah	He says. But it is he who moves towards me. And I look into my father's eyes There is something else now apart from fear. I want to say "No, Daddy. Don't beat me and I will never see him again." But the words don't come. They cannot. A draft creeps in under the door across the floor, around my ankles And up under my skirt. I shiver. Then I say to myself, "It is *his* touch, in the big pasture When I ate strawberries and kissed him My mouth full of the sweet taste." He grasps the belt in the necessary place. I hear her draw breath.
Ruth	Now you'll listen.
Sarah	She says. First crack of pain Flying forwards Left arm across my chest Winded flying backwards Slam onto table I close my eyes. Make no sound He is breathing hard

Second third fourth crack come down across my spine.

He stops after each blow
Waitin
For a tear, a plea, a cry
I give him nothing.

Ruth   Enough now.

Sarah   He's not listenin
I hear buckle clunk on floor
He tosses belt to one side
Grabs me by shoulders
Throws me backwards
We are dancin.
One and two and three and cut
And back and back and one two three four.
Round the room
I travel
Little Fall leaf blown about on gusts of rage.
Hittin me now with hand open
Bang on this side of the head
Bang on the other
Round and round we go

Ruth   Enough, now! Hugh!

Sarah   Against the wall.
Against the floor.
Against the door
Under table
Tumblin on my back
Feet chase me to the other side
Hands drag me up again
And bang on this side of the head
And bang on the other
And bang in the face
Mouth fills with thick salt taste
She is screamin now

Ruth   Stop! Stop!

Sarah   He does not stop
And back and back and fall to the floor . . .
It is cold.
Soothin
I open up one eye.
The little ones are at the doorway.
I hear them
Cryin.

Hugh crosses to pick up his belt. Ruth addresses the crying children.

Ruth   Go now, up to bed the lot of you. Upstairs this minute or I'll give youse all somethin to cry about.

Sarah still lies on the floor.

Ruth *[to Sarah]* Sit up.

Sarah raises herself off the floor.

Hugh   You don't see him no more.

Ruth   Sarah?

Sarah   Yes, Daddy.

Hugh   D'ye hear me?

Ruth   She hears you. She hears you.

Sarah remains lying on the floor.

Scene Nine

Spring 1919. The Donaghue farmstead.

Peter   A man maybe he uses up all he has, maybe he didn't have much to begin with, or maybe he just wants more. So what's he do? He goes exploring. He comes across something good, rich – a big diamond ring say. "I'll have that for myself," he says. Now what do we call that?

Michael   Dad, I'm late already.

Peter   Then be late. When it comes to a good piece of land, we call that pioneering. Now this pioneer gets caught red-handed by the man was there before him – the owner. Or we'll call him the owner at present because he probably stole the ring off of the man who came before him. But our pioneer y'see, he doesn't want to back off because he wants to keep this good thing he's found. So he fights the owner, beats him back or kills him.

Emer   How's Sarah?

Michael   I don't know.

Peter   Finally, our settler, he looks at this beautiful gold ring and he thinks to himself, "What use is the ring to me like this, I'm not gonna wear it. I want some hard cash." So he melts it down, breaks the big stone into little pieces, sells it off and makes a profit.

Emer *[to Michael]* Have you had a falling out?

Michael   No.

Peter   Now the previous owner might see that as destruction . . .

Emer *[to Michael]* That's good.

Peter	. . . but to the settler that's progress.
Michael	And that's what happened in Ireland.
Peter	And what are we doing here except farming land that never belonged to us?
Emer	It's not the same thing at all, Peader.
Michael	This country belonged to land agents.
Peter	And before them?
Michael	You didn't fight the Indians for the farm, Peter.
Peter	No. The French took the land from the Indians and then the English took it from the French. There were a few Dutch mixed up in it somewhere too. Whichever way you look at it, I bought a little piece of the diamond. So what do you want to do, Mike? After I'm dead, you want to trek up north to the reservation, find the big chief and give him the deed to the farm?
Michael	No.
Peter	No?
Emer	Leave him be.
Michael	Alright then, yes! Yes I do.
Peter	Good for you! That's integrity. But which one of the Plains owns it? The Metis, or is it the Cree or the Alongquipin?
Michael	I'll give it to them that originally owned it.
Peter	They all owned it one time or another. Be careful what you're getting into Michael.
Emer	It's only meetings. *[to Michael.]* Go on now.
Peter	I've heard whispers that there's more planned than talk.
Michael	What've you heard?
Peter	That they've been burning barns over near Hamilton.
Emer	He'd never get mixed up in all that.
Michael	That was in retaliation for –
Peter	If you're going to fight, do it out in the open.
Michael	For an attack on a Catholic farmer's livestock by a group of Loyalists.
Peter	None of this jumping about in shadows.
Michael	You're sounding like McCrea.
Peter	We don't disagree on everything.
Michael	He beats her.

Emer   For friendship with you?

Michael   He tells her that if I go there, she will suffer for it.

Peter   That's hard.

Michael   What do I do about that then, father?

Emer   Just what you are doing – let it go.

Michael *[to Peter]* Tell me, honest.

Peter   Is she a good girl, Michael?

Michael   I believe it.

Peter   Does she believe the same of you?

Michael   More than I believe of myself.

Peter   Then if you want her, take her to you and let no one come between.

Michael crosses to where Sarah still lies, picks her up and holds her.

Scene Ten

Autumn 1919.

Sarah   Day to day
Small army marches farm to farm
Harvesting
They come
Bagging hook and basket armed
Under blue so big
Hazy heat broods over
Red wheat splashed white with barley
All hands to
Reap and bind and bale
Scalded green lies the plain
Fruits of the earth in their season
Gathered in
Safe in the big barn it lies
And thank we all our God.
But we do not live by bread alone
Not us

Scene Eleven

Late September 1919. Harvest Fair, Yorkton.

Sarah   For now comes
The Fair
Cold sunshine
Sweet breeze

                    Apples pears plums
                    Taties carrots cabbages
                    Barrow by barrow
                    All in a row
                    Our barrow
                    Butter and eggs

Ruth   Twelve dollars and forty eight cents.

Sarah   Is that all?

Ruth   Enough to buy a few bits of groceries for the winter.

Sarah   Swarm
                    Stanley
                    Six road ends
                    Do I hear
                    Trading
                    Twelve dollars
                    Twelve
                    Fourteen dollars
                    Do I hear
                    Fourteen
                    Clydesdales
                    Apaloosians
                    Fourteen
                    Ponies
                    Steers
                    Stallions
                    Street running
                    Up and down
                    Sixteen dollars
                    Eighteen dollars
                    Eighteen
                    Do I hear
                    Twenty
                    Twenty dollars
                    Black stallion
                    Twelve hands high
                    Rearing

Hugh enters.

Ruth   Well?

Hugh   They're sold.

Ruth   How much?

Hugh   Twelve dollars each.

Ruth   That'll not pay even interest on the note.

Hugh   Look, missus I know that, but the two animals was near done out. Donaghue has offered me for the pasture land – six hundred dollars.

Ruth   We must sell the machinery.

Hugh   Who'll buy it? Samuel says that he'll make us a loan if we need it.

Ruth   We cannot take it.

Hugh   What would you do? Starve.

Ruth   You've accepted then? *[to Sarah]* Go and give two pennies each to the boys for spending. Tell them not to be wasting it.

Hugh   I've told Robert Milling that you'll dance wi' him the night.

Sarah   Why?

Hugh   What d'ye mean why? Because he asked me and I said yes.

Sarah   I don't want to go to the dance.

Hugh   Aye, ye do! Girls love the dancing.

Sarah   Ma?!

Ruth   She's tired, Hugh. We've been working all day.

Hugh   After all the Millings have done for us?

Ruth   That doesn't make a match.

Hugh *[to Sarah]* In the name of God, just dance wi' the fella.

Ruth   Let her alone, Hugh.

Hugh   I've told him now.

Sarah   So I walk with him
My cousin
Heavy arm on my shoulders Organ grinding rusty tune
Round roll-a penny booth
Round merry-go-round
Up and down
Swing boats
Pull on a rope
And up up we go
And down down
Sick I am
His chimney breath
Choking me
I will not dance with you
Says I.
You will, says he
And lifts me up

> And so it begins
> Turning me
> Burling me
> Round and round
> Til I can hardly stand
> Never mind
> Place one foot in front of the other

Michael   Enjoying yourself?

Sarah   Do I look like I'm enjoyin myself?

Michael   That's a handsome young man you've got there.

Sarah   He looks like a pig.

Michael   Now you must have him if daddy says you must.

Sarah   I will not have him.

Michael   I think you will.

Sarah   Dance with me.

Michael   No . . . Here?

Sarah   Yes, here. Why not here?

Michael   No.

Sarah   Why not?

Michael   Alright then. When Conor the King heard of the lovers' flight he said

Sarah   Let them return to Emain Macha.

Michael   He sent Fergus, a warrior of honour, and his own son, Cormac, to meet them.

Sarah   But on the way he laid a trap for them. What's that smell on you?

Michael   Nothing.

Sarah   Smoke.

Michael   We were burning up the chaff yesterday is all.

Sarah   James Lightbody's hay rick was burned last night.

Michael   Was it?

Sarah   He ambushed the lovers and a bloody battle raged. Naiose was slain, but not before he had pierced Cormac's throat and killed him.

Hugh breaks into the dance and whisks Sarah away. He dances with her.

Hugh   Isn't he some dancer now? Shift you!

He dances Sarah away from Michael.

Hugh	What're you doin? Heh? What?
Sarah	I'm only dancin.
Hugh	D'ye know what he is?
Sarah	No. What is he, Daddy?
Hugh	Don't try an' make a fool out of me.
Sarah	I'm not the one doin that.
Hugh	You will dance with Robert Milling.
Sarah	I won't.
Hugh	By Christ, I'll kill ye.
Michael	Mister McCrea!
Hugh	Get away from me. Get away and stay away.
Sarah	Mike –
Hugh	Shut up!
Michael	I'm telling you, Mister McCrea.
Hugh	Somebody better go quick and get this wee bastard's da.
Ruth	Now, Hugh, there's people looking.
Michael	I'm no bastard.
Hugh	Aren't ye? That's no' what I heard. I heard your mammy was a travellin stage whore who'd been tossed by every man up in the Klondike.

Michael goes for Hugh.

Peter	Mike!
Michael	Did you hear what he said?
Peter	Let him have his opinions. It makes no difference to me.
Hugh	Right, Big Man, get this wee fella of yours to hell's gates or I'll send him there myself.
Peter	Let's go, son.
Hugh	And keep him away from me and mine.
Peter	He goes where he wants. I put no rein on him.
Hugh	Well you tether him or I'll leather him! You, thinkin so much of yersel'. So right about all things.
Michael	Did you hear what he said. Do something!
Peter	What would you have me do, Mike?

Michael	Defend us.
Peter	Against what? Ignorance?
Hugh	D'ye think? I know all about you. And I'm telling you, I'll not have my line soiled with that.
Michael	Damn you!
Ruth	Sarah, come here.
Emer	Hugh McCrea! Hugh McCrea. Take your hands off my grandson . . . There'll be no more of this. *[to Michael.]* Get over here now and stand beside me. Sarah, go to your mother.
Hugh	Keep out of this!
Emer	I will not.
Hugh	I do not want to lay eyes on this young Fenian near my daughter in future.
Emer	If you would listen a moment.
Hugh	Tell the oul woman to shut up!
Emer	I'm no oul woman . . .
Hugh	Look, missus. This isn't an argument for you.
Emer	Oh be quiet man, I'm agreeing with ye. I certainly want no more of my blood mixed in with your sort. One of your lot was enough.
Peter	If you shame me in public, mother . . .
Emer	You can do that with no help from me, standing there letting this Puritan talk to you like a child. It's the two of you that's at fault. You let it run on too long. Do you see what happens? If I thought a marriage would come out of this . . . Mharaodh se me. An glsoiseann tú méa, Mhicil?
Peter	Don't blackmail him.
Emer	Do you understand me? I want an end to this business. Here's what will happen. Michael will keep away from Sarah. I will see to it if I have to chain him to my wrist, I'll see to it.
Michael	Mamo.
Emer	I didn't ask you to speak. What a carry on this is! And if he doesn't keep to it, then we will send him away to work.
Peter	Am I allowed to speak?
Emer	Indeed not. Sure what have you ever said that's any use at all. *[to Hugh and Ruth.]* The rest is your concern. There will be no more lending of tools or helping hands or even a word spoke between us from this day on. Fair enough?
Hugh	Fair enough.

Emer	Good. *[to Sarah.]* Now you, go home with your mother and father and do as they tell you. *[to Hugh.]* That girl you have's a fine, clever, honest, young woman. And if I hear you've been less than good 'til her, I'll come after you and rattle your skull for you, Hugh McCrea.

Scene Twelve

Spring 1920. Night. Outside the Donaghue house. Sarah waits hidden.

Peter	I told him to be back here before midnight.
Emer	Why would he hurry back? To get more of your lecturing him?
Peter	Will you go inside? It's too cold to be standing about.
Emer	I'm warm enough. You never leave him alone
Peter	I won't have this anymore.
Emer	He's of age. He can do as he wishes.

Emer takes a fit of coughing.

Peter	Are you alright?
Emer	Nothing but a cough and a splutter.
Peter	Here, sit down.
Emer	There's nothing to worry about, Peadar.
Peter	Where is he?
Emer	He's gone into Stanley for a meeting.
Peter	Again?
Emer	It's good for him to be interested?
Peter	In what? Getting himself killed?
Emer	Don't talk such nonsense.
Peter	Joseph Trimble's bull was found lying in a ditch with its throat slit.
Emer	Who'd do a thing like that?
Peter	You tell me. And what about these fire-settings?
Emer	Families feuding . . .
Peter	It frightens me. He doesn't tell me where he goes when he leaves the house anymore. He won't even lower himself to lie about it.
Emer	It happens when you let them run free.
Peter	I know the fault lies with me: leaving him to you for all these years to go filling his head with romantic nonsense about the Old Country and coffin ships and martyred rebels.

Emer	I only told him his history?
Peter	That's not history.
Emer	Ah, what more should I expect from you who hasn't been to mass this past twenty years.
Peter	I will not attend the church that refused to recognise my marriage.
Emer	She was married before.
Peter	And mistreated, deserted, divorced. Mine to marry by law.
Emer	And a Protestant.
Peter	Still on at that. Over twenty years ago!
Emer	How could it recognise such a marriage?
Peter	Well, I recognise it! And to hell with you and the Pope and anyone else who doesn't!

Emer's coughing fit returns.

Peter	Come, inside.

Emer goes inside. Peter waits a few moments. Then he goes into the house. Michael appears. He is tired. He looks to see if lights are on in the house.

Sarah	Hey, Donaghue.
Michael	Where are you?
Sarah	Over here! You're gettin warmer, warmer, hot, hot, hot!
Michael	Sssh! What're you doin here?
Sarah	Aren't you pleased to see me?
Michael	Your fathers give you the gears.
Sarah	He'll be late home and he'll be full. There's a lodge meetin tonight.
Michael	Well my grandmother'll kill the both of us if she catches us.
Sarah	I had to come.
Michael	It's okay.
Sarah	Where've you been?
Michael	At the parish.
Sarah	What for?
Michael	Just a meetin.
Sarah	Ah, Michael!
Michael	One of De Valera's right hand men. The room was packed wall to wall with men

come to hear him. I had to pull myself up onto a table to stop myself getting crushed. You should've heard him, Sarah! "Ireland as tirelessly struggled for her freedom since the hour she was first put in chains. Now our day has come at last. A parliament has been set up, the true government of the Free Nation of Ireland. The organisation of which you are members has set up a committee to arm the Defenders of Ireland. I see young men in this room, and it fires my blood. Young exiled sons of Ireland, do not despise your youth. Young comrades in Canada, join us in our struggle . . ." You're not listening to me.

Sarah	I am.
Michael	Sarah, I was right there in the room with him.
Sarah	He's just a man, Mike, like any other.
Michael	He fought right beside James Connolly during the Uprising. He reloaded his gun for him.
Sarah	Good for him! I'm listening.
Michael	And we all stood up and waved our fists in the air, and someone started singing, "A nation once again, a nation once again". And we all joined in, "And Ireland long a province be a nation once again." It was brilliant.
Sarah	My father says the Bolsheviks are takin over the whole world.
Michael	Loyalist bastard!
Sarah	Don't call him that.
Michael	You're defending him?

She moves towards him.

Sarah	What's happened you?
Michael	Nothing.
Sarah	Don't give me nothin, Mike, you're hurt.
Michael	I got into a fight.
Sarah	Who with?
Michael	Your sweetheart, Robert Milling.
Sarah	He's no love of mine.
Michael	And John.
Sarah	John?
Michael	Them and six others. They sort of bumped into me on the way back home.
Sarah	Were they drunk?
Michael	Stone cold sober.

Sarah	I'll gut him! I told you nothin good would come of all this Deval, Davel, De Van . . .
Michael	De Valera.
Sarah	Aye, whatever his name is
Michael	"What sort of meetin's this?" Johnny boy says. So I told him. "Youse are raisin money to buy guns for murderers," he says. Then they laid into me. Feet and all.

Peter enters.

Sarah	Will you come tomorrow to the stream?
Michael	I can't.
Sarah	Will you come?
Michael	Yes! Go home.
Sarah	I'll wait for you.

Sarah exits.

Peter	Where've you been?
Michael	Into Stanley.
Peter	To do what?
Michael	To meet with friends.
Peter	We're calling them friends now? I thought we agreed no more meetings.
Michael	You may have done so.
Peter	You know what kind of a district we live in.
Michael	I'm going to bed.
Peter	I haven't finished yet. Michael! Don't walk away from me! *[Noticing his wounds.]* What's happened to you?
Michael	I got in a fight coming out of the meeting is all.
Peter	With who?
Michael	Some of the lodge men. John McCrea.
Peter	For God's sake, Michael! You won't go anymore. Is that understood?
Michael	You can't tell me that.
Peter	Listen to me. Please.
Michael	Good night.

Michael walks away from Peter.

Scene Thirteen

Spring 1920. A churchyard.

Sarah   Lord, have mercy
              Christ, have mercy
              Lord have mercy.
              Ding dong
              Snaky procession black
              Through stones grey
              Open earth
              To swallow it up
              Seed of life
              Departed
              Will not grow again.
              Lord Jesus Christ
              Deliver
              Souls of all faithful
              From pains of hell and deep Pit
              Mumble word jumble
              This is the sign
              Of the cross
              Amen.
              Silent staring
              Stands he.
              Through fingers
              Running
              Memory dust.
              She had a good
              Crack of the whip
              She had.
              Slap backslap
              Shake handshake
              Bye goodbye.
              May Hell not swallow up
              Shovel it all in
              Dirt.
              Bring her into
              Eternal light
              Shine upon her
              Holy light
              Once promised
              To Abraham and his seed.
              Eternal rest grant unto her
              With your saints forever
              For you are merciful

Sarah   Is it alright that I came?

Michael   Someone will see you.

Sarah	For a full year Deirdre did not smile or speak or lift her head to look upon the faces of those who had done this shameful deed. Her heart was broken and nothing would ever mend it.
Michael	We killed her.
Sarah	It was the influenza, Michael.
Michael	Go home.
Sarah	Conor the King sent Deirdre away to dwell with the evil Eogan.
Michael	Stop.
Sarah	On the way, she hurled her body from the chariot into the way of a huge boulder, dashing her head against it . . . Finish it.
Michael	You know the ending.
Sarah	Please.
Michael	The true friends of Naiose and Deirdre claimed her body and gently they laid it in the earth close to her lover. In time, in time . . .
Sarah	Two yew trees grew up from out of their graves and did not cease to grow until their branches entwined . . . Where's your father gone?
Michael	To start the planting. I can't stay here.
Sarah	I'll go with you.
Michael	No.
Sarah	You can't go without me.
Michael	Where?
Sarah	Toronto.
Michael	Not yet.
Sarah	When?
Michael	Soon. I will come for you.

Scene Fourteen

Spring 1920. The McCrea farmstead.

Sarah	I lay deep drifting, dreaming of Toronto-we-will-go And calico And Silverwoods ice cream. He comes calling up at my window.
Michael	I have come, true to my *geis*
Sarah	He says.

We strawberry kiss and I says, he says . . .
Strange scent
Oven bread
Who would be baking bread this time of night?
Sleep
Silverwoods dairy . . .

Michael Sarah!

Sarah I am sure.
Calling
Under my window,

Michael Come!

Sarah Crystal clear.
I come . . .
Quiet.
Too quiet.
No dog-bark.
Through night eyes
I see
Shadows moving in shadows
Men of the night: masked men.
Light at the window
Bright not moonlight
Orange
It is old but it is beautiful . . .
Crash of glass smash on wood.

Hugh "Jasus!"

Sarah Rattle, rattle, rattle, bedsprings
Thud trip bang bang

Ruth "What's there?! Who?!"

Sarah Smell of
Bread burning.
Smell of

Hugh "Fire! Fire in the barn! Fire!"

Sarah Awake I am and
Running
Out into the Nightmen Night
Frozen I
Eyes on fire.
I see
Our barn roaring flames.
Doorposts of my brother's burning
Rafters of the lodgemen snapping

Little shingle where my nail went in
Father's pent-roof
Crashing down into
Burning, popping grain.
I see
Mother father oh mammydaddy water dancing

Peter   And one and two and three

Sarah   And splash
And back and back
And one, two, three, four
I hear
Singing
A man singing.
Is he?
No screaming
I see
In the fire
Man
Orange Man
Leaping
Flinging arms updown
Crackle crackle crackle jig
I know who he
Can't be –
Smell of smoke on topcoat
Can't be –
Sweet strawberry juice on my lips
Toronto and Silverwoods ice cream
Splash him down
Oh mammydaddy
No
Please God
No
Hands grasp shoulders hurling me back
No
I will go forward
Break through hands
To see him.
I see
Black burning skin like potato leaves
Crumble into black ashes

Emer   That destroyed Ireland

Sarah   His granny said.
Hands white
Waxy white mash melting

Under red burned blood
Charred all through to the bone
Feet still jig-dancing
Muscle blackened meat, all spoiled.
His hair
Sour smoke rising
His no lips gasping fear-wide eyes.

Hugh   Come on boy, breathe!

Sarah   No.

Hugh   Don't look at him.

Ruth   Sarah, come away with me into the house.

Sarah   Come back to me.
Dance! D'ye hear me?
Get up to your feet and dance!

Scene Fifteen

Just after the fire. The McCrea farmstead.

Hugh *[to Sarah]* He wasn't on his own. I saw two or three more runnin away. D'ye know who it was?

Ruth   How's she going to know that?

Hugh   Well, she knew him didn't she? She knew him. *[to Sarah.]* Will you answer me?

Ruth   Leave her in peace, Hugh.

Hugh   No one ever raised a barn as quick as that.

Ruth   We can build another barn.

Hugh   With what? Ashes?

Ruth *[to Sarah]* You'll be alright.

Hugh   Everything I have. My whole. And she sits there and will not speak to me.

Ruth   Leave her alone. *[to Sarah.]* What're you crying for?

Hugh   She's cryin for him.

Ruth comforts Sarah.

Ruth   Leave her alone now I tell you. *[to Sarah.]* There now. You'll be alright . . . I know . . . The Lord is my shepherd, I shall not want. He maketh me to lie down in green pastures . . .

Sarah   No more.

Ruth   He leadeth me beside the still waters . . .

Sarah   Mine
Black ashes
All mine

	Shouldn't be forgotten None can redeem
Ruth	I know . . .
Sarah	Dubadum No more
Ruth	He restoreth my soul,
Sarah	Boom boom
Ruth	He leadeth me in the paths of righteousness . . .
Sarah	Kentucky coffee Sassafras Sugar maple Twisting strange boughs
Ruth	I will fear no evil
Sarah	Entwined Knife wind Cuts through It is cold
Ruth	My cup runs over . . .

Scene Sixteen

Sarah	Bitter Not me It is old Old So old Not beautiful Sharp shins wheeling Turning Will I Home Not home Not beautiful No more Shouldnae be remembered Sludge heavy boots Through soil Sun bleeds Awake Township of Stanley Six road ends Which Nearly day

Activities

Adolescence – pages 68–73
Role Plays

A role play in groups of two. One is a television presenter who is interviewing Sarah for a programme entitled 'Funny What Kids Say', the other is Sarah.

The presenter has asked Sarah a lot of questions. Sarah now feels safe with the presenter and is less embarrassed. When the role play starts the presenter is about to ask Sarah about boys.

Allow around five minutes for this exercise, see some if you wish or have a discussion of what Sarah has told the presenter. This discussion should highlight the story Michael has told and also the innocence of their relationship but their obvious attraction even at this young age.

Bigotry – pages 94 & 123
Conscience Alley

Ask the group to form the conscience alley and have Ruth walk down it.
Use the words and atmosphere created here to discuss Ruth's attitude and her part in the bigotry.

Domestic Violence – pages 128–130
Diary Extract

Sarah is taken to her room by her mother and laid on her bed. She cannot sleep because of the pain she is in. She lifts her diary and begins to write.
Each member of the group becomes Sarah (male or female) and writes an entry in the diary.

If appropriate, ask each person to pick out a line in their version of the diary that they think sums up the situation or the emotion that Sarah is experiencing and read it aloud. Go right round the class without stopping for comment until the end. Discuss.

Love and Death – pages 143–146
Role on the Wall

Split the group into two and have one half complete a ROTW for Sarah and the other half for Michael. Put both on the wall, discuss with the whole class and add to it. Make comparisons with other literary figures in the same situation.

Character Studies

Sarah

The play spans a six-year period. Sarah is the main character; she is telling us her story. She takes us on a journey that at times we can identify with and at others we cannot. Throughout the play she displays great maturity, even at the age of 14. She is imaginative and inquisitive. She is interested in life and politics.

Although at 14 she seems childlike to us, we must remember that in 1914 life and attitudes were different. Sarah learns a lot about life and people as the play unfolds and we encounter with her the many aspects of her character and her growing up. Amongst these characteristics are: strength, rebellion, love, hurt, disobedience, hate and courage.

Strength

Sarah has a strong character; others do not easily sway her. When she first meets Michael she shows this *(page 69)*.

MICHAEL

> *This land belongs to the Carew's who have gone up to Vancouver. It's not sold yet.*

SARAH

> *It's as good as. My father has gone to the land agent today to bid for it.*

MICHAEL

> *So has mine.*

SARAH

> *My father has one hundred acres this side of the water.*

MICHAEL

> *My father has two hundred on this side.*

SARAH

> *Get out of our river!*

Here we see the childlike argument, but also a stubbornness that will follow her throughout the play in her dealings with all around her.

Sarah shows strength and intelligence when her father tries to match her with Robert Milling. She initially does not cause a fuss when she finds out what her father has said.

Robert Milling has approached Sarah's father *(page 92)*:

HUGH

Then he asked me if he could coort ye.

SARAH

And what'd you say?

HUGH

I told him ye were too young yet. "Come back when she's Forty," says I. "That'll be time enough for her to be thinkin of coortin."

Religious

Very quickly, Sarah and Michael establish their relationship and where they stand with their religions *(page 70)*.

SARAH

How do you know my brother?

MICHAEL

I fought him once.

SARAH

What for?

MICHAEL

He called me a Papist bastard.

SARAH

Are you?

MICHAEL

I'm a Papist; but no bastard.

Loving/Trusting

She is her daddy's girl *(page 74)*.

SARAH

I was watchin out for you.

HUGH

I'm glad you was for I've plenty news to tell ye. Oh, yes indeed I have.

HUGH

The wee boys all in bed?

RUTH

Long ago. Which is where this one's goin now.

SARAH

Ach, Mammy!

HUGH

Sure, let her sit up a while and have a yarn.

She has a special relationship with her father. He confides in her, perhaps because Ruth seems to be a harsh, unforgiving woman who is not open to new ideas.

When Hugh is dictating a letter to his brother it is Sarah who is writing it down, but he is playing with her. Instead of coming right out with the news he does it through the dictation *(page 78)*.

HUGH

Is it now? [to Sarah.] Set this down … Brother, I come back from the agent in Yorkton today havin bought another thirty acres of good land.

SARAH

You got it!

HUGH

I did so.

RUTH

You did what?

HUGH

I've bought part of the Carew place. That makes one hunder'd and ninety acres of good fertil' soil. I had to bid against our neighbour Donaghue.

SARAH

He's a Catholic, isn't he?

HUGH

He is. [to Ruth.] What's that face for? You're not anger'd?

RUTH

You would talk it over with a child before your wife?

Sarah's love for Michael continues to grow with every meeting. First it is childish teasing and taunting, quite literally testing the water, letting him know that because she is a girl she is not stupid and that no one can pull the wool over her eyes.

Their first kiss is when Michael gives Sarah his grandmother's handkerchief for her birthday.

The relationship is mirrored and developed through the story of *Deirdre of the Sorrows*.

Sarah's love for Michael leads her to make contact with his family. At this point we don't think she fully realises the consequences of her actions but she visits his home on several occasions, to learn to dance and for tea. Are these innocent visits or is she making a point?

Her great love for Michael is shown in the many ways she teases, protects and guides, and finally, at 18, they consummate their relationship.
Her description in the poem shows her all-consuming love for 'her boy' and the sacrifice she is making. We must remember it is 1918 and good girls saved themselves for marriage.

> *Oh he is beautiful!*
> *Scent of his hair all meadow perfume.*
> *Eyelash tickle on my cheek*
> *This is not a bad thing.*

Vulnerable

Sarah is often hurt by her mother.

Ruth and Sarah are sewing *(page 92)*.

RUTH

> *You want holes in your clothes do you?* [to Sarah.] *Give it to me.*

SARAH

> *I can fix it.*

RUTH

> *Just let it be.*

SARAH

> *I'll start over.*

RUTH

> *Leave it alone I tell you. Leave it alone. It's a disgrace you are to me a disgrace.*

She is also hurt by her father. She shows strength of character when she takes a beating from her father, but the emotional hurt she feels must be unbearable. Daddy's girl has been caught disobeying and her father finds it necessary to use this very public way (bruises and cuts) to discipline her.

She is hurt by Michael. She feels hurt by his deception when he tells her he is going to Vancouver but instead is involved in burning her father's barn and, in the process, is killed. Leaving her behind with her family being proved right about him and his terrorist involvement.

Rebellious

Sarah is a rebel.

Sarah asks about joining the Orange Order *(page 93)*.

RUTH

> *Don't be stupid! You know women cannot join.*

SARAH

> *Why not?*

RUTH

> *Because it's only for men.*

HUGH

> *In case we have to fight.*

SARAH

> *For what?*

HUGH

> *For the Empire.*

SARAH

> *I don't see the need for it.*

HUGH

> *There's need for loyalty everywhere in the Empire, Sarah.*

RUTH

> *Who's been filling your head with talk like that?*

HUGH

> *With the war on and the Home Rulers trying to break up the Union.*

SARAH

> *It's my own opinion.*

HUGH

>*She's havin opinions now!*

RUTH

>*That's what comes from too much talk!*

Michael also sees the rebel in Sarah.

SARAH

>*Then to hell with the Pope!*

MICHAEL

>*Shhh! Don't say that, Sarah .*

SARAH

>*Why not? He can't hear me.*

MICHAEL

>*You're a rebel, d'you know that? You're a hardened revolutionary, Sarah McCrea.*

Courageous

She shows courage in her relationship with Michael.

She stands up for what she believes in and despite her parents' mocking of her, declares she has an opinion. (See Rebellious above).

She shows courage in her defiance of her father over Catholicism, Michael, and Robert Milling.

She is willing to give up her family to go to Vancouver.

Disobedient

Sarah disobeys her father and pays the price *(page 127)*.

HUGH

>*Where'd ye go?*

SARAH

>*Out walking across the fields*

HUGH

>*On your own?*

SARAH

> *You know I wasn't. She saw me.*

RUTH

> *Who do you call "she"?*

HUGH

> *Ah, Sarah. Sarah, what did I tell ye?*

RUTH

> *Remember what ye said, Hugh.*

HUGH

> *What possessed ye after all we talked about?*

RUTH

> *Hugh?*

HUGH

> *I know what I said.* [to Sarah.] *What did I say til ye?*

SARAH

> *That I was to walk out with Michael Donaghue no more.*

HUGH

> *But you did so.*

SARAH

> *I did.*

She again disobeys her father.

HUGH

> *You will dance with Robert Milling.*

SARAH

> *I won't.*

Disillusioned

She hears of her brother's hatred when he beats Michael up for being a Catholic.
She witnesses first hand her mother's hate of Catholics.
She hears how her father is willing to fight for the Orange Order.
She hates what all of this has done to 'her boy'.
She possibly hates what Michael has become.

Disappointed

Sarah suffers a lot of disappointment.

Firstly with her family – her mother's rejection, her father's refusal to acknowledge her intelligence, both parents' view on religion – but secondly and more importantly with Michael.

She loves Michael. She knows that he is involved with terrorism in some way but does not want to believe it. We get the impression that she feels it is a phase that he will get out of his system.

She is further disappointed when they meet in the graveyard and she tries to bring him back to her by rekindling the Deirdre tale, but he shakes that off, giving the impression that there are more important things in his life.

Her final disappointment is in Michael's death. She is now left alone; there is no move to Vancouver to start afresh as she had dreamed.
She had given Michael her all, and now he has left her for a cause he felt was more important than their love.

Michael

Michael grows up throughout the play. He is older than Sarah, displaying his 'maturity' when he addresses her in the earlier parts of the play.

He is attracted to her and shows his affection openly when he asks for a kiss if he makes it across the river.

Michael is second-generation Canadian, whereas Sarah has come straight from Ireland, but it is Michael who appears to have the deeper sense of Irish heritage. Even as a young lad he talks of fighting for the cause and being part of the struggle. His father does not seem to encourage this but his grandmother has a deep-seated sense of being Irish.

Michael brings Sarah a birthday present and this prompts their first kiss.

He lives their relationship through the tale of *Deirdre of the Sorrows*, perhaps being able to show his love through the tale rather than having to say it as himself.

He acknowledges Sarah's rebellious nature and seems at times envious of her forthright opinions.

He loves her deeply and this is shown when he tackles her father when he demands that Sarah dances with Robert Milling.

His life experiences have been different from Sarah's, being beaten up as a young boy then later as an adult because he is Catholic.

He makes a choice later in the play – a choice that eventually kills him.

We do not know if he really intended to leave for Vancouver or whether he really intended Sarah to follow.

We feel that when he meets Sarah in the graveyard that he is trying hard not to let her persuade him from his duty. At this point he is building a wall between them, perhaps to make what he is doing seem right or easier.

Ruth

Ruth is Sarah's mother. She is a harsh woman who quotes the bible but does not live as a true Christian. She is hard on her daughter, perhaps because she knows the realities of life.

She does not show any tenderness or warmth to Sarah, but constantly chides, comments on and corrects her.

She is jealous of the special bond between her husband and Sarah and feels left out of their talks and secrets. She is the most bigoted.

RUTH

> *I've never made friends of a Cathelicke in my life. Their bigotry is too much.*

She hides behind her husband's membership of the Orange Order *(page 116)*.

RUTH

> *Harm?! Making love to a Catholic.*

SARAH

> *I'm making love to nobody.*

RUTH

> *Your father a leading member of the Order.*

Her hatred of the Catholic faith is so great that she goads her husband into fulfilling his promise of beating Sarah if she ever went out with Michael Donaghue again *(page 128)*.

RUTH

> *I tell you this and I tell you no more: you give in to this one here the night and ye'll surely have a Fenian for a son-in-law. I will not stand by and see our blood mixed in with that. Now either you do what you said you would or I'll do it myself.*

Hugh

Hugh is Sarah's father. He is a hard-working man who wishes to do well. His trials over land are not only to please his wife but to be able to report back to family in Ireland that he is prosperous.

He loves and admires Sarah. He confides in her and enjoys her company out in the fields.

However he is two-faced. He is happy for his Catholic neighbours, the Donaghues, to help him with his work, but not happy about Sarah's relationship with Michael (although he does turn a blind eye at times).

We often feel the phrase 'anything for a quiet life' typifies him.

In a lot of ways he is a weak man. He doesn't always have the courage of his convictions. At times he has it within his grasp to change attitudes and conventions but he lacks the strength and courage to do this. He reverts to type when things become too complicated or when the pressure from Ruth becomes too great.

Peter

Peter is Michael's father. He is much quieter than Hugh. He appears to have seen it all before. He is strong and is not afraid to say or do what he feels is right.
Michael's mother is only mentioned briefly by Emer and we can deduce from this that she was not a Catholic. Peter really loved her. This is shown when Michael asks his father's opinion of his relationship with Sarah *(page 132)*.

MICHAEL [*to Peter.*]
> *Tell me, honest.*

PETER
> *Is she a good girl, Michael?*

MICHAEL
> *I believe it.*

PETER
> *Does she believe the same of you?*

MICHAEL
> *More than I believe of myself.*

PETER
> *Then if you want her, take her to you and let no one come between.*

We don't know if Peter knows of Michael's activities; we can only assume that he would not condone them.

Emer

Emer is Michael's grandmother. She is unwell but she is a strong member of the Donaghue household. She has obviously come to live with Peter to look after Michael. Both men love her very much. She is less forgiving than Ruth although not as openly bigoted. She encourages Michael to attend the political meeting which supports a free Ireland, when his father is more wary.

She plays the role of a wise sage who can only see harm coming through the relationship Michael has with Sarah. She does not openly speak of religion although she does hint at it when discussing Michael's mother.

EMER

> *A Dhía dhilis!* [My God] *Goin' the same way. Just like you, every bit of him.*

Emer and Ruth strike an understanding about their offspring's relationship and almost silently agree that they can be kept apart. There is no love lost between the women.

CHAPTER FIVE

SEA URCHINS
BY SHARMAN MACDONALD

Background Information

Sea Urchins started life as a radio play, subsequently heard by Tron theatre's artist director, Irina Brown, who then staged it at the Dundee Rep and Tron in 1998. Set in the 1960s, the text combines lively accessible dialogue with the popular music of that period to create a drama which will 'come off the page' well when read in the classroom. The stage directions, while simple and straightforward and often making reference to what is heard rather than seen, are still 'theatrical' enough to draw students' attention to the three-dimensional nature of a stage production. It should still be possible to have a fairly flowing reading of the text 'round' the class, although students taking part will need to be fairly alert to how the dialogue is being directed. Sharman Macdonald deploys some interesting techniques (accredited to Caryl Churchill) in her presentation of the dialogue, which should provide scope for students to achieve some depth in their analyses of the text.

Both plot and character should appeal to a young, contemporary audience as the play deals sensitively and imaginatively with family tensions. It also confronts frankly the difficulties facing young people in coming to terms with growing up, not least in understanding and relating to the adults around them. The central character, Rena, must learn the family's 'dark secret', which is hinted at throughout the play and finally made clear in the closing stages. This is a strong narrative 'hook' which keeps an audience involved as the drama unfolds.

The opening monologue by Rena is edgy and discordant as she tries to summon a notorious murderer to sort out her family. Her self-absorbed communications to Mr Manning are a mixture of mundane detail, childish awe and adolescent angst. In Act One, it's clear that Rena does not want to have to confront what she doesn't like about her family so she avoids them, talks to herself and refuses to listen. Rena says:

> *Noelle. She's going to tell me something that I don't know. And once she's told me I'll know it. And I'll not be able to unknow it. And my whole life'll change. I don't want that.*

In Act Two, the interchange between Rena and Noelle about the twin brother that died at birth marks a turning point for Rena. Noelle forces her to listen to the story which then pushes Rena into asserting her own identity and declaring her own love for her father:

> 'I can do anything I want ... I'll never take any other man's name but my father's.'

By contrast, the worldly-wise Noelle has already absorbed the rhetoric of 'femininity':

> 'A man likes a woman to be modest in her endeavours and her achievements and to show a proper respect.'

Like their mothers, both girls will have to come to terms with the fact that John is their father, but unlike their mothers there are still major decisions for them to make about the kind of relationships they will have with men when they are adults. While Noelle seems to have everything 'sussed' just now, there is a sense that she sees her own future mapped out already in her mother. Rena on the other hand is intelligent and different enough to forge a life that's a bit more individual. As Ailsa poignantly remarks at one point in the play:

> 'Nothing is the worst thing that can happen to you.'

There are two acts in the play but no separate scenes. This creates an ebb and flow of characters, dialogue and music. Lines of communication cross, are broken and then picked up again. The use of slashes (/) to indicate an interruption and asterisks (*) to indicate that the dialogue travels from star to star, adds to the sense of self-absorbed characters whose music and chat run in parallel to one another, rather than in direct communication with one another. These formal devices also draw attention to the need for straight talking to sort out dysfunctional family relationships.

DAVID

> True member of this family / you've got here John.*

JOHN

> Four guitars we / can muster now.

RENA

> *I can't play.

DAVID

> No such word.

For example, in the above exchange David starts off by addressing John but John doesn't wait for him to finish; he's absorbed in his own 'musical agenda' and interrupts David. Rena then ignores what her father is saying and interrupts him as she responds to David's statement with the line: 'I can't play.' David then replies directly to her: 'No such word.' It's worthwhile taking some time to work through these quite complex moments to consider how the lines sound when they are read together. What conclusions can an audience draw about the relationship between characters from how they engage in communication with one another? The short exchange highlighted here suggests most strongly that the two brothers do not communicate well with one another and that Rena is desperate for her father to hear what she has to say. Those points in the play where Sharman Mcdonald uses the (/) and (*) require careful reading and so provide 'natural' stopping points for discussion. These techniques also highlight the importance of performance in drama and reminds us that what is actually said is only part of dynamics of communication.

John's desire to have a 'musical' daughter means he insensitively shuts out any comments by Rena which deny her ability. This tension is heightened as we learn that what attracts John to his sister-in-law is her attractive singing voice. Music and song are used skilfully in a number of ways in Act One. One function is to evoke nostalgia. As Sharman Macdonald comments in her short introduction:

'The music is as I remember it. There must be sheet music somewhere that would mend the idiosyncrasies of memory.'

John uses his guitar playing, mainly of the Blues, to escape from direct communication with Ailsa and to get at her. It becomes a commentary on his relationship with Rena.

JOHN

    Don't you listen / to your mother Rena.*

AILSA

    Have I smudged my mascara? Have I?

John sings.

JOHN

    * She's driving me crazy /
    What am I going to do?

Ailsa, still very much in love with John, uses, for example, the George Gershwin song, … *My Sweet Embraceable You* to hark back to a better time in their relationship.

It's largely through music that John connects with Dora as he urges her to sing duets with him in front of his wife and brother. However, the music unites the family as well when David, Gareth and Rhiannon join with John and Dora to sing Hawaiian songs, significantly Ailsa is left out of this as she organises food elsewhere. In the closing stages of the play it's music that unites the adults in the family and this time it's David and Dora that lead the final duet.

In Act One the slash and asterisk are much more frequently because at this point each of the major characters is pursuing their own agenda, which often leads to them shutting out what they don't want hear or leaving unsaid what they don't want to face. By Act Two characters are forced to communicate much more directly with one another. Rhiannon confronts Ailsa about whether her father is John or David. Ailsa has already made passing reference to Rhiannon having 'John's eyes'. Eventually Ailsa can only be honest:

> *'I know nothing. I surmise that's all. I know no more than you.'*

Like Dora's husband David, Ailsa has lived with the knowledge of John and Dora's relationship. Unlike David, who locked it all inside, Ailsa's pride has meant that she's 'paid (John) out'. Sharman Macdonald provides no trite, easy answers, nor is judgement neatly passed on each character's behaviour. But there is a strong sense that, between Ailsa and Dora in particular, a new understanding has been reached which will allow them to

> *'dig a hole in this beach and bury the past in it'.*

Sea Urchins

by *Sharman Macdonald*

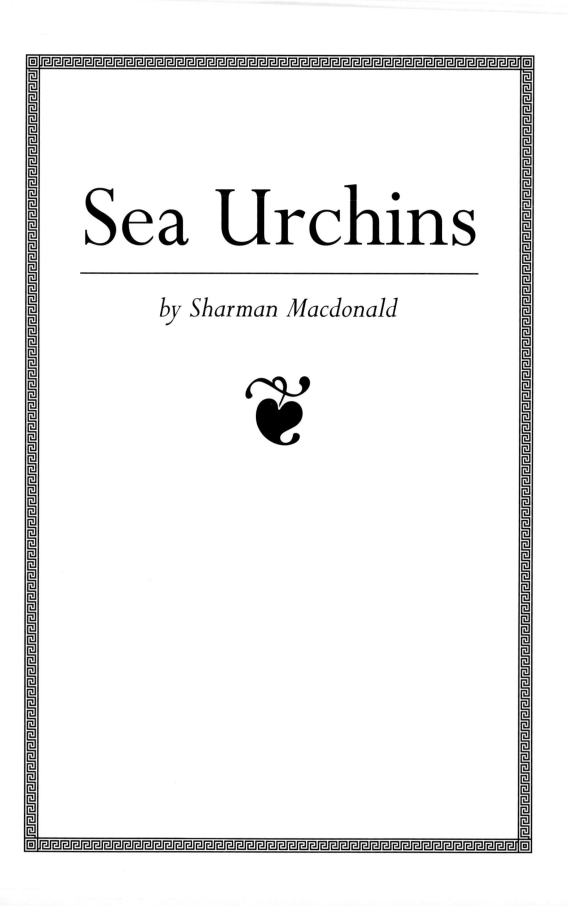

Sea Urchins

By Sharman Macdonald

SETTING

The play is set on a coved, pebbled beach, below a cliff near David's home on the Atlantic Coast of Wales.

*/ indicates an interruption; * indicates that the dialogue travels from star to star.*

CHARACTERS

Martin   An English boy. Twelve or thereabouts.

Rena   A Scottish girl. Eleven.

Ailsa   Her mother.

John   Ailsa's Welsh husband.

David   John's brother.

Dora   David's wife.

Gareth   Their son. Twenty-one.

Rhiannon Gareth's sister. Eighteen.

Noelle   Rhiannon's sister. Rena's cousin. Eleven.

Man   A Glaswegian.

Act One

Distant shushing of the waves on pebbles.

Feet rushing. Pebbles rolling. Martin slipping and slithering over the slopes of the beach, looking for his brother. Yelling. His yells make the place vast and empty.

Rena's watching.

Martin   George! George. George!

Twists an ankle.

        Damn. Damn. Damn. Damn.

Runs on.

        George.

When he's gone Rena twists round onto her back. Looks up into the vast blue of the sky. She's lying in a pebble hollow. Rough sea grass blows around her. A private voice.

Rena   Aberrhyll. That's where I am.

In the distance Martin's running feet.

> OK Mr Manning? June 16th. 1961. Synchronise watches. Three, two, one. Eight a.m. precisely. There are white horses on the waves and the weather's fine. Mr Manning? I'm calling you. They say you're the best. A clean killer. Is that not right? A man of business. I read the papers. Even the police, my Dad says. They speak of you with awe in their voices. You've got to leave Glasgow right away and get yourself down here. Aberrhyll. The beach below the cliff. Have you got that? I'm at the end of my tether. You're my last hope. Mr Manning, I've got some business for you.

Martin's feet clatter across the stones. Closer and closer. He doesn't see Rena. She doesn't see him. Flesh bumps on flesh. Rena yells.

> Mind it.

Martin   Sorry.

Rena   That's just a word.

Martin stares. Rena stares back. It's a stand off.

Rena   Well?

Martin   What?

Rena   See me, see Beethoven.

Martin   What?

Rena   Don't you understand English?

Martin   Beethoven?

Rena   It's rude to stare. Did your mother never tell you that? I haven't got time for this. Go away. Go on, get.

She watches him back off up the beach. Goes back to her private voice.

> Please forgive the interruption, Mr Manning. Some boy that's all. I don't know him. He's not part of it.

Martin's staring from a safe distance.

> I don't want any mistakes. See me before you murder anyone. I'm the boss. I'm still feeling a bit sick but fully compus mentus, so don't you go trying anything off your own bat. I spewed up three times on the drive down but I managed to get out of the car. So no one was cross with me. We'll have a Hillman next year by the way if we're all still alive. There are hermits on the Rest and Be Thankful. Which I was glad to see. That's where I'm headed if you fail. I'd rather be a hermit than on this beach waiting for Noelle to get here. She's it Mr Manning. Kill her. She's the same age as me, only she's got breasts but. Note that down in indelible pencil Mr Manning. B.R.E.A.S.T.S. God help me I never hear the end of them. Of course we may be talking about a multiple killing Mr Manning. We'll see how the day pans out. Families Mr Manning. They're the very devil at the best of times. But on

holiday they really do take the biscuit. Payment will be by IOU. I intend to be rich in my own right by the time I'm twenty-five. So you can collect then, provided you've not been hanged / OK Mr Manning? OK? OK?

Ailsa's walking down the beach. She calls to Martin.

Ailsa   Hello there.

Martin   Hello.

His reply catches Rena's attention. He ducks down into a hollow. Creeps round nearer to her.

Ailsa laughs in delight at the wind in her hair and the warmth and the blue blue day.

Rena's watching Ailsa from her hollow.

Rena   That's my mum Mister Manning. She's part of it. Not the worst part. Not by a long chalk.

Ailsa's right at the sea's edge. The gentle waves push at the stones at her feet.

Ailsa   Oh yes. / Yes, yes.

Rena's watching Ailsa.

Rena *[whispers]* Oh God. Oh no. Oh shite.

Ailsa begins to sing. Her voice embraces the whole coastline.

Ailsa   There'll be a / welcome in the hillside.

Rena *[whispers]* Christ, don't sing.

Ailsa calls.

Ailsa   Come down here John.

John's in the grassy wind-sheltered cove far behind her. He's filling the primus with paraffin. The fuel glugs into the base of the stove. Metal grinds against metal.

John   God save us.

He pumps up the fuel with the metal plunger.

Ailsa *[calls]*   Come on and I'll hold your hand by the sea's edge and we'll pretend we're winchin'.

John *[calls]*   I'm doing something en' I. Sing your song Ailsa. *[to himself]* Let's get it over with.

Ailsa's voice is high, strong and Scottish. She's gloriously sentimental.

Ailsa   There'll be a welcome in the dale
                This land of ours will / still be singing*

The song continues.

Rena *[whispers]* Shut up. Shut up. Jesus.

Rena wriggles forward on her stomach. A bird cries.

Ailsa   * When you come home / again to Wales.

Rena [whispers] Shut up, shut up, shut up, shut up.

Martin's foot slithers on the shingle. An intake of breath. A loose stone slithers and clatters down the slope.

Martin   Hey!

The stone hits Rena on the shoulder.

Rena   Jesus. Did you throw that?

Martin slithers down the stony slope.

Martin   It was an accident.

Rena   Clumsy wee shite.

Martin   I shouted.

Rena   I had my fingers in my ears.

Martin   It was only a pebble.

Rena   It was a rock by the way.

Rena twists round to look at her shoulder.

        I've got a bruise.

Martin   Can I see?

Rena   Help yourself.

Martin crunches across the stones.

Martin   It's quite big.

Rena   You don't have to prod it do you?

Martin   Looks sore.

Rena   I bruise easily.

Martin   That'll be your hair.

Rena   What's wrong with it?

Martin   People with red hair bruise easily.

Rena   D'you want a punch in the mouth?

Martin   Delicate skin that's all. Red hair.

Rena   Auburn.

Martin   I don't dislike it.

Rena   That's big of you.

Ailsa's singing reaches them from the sea's edge.

Ailsa	They'll take away each hour of heiryth When you come home again to Wales.
Martin	She looks sad.
Rena	Mind your own business.
Martin	She's very attractive.
Rena	Eh?
Martin	Like mother, like daughter.
Rena	D'you mean that for a compliment?
Martin	She is your mother isn't she?
Rena	Oh my God.
Martin	What?
Rena	She's stopped. Silence. Feel the smell of it.
Martin	You can't smell silence.
Rena	I can. Don't you just love it.

A bird cries. The wind blows. The waves break on the beach.

Martin	The waves make quite a racket.
Rena	See that song. She sings that for my father. I'm never going to be a woman.
Martin	D'you come here every year?
Rena	Every year of my whole life.

George begins to cry. Martin's head turns.

Rena	Who's that?
Martin	George.
Rena	Who?
Martin	My brother.
Rena	That's sore crying.
Martin	He starts sometimes and he can't stop.
Rena	We all have our burdens in this world. You have yours and I have mine.

John calls down from the cove.

John	Rena!
Martin	That your / dad?
Rena	Your brother's breaking his / heart.

Martin   Aren't you / going?

Rena   See him. See him crying. Takes the soul out of you, that. Can't you stop him?

Martin   My mother can.

The crying turns to sobbing.

          See.

The sobs lessen.

Rena   He must love her.

Martin   Would you like to come swimming with me?

Rena studies him quite carefully. Till he can't meet her look.

          I mean, if you want.

She's about to answer, on the edge of a smile.

John *[calls]*   Get yourself over here.

Rena runs off. Her feet sliding on the stones.

Rena   Aw. Jesus, Jesus, Jesus.

John *[calls]*   Shift, Rena.

Martin yells after her.

Martin   What's your name?

Rena   You stupid or what are you?

John *[calls]*   Rena!

Rena   The whole of bloody Wales knows my name.

Martin   Rena?

Rena   What, for God's sake?

Martin   See you later?

Rena   Alright.

Martin   Promise?

Rena   Uh huh.

Martin runs over the stones.

          See him, Mr Manning? Don't you lay a finger on him. Do you hear me?

John *[calls]*   Chop chop. Banana banana.

In the cove John plays the introduction to Leadbelly's 'Good Morning Blues'. Rena runs over the stones onto the grass. Throws herself down.

John	You took your time.

Fat spits in the frying pan. The primus roars. There's an angry sizzle as bacon hits the fat. Martin's creeping round so that he can watch them.

Ailsa	Why can't they get here first? Why can't they do that?*

John sings.

John	Good morning Blues Blues how / do you do? Good morning blues Blues how do you do?
Ailsa	* They'll get here when the bacon's right crisp and not a moment before. Then they'll thunder up, the whole damn herd of them. Why should this year be any different?
Rena	You like them though.*
John	I'm doing alright Good morning how are you?

The guitar plays on.

Ailsa	* There's no surprise in my life and very little pleasure.
Rena	Don't say that.
Ailsa	When I was wee we went to Dunbar for the Glasgow Fair fortnight and your grandfather hired a cottage and we took your grandmother's charlady with us. Auntie Mac. She cooked the breakfast. Look at me. I've come down in the world.*
John	You've come down in the world?
Ailsa	* Never marry a Welshman.
John	I sold my birthright for a plate of porridge.
Ailsa	My father ate his porridge with salt and put pepper on his strawberries. He suffered from kidney stones. From the rhubarb they said. Your grandmother's rhubarb was legendary. There's nothing legendary about your father's family. They're Methodists.
Rena	Say you like coming here.
Ailsa	I come here for him.
Rena	Say it. Please.
Ailsa	Oh my God.
Rena	What is it? What's wrong?
Ailsa	Bloody bacon spat in my eye. / God's greatest invention was the electric cooker. And I'm down on my hunkers at a bloody primus stove arguing with a rasher of streaky.*

John	I laid down last night Turning from side to side I laid down last night Turning from side to side

Speaks.

       Pick up your guitar Rena. Rena I need you.

Fingers slide on the strings.

Ailsa	* I'll have a bloodspot. Is that inflamed is it?
John	C. C. That's D. C.*

Another guitar strums almost in rhythm.

Ailsa	I could be dying here for God's Sake.

John sings.

John	* But I wasn't sick. Just / dissatisfied.
Ailsa	John?
John	I woke up this morning Blues sneaking round my head I woke up this morning.

Speaks.

       C. D. G.

Sings.

       Blues sneaking round my head.

Speaks.

       G. G, Rena. G.

Sings.

       I couldn't eat
       Blues all in my bread.

Speaks.

       That's not a left hand Rena. That's a rollmop herring.

John picks. Rena strums.

Ailsa	You drive that girl too hard.
John	She's my harp of joy.
Ailsa	Is that what she is?

John	Don't you listen to / your mother Rena.*
Ailsa	Have I smudged my mascara? Have I?

John sings.

John	* She's driving me crazy / What am I going to do?
Ailsa	He thinks* he's awful funny.
Rena	Your mascara's fine.
John	* She's driving me crazy What am I going to do? I ain't got nobody To take my troubles to.
	C, Rena. C, Rena. C. C. C. You glean knowledge in this world.
Ailsa	Here we go.
John	It may not be much but it's all I have to leave you Rena. The knowledge that I've gleaned.
Ailsa	Planning on dying are you?
John	Who knows what the future holds?
Ailsa	We've a long way to go yet, you and me.
John	Not so long as we've been.
Ailsa	Planning on leaving me?
John	You're driving me crazy What am I going to do?
Ailsa	I'm asking you a question John Williams.

John sings.

John	I need somebody To take my troubles to.

His voice fades. His picking fades. Rena's stuttering strum comes to the fore and her private voice.

Rena	Manning come here and murder me where I sit. I'd like that. Manning. Mr Manning. They're at their damn games again. Don't leave me to listen to them. Come on now. Right now.

She whisper-sings. Still in the private voice.

Come on Mr Manning
You can murder me any time
Come on Mr Manning
You can murder me any time

Cause I'll be so glad
To be your number nine.

Strings jar.

John	What do you call that?
Rena	What?
John	Don't look at your fingers. What's that chord? Know it in your soul Rena.
Rena	G? G seventh. It's D seventh. D seventh, Dad. Sorry. Sorry.
John	What should it be?
Rena	C?
John	Don't ask me. Tell me.
Rena	I don't know. / I don't know.
Ailsa	She can't play.
John	You've never strummed anything more than a bloody ukelele, Ailsa. / Don't you start talking to me about the guitar.
Ailsa	You can't put there what's not there in the first place. / Practise she ever so.
John	I thank God for one thing.
Ailsa	What's that John Williams?
John	She hasn't inherited your voice.* On my bended knees I thank God for that.

Rena's private voice whispers through the bitter words.

Rena	Manning come on. Come on quick. I need you Manning. I need you now.
Ailsa	* I'm warning you John. / We both know you can hurt me.
John	I'll tell you something about your voice. It's not this world it belongs to. And I'm not talking about angels. Your voice belongs in the other place Ailsa. Buried deep.
Ailsa	You always preferred a contralto. / You've made that perfectly obvious.
Rena	Don't. Don't, don't / don't don't.
Ailsa	He likes your Auntie Doe's voice best. Amongst all the other things he likes about your Auntie Doe. / And I'm not talking about her Welsh cakes.
John	Enough.
Ailsa	It's the God's honest truth.
John	Truth tellers are the salt of the earth and they should be buried in it for the harm that they do.*

Rena's whispering.

Rena	God Manning. Stop them. Stop them.
Ailsa	* You're a romantic John Williams.
John	Romantic / am I?
Ailsa	Whatever you can't have. That's what your heart desires.
John	You tell me something Ailsa. If I'm romantic how come I married you?
Ailsa	That's cheap.
John	You should know.
Ailsa	A true singer sings with her heart. And when the heart goes out of her she sings no more. I'm begging you to leave me with something John.
John	This is not about you.
Ailsa	I'm what you've got. Nobody twisted your damn arm. I'm what you've got. You tell me. Out loud. So that it's in the air between us. I'm what you've got. What is it that you cling to? Answer me that. As if I didn't know. My God, I wish I didn't know.
John	Pick up the guitar Rena.
Ailsa	Leave her.
John	Pick it up Rena.
Rena	My fingers are sore.
John	Feel. Feel there. Tips of my fingers. Callouses, see. Feel how hard they are. Your fingers will be like that one day. They won't hurt you then.
Rena	I'm no good at the guitar.
John	You will be.
Ailsa	How will she?
John	One day. When I'm gone and you've got a man of your own Rena. That you'll love and care for more than you ever have me. You'll play for him. And your children Rena. You'll teach them what I've taught you. See this. Feel it. Feel the sun on the wood. That's my Gibson Kalamazoo you're touching there.
Rena	I won't marry.
John	You will.
Rena	I won't leave you.
Ailsa	I used to say that to my Father.* I'd sit on his knee, I'd clap his head. He'd give me anything I wanted. The moon from out of the sky he'd give me on a plate or a new silk dance dress from Pettigrew and Stevens.
John	* You'll leave me and my name will go out of this world.
Rena	There's Gareth, isn't there?

John	He bears your Uncle David's name.
Rena	Same difference.
John	Not to me. See my guitar. This is what you'll have, Rena Maeve. All through your life you'll have it. And when I die I'll die happy knowing that you've got my guitar and the skill to play it. That's what'll be left of me on this earth when I leave it. Ring finger, E string, third fret.

A steel string complains.

Ailsa	Rena Maeve'll be left will she? Rena Maeve and your Gibson Kalamazoo?
John	Enough, Ailsa.
Ailsa	Is that all that'll be left?
John	I'm warning you.
Ailsa	You're not the clean potato John Williams.

The hissing and sparking of the bacon fades. Rena whisper-sings.

Rena	Dear Mr Manning
	Hear me calling to you
	Dear Mr Manning
	Hear me calling to you
	I've got some troubles
	You can help me through.*

The guitar stumbles.

John	Don't fight it darling. It's your lover, not your killer.

The guitar hits a smooth patch.

	You're my daughter and you're special. Never you forget that. You can do anything you want in this life. Be anything that you want. You just have to want, Rena Maeve. You just have to want.
Rena	* Pick up your knife now
	Plunge it in to my breast
	Pick up your knife now
	Plunge it in to my breast
	I got the blues Mr Manning
	I need to get me some rest.

Rena's guitar stutters on. John's joins.

David, Dora, Gareth, Rhiannon and Noelle Williams walk along the cliff path. The wind's blowing up there. The grass is rustling. The music's distant.

David	He's got her playing.
Gareth	What's she playing on?

David	He'll have made her that.
Gareth	You can't tell that from up here.
David	Left handed guitar Gareth. Done no less for her than I did for you.
Gareth	She can't play Da.
David	Sausages for fingers.
Noelle	Oh God these summers. These summers.
Dora	Don't be affected Noelle Williams. I never liked an affected child.
Noelle	You telling me you're looking forward to it are you Mam?
David	It's family right. Right Noelle? Right?
Noelle	Ttttt.
David	You'll behave Noelle. I'm not asking you, I'm telling you.
Noelle	I'm promising nothing.
Gareth	You let her away with murder.
David	Nothing wrong with a bit of spirit.
Dora	When they were babies that was the best time. I only ever wanted babies. Catch up Rhiannon. Come on.
Noelle	I'll get her.

Noelle runs down the sunbaked mud cliff path. Dora calls.

Dora	Not so fast Noelle.

Noelle runs at Rhiannon.

Noelle	Rhia aa aa non.
Rhiannon	For God's sake.

Noelle charges into Rhiannon. Knocks the breath out of her.

Stupid cow.

Noelle's laughing.

Noelle	Joke Rhiannon.
Rhiannon	You could've bloody killed me.
Noelle	How could I?
Rhiannon	You're no light weight Noelle. Suppose I'd gone over?
Noelle	You'd be lying squashed at the bottom of the cliff and there'd be one less nuisance in the world. You think you're so great.

Pause.

You're up to something Rhiannon Williams.

Rhiannon   Don't talk daft.

Noelle   You want watching.

Rhiannon   You've got an over-active imagination.

Noelle   Sweetness and light they think you are. I know better. You're waiting for someone.

Rhiannon   I am not.

Noelle   What're you looking up there for?

Rhiannon   Cliff's beautiful in the sunlight.

Noelle   Since when have you been a nature lover, Rhia Williams?

Dora calls.

Dora   Come on you two. Don't lag. Gareth, go and make them come can't you?

David   You're alright aren't you Dora?

Dora   'Course I am. Why shouldn't I be?

David   You'd tell me wouldn't you?

Dora   Tell you what Dai?

David   I don't know.

Dora   Well if you don't know, heart, how should I?

David   If you weren't alright you'd tell me. If you were sad like?

Dora   * What have I got to be sad about? On a day like today? I've got nothing on this earth to be sad about Dai. Neither have you, my love. Neither have you.

And she walks on down the hill into the music in the cove.

John   * Blues you're driving me crazy
What am I going to do?
I ain't got nobody
To take my troubles to.

Rena!

A sequence of chord changes more or less in rhythm, rather less stumbling than they have been. John puts a two chord stop on it. Applause.

Dora   Clever, / clever girl.

Rena   Don't Auntie Doe.

David   True member of this family / you've got here John.*

John	Four guitars we / can muster now.
Rena	* I can't play.
David	No such word.
Rena	I'm useless Uncle David. You know that better than anyone.

She runs. John calls after her.

John	Rena?
Gareth	Women!

Martin slides out from his hiding place in the grass and follows Rena. The bacon sizzles.

Ailsa	You can have bacon. You can have black pudding. You can have sausages. / Gareth, look at the height of you.
Dora	Spoiling us Ailsa heart.
Ailsa	You look well Doe.
Rhiannon	Good to see you Auntie Ailsa.
Ailsa	She's growing into the family look. I see my husband in your eyes Rhiannon. She's John's eyes Doe. God help us all. You see your age in the young ones Dora.
Dora	See your age in the faces of your friends Ailsa. Least that's where I see mine.
Ailsa	I hope that's not me you're referring to.
Gareth	The whole world fancies you Auntie Ailsa, specially when there's bacon on the primus.
Ailsa	You're a sweet talker.
Dora	I could live in Scotland for their baps. Though the people scare me to death.
Ailsa	Of course Wales is famous for its saints, Dora.
Dora	Is that a fact?
Ailsa	You should know.
Dora	I beg your pardon.
Ailsa	You've your own Welsh saint that you're married to.
Dora	I'll have my bacon well done.
Ailsa	It's always good to see you in the flesh Dora.
Dora	I look forward to your visits.
Ailsa	There's a masochist in all of us then.
David	Girls. Girls.
Ailsa	Is that well enough done for you?

Dora	You were always a good cook.
Ailsa	I have many talents Dora. Many, many, many.
Dora	We must all thank God for that.
Ailsa	Your wife doesn't change David.
Gareth	You give as good as you get Auntie Ailsa. You always have.

The sizzle of bacon fades into the sound of the sea and the cry of a bird.

Rena runs along the beach. Lies down flat on the stones. She's crying.

Martin stops running when he sees her. Listens to her crying. Walks softly over to her. Stands looking down at her. Rena stifles her sobs.

Martin	You crying?
Rena	Feel the stones. You could fry eggs on them. Don't you just love the heat. I haven't a hankie.
Martin	Here.
Rena	Jesus. The bloody thing's clean. Mammy's boy. Won't even say shite. I hate Mammy's boys. You can't trust them.
Martin	Shite.

She applauds.

Rena	There's a big man.
Martin	I'm not the one crying.
Rena	I get bad hay fever sometimes.

An English woman's voice calls.

Maureen	Martin?
Rena	That you is it? Martin? That your Mother calling you?
Martin	She just wants to know where I am.
Rena	Wave then. There's a sweetheart.

She starts to laugh.

Martin	What's funny?
Rena	Martin?
Martin	So what?
Rena	She can't have liked you much, your mother, to have called you that.
Martin	Are you always like this?
Rena	Say I wasn't crying.

Martin	'I wasn't crying.'
Rena	You weren't crying say.

Pause.

Bugger you then . . . Martin. You're an awful Nosey Parker by the way. You were watching us weren't you. You were in the grass spying on us. Don't think I didn't see you. What's the big fascination, eh?

Martin	We don't play guitars in my family.
Rena	What do you do?
Martin	We play board games on Sunday afternoons.
Rena	Monopoly?
Martin	Ludo.
Rena	I quite like Ludo.
Martin	I like guitars.

Pause.

Rena	Why does she hold your brother like that, your mum?
Martin	Don't you like being held?
Rena	Depends who's doing the holding.

Beat.

What's wrong with your brother Martin?

Martin	My mum and dad were too old to have another child. That's what the girls down my road say. They say it's disgusting at their age and they got what they deserved.
Rena	Girls can be cruel.
Martin	George is alright.
Rena	I'm cruel.
Martin	I know.
Rena	Why do you like me then?
Martin	What were you crying for?
Rena	My cousin's imminent. Noelle, for she was born on Christmas day. So she started out special. Doesn't that make you sick. If you like me. You mustn't like her. Promise.

Pause.

Martin	Where is she?

Rena   She takes her own sweet time about everything. She's spoilt. People think only children are spoilt. They're not. See only children, they have an onerous burden on their shoulders. They're never spoilt. I can always tell an only child.

Martin   Is that what you are?

Rena   See skeletons. They're supposed to stay in cupboards by the way. See our skeletons, they keep popping out to join the party.* They're particularly fond of Wales.

Up in the grassy cove one guitar's strumming. John's singing.

John   Out in Arizona where the bad men are
          And the only friend to guide you is an evening star
          The roughest, toughest man by far
          Is ragtime cowboy Joe.
          He got his name by singing to the cows and sheep
          Every night they say he sings his herd to sleep
          In a voice so rich and deep
          Creening soft and low
          * He used to sing
          Raggy music to the cattle as he swings
          Back and forward in a saddle on a horse
          That is syncopated gaited
          And there's such a funny meter
          To the roar of his repeater
          How they run
          When they hear that feller's gun
          Because the western folk all know

Three guitars picking and strumming.

          He's a hi falutin' rootin' tootin'
          Son of a gun from Arizona
          Rag time cowboy
          Dirty old cowboy
          Rag time cowboy Joe.

They go from 'Cowboy Joe' into 'The Hawaiian War Chant'. Gareth's singing. The men are the chorus. The steel string modulates to a bottle-neck Hawaiian sound.

Gareth   Hic a hooera
          A tac a hac a hooera
          Hic a hooera
          A tac a hac a hooera
          O wooera

David and **John** Wuh, wuh, wuh

Gareth   Hic a hooera

David and **John** Wuh, wuh, wuh

Gareth   O wooera

David and **John** Wuh, wuh, wuh

Gareth   Hic a hooera

David and **John** Wuh, wuh, wuh.

David   Doe-Doe. With me now.

Romantic slow slides on the guitar.

Dora   Sing me a song of the islands
My serenade where the trade winds blow
Sing me a song of the islands*
Where hearts are high and the moon is low.

Ailsa calls down from the cove to the beach.

Ailsa   * Rena, I've a roll for you.

Rhiannon joins Dora in harmony.

Both   Where rippling waters seem to sa aaaa yeee*
Oh ah oh ee alleee ayeee.
Bring me the / fragrance of ginger
Strum your guitars while I sing away
Sing me a song of the islands
Oh ah oh ee allleee ayee.

A wave breaks. The guitars are in the distance and the singing. The stones crunch under Rena's feet.

Martin   * Don't go.

Rena   I'll be back.

He calls after her.

Martin   What's their burden, only children?

Rena   Their parents, for God's sake.

Martin   My mother said George'll be the saving of me.

Rena   Do you need saving?

Martin   From her she said. I've always to protect him and stand up for him. The neighbours say his death would be a mercy. 'After all,' they say. 'He's quite sweet now,' they say. 'He won't be so sweet at six-foot-four and still in nappies.' The men in our family achieve a great height.

Rena   The men in our family play the guitar. The women sing. I'm genetically unsound so they tell me for I do neither.

Martin   I heard you playing.

Rena   I can't play. I'm a disappointment. Noelle's never disappointed in her life.

Martin	You sounded alright to me.
Rena	It's just a noise, music. Leadbelly and Brownie Mcghee, they're a noise. My Dad plays me Beethoven on the gramophone. Tchaikovsky he plays. Bach. It's a noise and it hurts my ears. See. In any other family it wouldn't matter. I'm a changeling in their nest. My hair's a flag that signifies that. I'm left-handed for God's sake. The devil took their proper child. My mother didn't see me for two days after I was born. My birth was very tiring. Noelle says I was swapped.
Martin	She's teasing you.
Rena	She's torturing me. That's her speciality.
Martin	Don't listen to her.
Rena	Everyone listens to Noelle. Even the skeletons dance to her tune.

Waves pull the stones down the slope to the sea.
In the cove.

John	Heart's ease. Rhiannon my love. Give your old uncle a treat.
Rhiannon	You're not old.
John	Do you still cry when you sing?
Rhiannon	That's my curse.
John	Come on my child.
Rhiannon	I'm no child.
John	You are to me.

Four soft chords.

Rhiannon	Lu la lu la lu la lu la Bye bye Does he want the moon to play with* The stars to run away with They'll come if you don't cry.
John	In her daddy's arms she's weeping.
Rhiannon	Soon she'll be a sleeping.
John	So close those pretty eyes.
Both	With a lu la lu la lu la lu la Bye.
Ailsa	* She's a beauty Doe.
Dora	Crocodile tears. She could sing 'Ten Green Bottles', they'd be rolling down her cheeks.
Ailsa	Still they break your heart.

Dora	John's always had a soft spot for Rhiannon.
Ailsa	God, I wish I was young. If I was young now I'd know what to do with it.
Dora	Would you have it different?
Ailsa	I'd have it better.

Ailsa's voice rises high.

> Once a native maiden and a stranger met
> Underneath a blue Tahitian moon.
> The stars were in her eyes
> Gardenias in her hair*
> And she vowed to care for ever.

Ailsa's singing fades into the distance. The waves are loud.

Martin	* There's someone watching.
Rena	Shite.
Martin	Rena!

Rena runs along the beach.

Rena	Noelle hey!
Noelle	Hay's for horses.
Martin	Rena!
Noelle	Who's your friend?
Rena	Why are you always so far behind?

They walk up the beach to the cove.

Noelle	Pleasure.
Rena	Eh?
Noelle	Rush at a thing, Rena, and it's over before it's begun. Who's he?
Rena	A friend.
Noelle	Sneaky.
Rena	How am I?
Noelle	I like the look of him.

Ailsa's singing drowns out the sound of the waves.

Ailsa	Then one lonely day the stranger sailed away
With a parting kiss that came too soon*
And now the Trade Winds sigh
As ships go sailing by

Underneath a blue Tahitian moon.

David	* Back to back. Come on now. / Noelle. I'm talking to you. Come on Rena.
John	We'll tell you who the tallest is but for the bonniest we'll leave you to fight it out between you. As for the sweetest natured we'll leave that for the future to decide. I've never met a sweet natured woman yet. Not after I've married one.
Ailsa	Been married often then have you?
John	There's married and married.*
Ailsa	What's that supposed to mean?
Dora	* That's enough John.*
Ailsa	I don't need you to fight my battles Dora.
Noelle	* I'm tallest see. Don't have to / stand back to back to tell that.
Ailsa	I may not be the first woman in your life John Williams. But I'll make damn sure I'm the last.
John	Is that a threat?
Ailsa	It's a promise.
John	Don't I have a say?
Ailsa	You had your say when you married me. You've said a couple of things since that haven't been so hot but I'm prepared to overlook them.
John	Here, Noelle. Here's a fried egg roll. Of my making, mind. Nice and hot and fresh out the pan. One for you Rena. Now. My advice to you. Take yourselves away. Don't let your sweet young selves be contaminated by this witch I married. Gareth don't you marry. Don't you ever marry.

He sings. David's guitar picks him up.

John	Oh I've got those mean mean woman blues
	I've got those mean woman blues
	She treats me so bad
	I've got nothing left to lose
	I work* hard to keep her
	But she throws my care away.

The guitar keeps the twelve bar going.

Ailsa	* I work, I might paint my nails red but I work my fingers to the bone. You show me a smarter woman when I leave the house in the morning. There isn't a smarter woman in our street. Nor any house with cleaner windows.* My windows shine. My baking tins are aye filled with gypsy creams and Empire biscuits. My stovies are unrivalled. You're living with a miracle John Williams. You're living with a miracle and you don't even know it.
John	* Oh I work so hard to keep her

But she throws my care away
The Lord will judge me willin'
When I come to him on judgement day.

Ailsa   Tell me you don't love me John Williams. Tell me that and I'll leave this cove and I'll leave this beach and I'll take my daughter and you'll never have truck with either one of us again. My God, sometimes I wish you would tell me. Tell me before I lose my looks John. Do me that favour. Then I can go out and I can find someone that'll appreciate me.

Dora   You'll never learn will you.

Ailsa   What the hell does that mean?

Dora   There was the wicked one and there was the good one. You got the wicked one.

Ailsa   And you got what you deserved isn't that right Dora?

John sings.

John   * Oh I've got those mean mean woman blues . . .

The guitar takes over. Another joins in and another. The girls slush through a shallow stream flowing over stones.

Rena   * Jesus this is freezing.

Noelle   Fresh water's colder than the sea of course.

Rena   You know everything I suppose.

Noelle   You have no idea.

Rena   Don't start.

Noelle   What?

Rena   Just don't start, right.

They wade through the stream. Rocks shift in the shallow water.

Noelle   Your Da makes great egg rolls.

Rena   D'you want mine?

Noelle   Don't you?

Rena   You can have it.

Noelle   Thank you.

Rena   Want a mud bath?

Noelle   What do you mean?

Rena   Lie down and I'll cover you with mud and it'll bake hard in the sun and it'll paralyse you.

Noelle	I'm eating an egg roll amn't I.
Rena	I'll start with your feet.
Noelle	Go on then.

She sits down with a splash.

Rena	Your skin's very dark.
Noelle	Jesus, he makes them salty.
Rena	Take a drink. You could bottle and sell it, this water. See, Welsh water. I love it when I come here.
Noelle	You never invite us up there.
Rena	My dad would live down here if he could. He's happy here that's what he says.
Noelle	Is that happiness? When I'm happy I hope I never look like he does.

The sound of mud slapping.

	Ow Rena. Watch it.
Rena	Hold still then.

The mud slaps and slaps.

	What're you staring at?
Noelle	You've got thin thighs. I wish I had thin thighs. I'm going to take after my mother. These are my best years. Depresses me sometimes. Why do you have to spend longer old than you do young?
Rena	Your waist's quite small.
Noelle	Do you think a man could get his hands round it?
Rena	Depends how big his hands are.
Noelle	I long for the feel of a man's hands at my waist. I want to feel small in his hands. Like a wild and delicate flower.
Rena	You've got yellow douk running down your chin.
Noelle	Tickles.
Rena	It's not very attractive.
Noelle	Some man might find it so. I might be sitting at breakfast with my husband one morning. And my breakfast egg will spurt and he'll come round the breakfast table, my husband will, and he'll lick the running egg from off my chin.
Rena	That's horrible.
Noelle	Only if you're Scottish.
Rena	A man licking your chin?

Noelle	The whole Scottish nation suffers from guilt and prudishness.
Rena	Says who?
Noelle	You want to remember you're your father's daughter.
Rena	What does that mean?
Noelle	He's licked some chins in his time.
Rena	Whose chin?
Noelle	Feel how hard this mud is. That sun's baking.
Rena	What d'you mean about my dad, Noelle?

Pause. A bird cries.

Noelle	The heat in this mud. I feel all lackadaisical. / I do really.
Rena	You'll feel dead in a minute. You'll get this mud in your mouth and you'll suffocate, Noelle Williams.
Noelle	Are you going to put it there?
Rena	Don't tempt me.
Noelle	You think you can take me on?
Rena	I know I can.
Noelle	I'll tell you about your father, I wasn't going to because I'm fond of you Rena and I'm not a cruel person. But you force my hand. You've got mud in my hair.
Rena	Jesus, Noelle.
Noelle	Blasphemy's common Rena. That's your mother's colours slipping through there. If you're very lucky your Welsh side might save you.
Rena	You are such a bitch.
Noelle	I've had yearly lessons, Rena Williams.
Rena	Are you going to tell me about my father or are you not?

Beat.

Noelle	I'm not. Not yet anyway.

Rena gets up and runs away along the bed of the stream. Noelle calls after her.

Careful Rena. Rena. You'll break your bloody leg.* Come and get this mud off me. Rena. Rena.

Her voice fades into the sound of rushing water and Rena's panting.

Rena *[whispers]* * Dear Mr Manning. Dear, dear, dear Mr Manning. I've a candidate for murder I want to introduce you to. I've got your number nine sitting in a fresh water stream in Wales waiting to have your knife plunge into her guts. Dear Mr Manning please don't take any other applications. This is important. Noelle Williams is the one for you. Please get yourself down here by the quickest method of travel. I'll reimburse any expenses you incur though it might take me a while. Girls can be bad bitches Mr Manning but Noelle Williams takes the biscuit. She'll make an awful woman when she comes to maturity. You'd be doing the world a favour were you to cease her being. About dinner time should suit. We'll all be gathered. You'll know the bitch by her yellow swimsuit and the rolls of fat on her upper arms. And the three necklace of Venus lines that circle her dark neck. She says they're a promise of the beauty that is to come. Don't go confusing the two of us. There's some maintain we look alike. I have no necklace of Venus round my neck as Noelle kindly pointed out last year. I have a red swimsuit, Mr Manning. Just so you know. It clashes with my hair but my mother says be brazen and be damned. She bought me the swimsuit. If only you were God Mr Manning. If you were God I would ask you to let me sing so that I could join them. I'm all alone here Mr Manning. My Father would forgive me the guitar if I could sing. Noelle can sing. And Rhiannon. I can hear it. I dream it, Mr Manning. I dream it so hard that when I wake up I can taste it. My own voice and it's lovely. Then I open up my mouth. And the sound that I hear. Mr Manning, it's an abomination. And it hurts my heart. Kill Noelle for me please. She only has to look at me. She knows all my misery. She knows it better than I do myself. That's not a thing any person should have to suffer. So you just kill her. We're all here on earth for a purpose. Your purpose is to rid the world of Noelle Williams and make me happy. No one's all bad Mr Manning. You do this death for me. It'll be your good deed. It'll get you into Heaven.

Martin	Who are you talking to?

A clink of flint on flint.

	Ow.
Rena	Don't you ever spy on me.
Martin	Don't throw stones.
Rena	Tit / for tat.
Martin	You / drew blood.
Rena	You stoned me. / So I stoned you.
Martin	Bloody sharp.
Rena	Not sharp enough.
Martin	You're sick.
Rena	You a wee skink are you, spying on me.
Martin	You're a cry baby.
Rena	Aye but you want to lick the tears from off my cheeks eh? Otherwise what are you doing hovering around eh?

The sound of the sea. The cry of a bird. The distant desultory strumming of a guitar.

Martin	Who's Manning?
Rena	What?
Martin	'Dear Mr Manning.' You talking to God?
Rena	Since when was God's name Manning? Don't you know anything where you come from?
Martin	We learn quickly. Who's Manning?
Rena	He's murdered eight folk so far. Everyone's waiting for number nine. My mum lives in terror. See, when the curtains are shut she thinks she hears him climbing up the rhone pipes. I hide under the kitchen table.
Martin	From Manning?
Rena	In the afternoon. When the cakes come out and the women talk. 'Manning' they say like they love him. Jesus they talk about nothing else.
Martin	Why don't the police arrest him?
Rena	See. What it is. The police know it's him. They trail him the whole time. They even drink with him in the club that he goes to. But they've got no evidence. He knows it and they know it. They have to wait for him to slip up. So far he hasn't. It's quite exciting. Used to be they scared you with the bogey man if you were bad. You know? Now it's Manning. 'Eat your mince or Manning'll get you.'
Martin	We could swim.
Rena	So we could.
Martin	Will we?*
Rena	What?
Martin	Swim.
Rena	If you like.

In the cove.

John	* Come on Doe. This is your song.

Three chords.

Dora	As I sailed my ship across the water When to Hawaii I said good bye All the world seemed sad and still as if It saw my grief and heard my cry.

Ailsa's soprano comes in in harmony.

Both	Farewell to thee.

The guitar breaks off.

John	I always preferred the single voice on that song.

Gareth	I'll help myself to black pudding will I?
John	Give me a contralto for a contralto sends shivers up and down my spine.
Ailsa	Maybe you should have married one.
John	Missed my chance didn't I?
Gareth	I'll help myself then. Da?
David	You're on your own son.
John	'Farewell to thee' Doe-Doe.

Three chords.

Dora	Farewell to thee
	Farewell to thee
	My passion flower for whom I long in vain*
	One fond farewell
	And faithful we will be
	Until we meet again
	Farewell.

Waves break on the stones at the sea's edge. The singing's far off.

Martin	* Right so. What you have to do. You have to stand with the water up to your neck. And you have to keep quite still and let the waves go right over your head.
Rena	How do you breath?
Martin	It's all in the timing.
Rena	I'm not allowed out of my depth.
Martin	In England we always do this.
Rena	You must think I'm awful thick.
Martin	No.

She imitates him.

| Rena | 'No.' Why can't you talk right? Say 'no'. |

He imitates her.

Martin	'No.'
Rena	Why can't you talk like that all the time?
Martin	You don't have to do the wave thing if it frightens you.
Rena	I'm not frightened of the sea. There's only one thing I'm frightened of.
Martin	What's that?
Rena	I'm not quite sure. But I'll tell you this by the way. Her up there, the

hippopotamus in the mud. Noelle. She's going to make damn sure I find out. What did I ever do to her Martin? You answer me that. For I must have done something. She hates me Martin. So she does.

Martin   Hate's a big word.

Rena   Popacatapetl that's a big word. Hate's easy learned.

Martin   Where are you going?

Rena   To the waves. Come on.

The waves break and break. The reflection of the sunlight blinds up from the water.

Blackout.

End of Act One.

Act Two

The heat shimmers on the horizon. It's almost audible in the grass cove.

Ailsa   For God's sake keep still Rhiannon.

Rhiannon   It's fidget time of day. Look see. Dad and Gareth are wandering. There's Mum and Uncle John on the cliff path.

Ailsa   Is there someone else up there?

Rhiannon   Why do you quarrel?

Ailsa   Your eyes are aye on that clifftop.

Rhiannon   Lying in bed when I was little, I used to listen to you all. The sound of the guitars floating up to my bedroom late at night. Made me feel safe.

Ailsa   Other days.

Rhiannon   I liked them.

Ailsa   Have you got St Vitus dance?

Rhiannon   It's hot that's all.

Ailsa   Go for a swim.

Rhiannon   Plenty time for that.

Ailsa   Who the hell are you looking for?

Pause.

     You must think I'm in my dotage.

Rhiannon   I'm not looking for anyone.

Ailsa   Have it your own way. Looking up there with your 'come to bed' eyes.

She sings at Rhiannon.

> Embrace me
> My sweet embraceable you.
>
> Don't tell me Rhiannon. I wasn't born yesterday.
>
> Embrace me
> You irreplaceable you
> Just one look at you my heart grew tipsy in me.
>
> We've all been there.

Rhiannon   I don't know what you're talking about.

Ailsa   Just one look at you brings out the gypsy in me. Is he nice?

Rhiannon   You have a vivid imagination Auntie Ailsa.

Ailsa   Don't come it Rhiannon. Don't you come it.

She lies back in the sun, still singing the Gershwin song. But to herself now. And it becomes about John. And there are tears in her eyes.

> I love all the many charms about you
> Above all I want my arms about you
> Don't be a naughty baby
> Come to Mama, come to Mama do
> My sweet embraceable you.

The wind soughs through the long dry grass by the side of the cliff path.

John   Come on into the long grass Dora.

Dora   What for?

John   Privacy.

Dora   No touching.

John   I'm offering you my hand so you don't fall. I'm offering you my hand, what's wrong with that Dora?

Dora   I know you.

John   Sit with me in the long grass. Talk to me, that's all.

Dora   Where does talk lead?

John   Wherever you want it to. You're in charge Dora.

Dora   Promise to be good John.

John   Come on. I'll be as good as you want me to be. Come on.

The grass swishes around them.

John   There's a hawk.

Dora   Take your hand off from round my waist.

John	Don't you want to see the hawk.
Dora	Where?
John	See how still he is.
Dora	That's a buzzard John.
John	I could drink that sky.
Dora	I'd rather drink a milk stout.
John	You haven't an ounce of romance in you.
Dora	I've been playing this game with you for the last – I've lost count of the years. If that's not romantic I don't know what is.

John kisses her and for a moment she's as passionate as he is. Then she breaks away from him.

	Who's there?
John	No one.
Dora	Is it one of the kids?
John	Rabbit maybe.
Dora	I don't want the kids seeing us.
John	There's no one there Dora.

His fingers tease at the bottom of her dress lifting it so that his hand's on her thigh.

Dora	I heard something.
John	You're jittery, that's all.

Music.

She lets him calm her. Allowing his hands free range. The music and the heat of the afternoon soothe. Then she pulls half away.

Dora	This is daft John. What we're doing.
John	Not doing anything are we? Not even talking. Not sensible talking. We could sit down Dora. We could at least do that. Be hidden by the grass then.

They sit.

Dora	Only for a minute.
John	Come here.
Dora	Oh God John. Listen.
John	What? What for God's sake?
Dora	Bach.
John	Bach?

Dora	David's playing Bach John. He's not happy.
John	Where're you going?
Dora	To his side.
John	What about me?
Dora	I'm thirteen stone and ten pounds John and my husband's playing Bach. Let me go.
John	What's your weight got to do with it?
Dora	There was a time once when I would have lain on a bed of nails with you and thought myself lucky. I'd have looked at the sky till my neck broke. Now heart, listen to me. It would be awful if we were found out now, you and me, when my passion's fulfilled by a hymn with the choir, a sit in a pub and a long cool glass by my hand.
John	Stay with me until I go and cook the curry. That's all. Let him play Bach. He's not out looking for us if he's doing that.

He takes her in his arms.

Dora	We're old for kisses.
John	No such thing.
Dora	I'm fat.
John	You're a river salmon.

She laughs.

Lush.

She doesn't leave him. She lets him coax her down into the grass.

Noelle's looking down on John's hollow from the top of the cliff.

Wind in the grass. A sharp scream.

Man	Spying are you?
Noelle	Get your hands off me.
Man	If you can see them they can see you.
Noelle	They're too busy to be looking up here to the cliff top.
Man	I don't like spies.

Noelle's startled but defiant.

Noelle	Your likes and dislikes mean nothing to me.
Man	That your Mammy?
Noelle	Everyone's Scottish today.

Man	You're not.
Noelle	Thank God for that.
Man	Eh?
Noelle	What I know of your lot I don't like.
Man	My my my.
Noelle	Who the hell are you?
Man	Go swim with your friends.
Noelle	They're no friends of mine.
Man	Your mammy's talking.
Noelle	Is that what you call it?
Man	You leave her to talk.
Noelle	Why should I?
Man	Spying's the act of a mean person.
Noelle	That's Rena Maeve Williams' father and he's holding my mother in his arms. Am I supposed to put up with that?
Man	They're not doing you any harm.
Noelle	I know exactly who you are. I could blow the whistle on you if I had half a mind.
Man	Go on with you. Go away.
Noelle	That's changed your tune.
Man	Go. Go, go, go.
Noelle	Make me.
Man	Yaaaaaaaaa.

Noelle gasps in fright and runs. The man laughs. It's not an unpleasant laugh. Not at all. Noelle yells from afar.

Noelle	Are you not ashamed of yourself?
Man	I'm not if you're not.
Noelle	You frightened me.
Man	You're easy frightened then.
Noelle	I'll tell on you.

The man's teasing laughter accompanies her running feet. Wind and sea and the cry of a bird. The sound of breaking waves. The water ripples around Martin and Rena. Loud panting.

Rena	My God. My God.

| Martin | Another one coming. |

Rena screams. The scream's muffled by water.

Heartbeats and the odd not quite silence of the underwater world.

Beyond the surface. Wind and sea and the cry of a bird.

Rena and Martin break the surface. Heave breath into their lungs.

Martin	What did you see? What did you see down there?
Rena	Jesus, I'm dying.
Martin	What did you see?
Rena	What did you see?
Martin	Took the heart out of me.
Rena	Was it Manning?
Martin	It was the devil. It was the devil coming in his chariot.
Rena	It was Manning. He heard my call. He's down in the depths come all the way from Glasgow. She better watch out Martin. Noelle. I've summoned him, Martin. Manning's nearly here. And if you're good to me Martin. I'll let you ask for a death too. Whose would you ask for Martin?

Beat.

Martin	Wave coming.
Rena	How long till you die for want of breath?
Martin	I don't know.
Rena	Are you scared?
Martin	Wave coming now.

Heartbeats fading into Rhiannon and Ailsa chopping vegetables on wooden chopping boards in the cove.

Rhiannon	Can I ask you something Auntie Ailsa?
Ailsa	Ask away. Asking's free. Do some more carrots.
Rhiannon	Am I my father's daughter?
Ailsa	Oh good. A riddle. I like riddles.
Rhiannon	If I had a child I'd like her to know who her grandfather was.
Ailsa	Are you expecting?

The sound of chopping fades into the sound of the waves.

| Rena | God I'm freezing. |
| Martin | Want a towel? |

Rena	Eh?
Martin	I'll get you one.

He runs over the stones. Rena calls after him.

Rena	Martin!

His footsteps fade into the sound of chopping in the cove.

Rhiannon	You know who my father is. Why shouldn't I?
Ailsa	The shock, Rhiannon, and me with a knife in my hand. You take my breath away. So you do.
Rhiannon	Who's my father?
Ailsa	David.
Rhiannon	It's between two people Auntie Ailsa. My mother's husband and yours.
Ailsa	Never mind the celery. Go and swim. Go on, go on. Give me the knife.
Rhiannon	I'm asking you a question.

Pause.

Ailsa	That's my knife. Give it to me.

Beat.

> Your mother would cry to hear you. And David. My God what would he do? Go and swim. Go on. I don't need you here. I don't want you. You're too thin and you're too young and you're bothering me. Give me my knife Rhiannon.

The Bach floods into the sound of the bubbling cold spring.

Noelle's in the stream splashing Rena. Noelle's laughing. Rena's shivering.

Rena	Stop it, / Noelle. Stop it.
Noelle	Only a bit of fun. / Where's your sense of humour.
Rena	I don't like being splashed. I don't think it's funny.
Noelle	Only being friendly.
Rena	People always say that when they hurt you.

A giggle and a splash.

> I'm warning you Noelle.

Noelle	Get your knight errant.

She shouts.

> Martin. / Martin. He'll save you.

Rena	Stop it.

She lobs a quick flint.

Noelle   Ow. No call for stones.

Rena   Don't say you weren't warned.

Beat.

Noelle   Your Mum had a son when she had you. But he died. Deformed he was.

Beat.

Rena   We could damn the stream. What about that?

She wades through the water grabbing rocks and heaving them down in a pile.

Noelle   Deformed horribly my mum says. I know you're listening.

Rena   See we could change the way the water runs. We could change it utterly.

A large stone clunks down on the rocky bed of the stream.

Noelle   The softest whimper he gave. Your brother. And then he died in Uncle John's arms. They went into mourning, your mum and dad. No one celebrated when you were born and your father mourns still. Because a girl can't carry on his name. So it's my brother that'll be the head of the family when your dad and my dad are dead and that means something, my mum says. If your dad died here on holiday you wouldn't even get to go to his funeral for women mean that.

She clicks her fingers.

                And girls mean less, my Mum says.

Rena   I'll keep his name.

Noelle   Well you can't so.

Rena   I can do anything I want.

Noelle   No woman can. Prisoners of their bodies women are.

Rena   Not me.

Noelle   Your mother can do anything I suppose.

Rena   Course she can.

Noelle   She can't get her husband to love her. She's stupid and you're stupid. You can't play the guitar and you can't sing. You've disappointed your father all the way down the line.

Rena   There was no twin brother.

Noelle   When have I ever lied to you?

Rena   My father loves me.

Noelle   Love's conditional Rena. It always was and it always will be.

Rena	I'll never take any other man's name but my father's.

Noelle   Your husband won't like that.

Rena   He'll have to take me as he finds me. He can have my body but he can't have my name and that's that. And if he doesn't like it I'll find one that does.

Noelle   You think a lot of yourself.

Rena   If I don't who will?

Noelle   A man doesn't like that in a woman. A man likes a woman to be modest in her endeavours and her achievements and to show a proper respect. See your attitude. Your attitude's the trowel that you'll dig your own slow grave with. You'll die alone Rena Maeve Williams. You mustn't be too powerful. Not obviously anyway. You must be subtle and devious. Dodge and weave, then you'll get your own way. Above all you must be clever.

Rena   I'll keep my father's name. That's my colour. I was born with it. I'll keep it for his sake and for my brother's sake that died though I didn't know it till this moment. I'll learn to play the guitar and when my father dies I'll play it in his stead every Hogmanay and the whiskies will build up under my chair as they do now under his. And I'll keep going till the morning light and I'll sing the old songs in my father's memory. I've got music in my soul. One day I'll find a way to let it out. When I do my father'll look down from on high with my baby brother on his lap and he'll love me very much and be proud of me for what I've become.

Noelle   It won't be legal.

Rena   Eh?

Noelle   You'll bear a pretend name. And he'll look down from on high with your baby brother on his lap and he'll say to your baby brother. 'She should have died, not you. For her name is a sham and she can't play the guitar to save herself and she's got a voice that slides between the frets and defies all keys and she's an abomination on the face of the earth and that's my Gibson Kalamazoo she's holding that should have gone to my son and heir and her fingers defile it that should never have touched it in the first place for they should be dead fingers and my Gibson Kalamazoo that a dealer offered me real money for and I said 'No,' should be in the hands of my living son and then I'd look down from up here and I'd be happy indeed.'

There's a sob in Rena's voice but it bites.

Rena   You've still got yellow douk running down your chin. It's dried and it's cracked. It's not the most attractive sight I've ever seen. Don't ever let a man see you like that Noelle, for you'll turn his stomach and then where will you be. I can stand on my own two feet. I can now and I always will. You're a clinging vine Noelle. You'll die on your own.

The sound of feet running away.

Noelle   Rena.

Noelle picks up water in her hands. Splashes her face with it. A private voice.

Noelle   You never get food on your chin do you Rena. One day I'll be as old as my Mother and then I won't know which chin I've got food on.

The sound of the stream fades. A knife chops on the wooden board.

Ailsa   Your eyes are aye straying to that hilltop.

Rhiannon   Mind your own business Auntie Ailsa.

Ailsa   It's alright for you to satisfy your curiosity is it? That's alright. But I can't ask a civil question in return. One brother or the other what difference does it make?

Desultory chopping.

Race you.

Rhiannon   What?

The knife's still again.

Ailsa   Onion. Catch.

The thud of an onion on the ground.

Butterfingers.

Rhiannon   I've a knife in my hand for God's sake.

Ailsa   Two onions each. First one to finish wins.

Rhiannon   These knives are sharp.

Ailsa   You win, I'll tell you all I know.

Rhiannon   You can't make a game of it.

Ailsa   Why the hell not?

Beat.

Take it or leave it.

Beat.

Go.

Ailsa's knife rapidly chews up an onion on her chopping board.

Rhiannon   I wasn't ready.

Ailsa   You have to be ready for anything in this life Rhiannon. Don't you know that by now. If I hadn't been ready. What I've had to put up with would have sucked the life out of me. But here I am. And here I'll stay. I'm battling against existence Rhiannon. And I'm winning Rhiannon. I'm battling against existence and I'm winning so far.

The chopping's furious and then it fades. The waves are sluggish now. Pulling at the stones. There's a football.

Noelle gasps in fright.

Martin	What are you doing?
Noelle	Sun bathing.
Martin	You were spying on Rena's mother.
Noelle	You gave me a heart attack.
Martin	I beg your pardon.
Noelle	Creeping around.
Martin	Sorry, I frightened you.
Noelle	I'm frightened of nothing.
Martin	Where's she gone?
Noelle	Who's she? The cat's mother?
Martin	Rena.
Noelle	You like her, don't you?
Martin	I brought her a towel.
Noelle	Give it to me.
Martin	I brought it for her.
Noelle	I'm wet aren't I?
Martin	I don't know you.
Noelle	You know her do you?
Martin	Rena?
Noelle	She's an evil cow.
Martin	What does that mean?
Noelle	Means she's my cousin. She's got red hair and green eyes and everybody turns their heads to look at her when she walks by. That's fine most of the time. Now and then it gets to me. Have I got the yellow off my chin?
Martin	I'm not that fond of red hair myself.
Noelle	You don't have to say that.
Martin	You're very pretty.
Noelle	You're a typical Englishman.
Martin	What's that mean?
Noelle	You've a smooth tongue and you can't be trusted.

Martin	You can have the towel.
Noelle	I only want to borrow it.
Martin	I didn't mean to keep.

The sound of the sea.

Noelle	Are you rich?
Martin	Why?
Noelle	You must be quite well-off.
Martin	How?
Noelle	We don't have towels like this to waste on the beach. That your Mum?
Martin	Uh huh.
Noelle	That your brother?
Martin	What if it is?
Noelle	He's big to be carried.
Martin	Is he?
Noelle	You look angry.
Martin	I'm never angry.
Noelle	I get so angry I could kill sometimes. You look angry watching your brother.
Martin	I love George.
Noelle	Funny that.
Martin	What?
Noelle	The look on your face doesn't spell out love to me.
Martin	What're you shivering for?
Noelle	I think you're quite a frightening person. Thank you for the loan of the towel.
Martin	We could find Rena.
Noelle	I was born on Christmas Day. They call me Noelle.
Martin	I know.
Noelle	Do we have to find Rena?
Martin	She's wild isn't she?
Noelle	I think she's common myself but you can call it wild if you like. People don't usually like their names. I like mine very much.
Martin	Come on Noelle.

Noelle	Sounds especially nice when you say it.

Just one pair of feet run up the beach slithering on the chuckies. Noelle stays where she is. Martin yells back.

Martin	Come on.

Noelle walks slowly up the beach.

Noelle!

Noelle	Keep your bloody hair on. I'm coming, look. See. I'm coming en't I.

The pebbles crunch and fade into two knives chopping furiously. One knife stops.

Rhiannon	I've won.
Ailsa	Have you?
Rhiannon	You tell me what I want to know.
Ailsa	This is the only dish my husband cooks. Every summer of your young life you've had Curry in a Bucket off him. Be honest with me Rhiannon. I know you want to beat me. Can you call to mind a lumpy onion in any one of the curries within your living memory? You can't, can you? Finely chopped they've been and this is the hand that chopped them.
Rhiannon	Know what made me question it, who my father was? It was you, Auntie Ailsa. The look in your eye. The way you watched Uncle John when he looked at me. We made a triangle him and you and me.
Ailsa	Nonsense.
Rhiannon	You're dead scared I'm going to win.
Ailsa	Are you chopping? Are you?
Rhiannon	I'm chopping. I'm chopping alright.

Frantic chopping on two boards. A caught breath. Then a scream.

Ailsa	What is it? / What's wrong? What's the matter.
Rhiannon	I've cut the top of my finger off.
Ailsa	Don't be / ridiculous.
Rhiannon	I have, / I have.
Ailsa	Where is / it then?
Rhiannon	Auntie Ailsa! / Auntie Ailsa!
Ailsa	If you'd cut the top off your finger it would be on your chopping board. Look in the onion. Look in the onion Rhiannon. Do you see a finger? Because I / most certainly do not.
Rhiannon	Auntie Ailsa.

Ailsa   You were always a tragedy queen Rhiannon. Show me what you've done.

A hiss of breath between teeth.

I'm not saying it's not nasty but you can dry your tears. At least it's all there. Hold your arm up for God's sake. Keep the blood off the onion. I've elastoplast in the picnic bag. Winning isn't everything Rhiannon. You should have been more careful.

The chords for Cole Porter's 'Miss Otis' from afar.

Rhiannon   Listen. David plays the sweetest guitar in the world but you wouldn't want to listen to him. Uncle John makes mistakes but you listen and you watch and you just love him.* Everybody does. Don't they Auntie Ailsa?

Ailsa   Keep that hand up. I don't want you bleeding to death.

An easy bluesy strum. David's soft sweet tones.

David   * When she woke up and found
That her dream of love was gone Madame
She ran to the man
Who had led her so far astray*
And from under her velvet gown
She drew a gun and shot her lover down
Madame, Miss Otis regrets she's unable to lunch today.

The wind rustles the dry grass. A far bird calls. A private voice.

Rena   * Dear Mr Manning. Mr Manning where are you? Mr Manning I can see them all from this cliff top. I'm like a bird up here in the wind and the air. I'm higher than the birds for they're all below me. I'm right on the very edge and I'm very nearly dizzy but I'm not quite. It's better than the waves Mr Manning. I'm battling against myself to stay on this cliff edge. Not to step forward and not to step back. That's my battle. My heart's beating Mr Manning. Can you hear it? I'm more excited than I've ever been in my life. This is the best moment I've had so far. Ever. Ever. Ever. Now I can sing. Now, now, now.

Hands grab Rena. She screams.

Man   Get away / from the edge.

Rena   I knew you'd come.

Man   Care / ful.

Rena   Manning?

Man   You'll fall.

Rena   I will not.

Man   The cliff could crumble.

Rena   I had taken that into consideration.

Man	Had you now?
Rena	Don't patronise me.
Man	I beg your pardon.
Rena	Get your hands off.
Man	Right you are.
Rena	You are him aren't you?
Man	Who are you?
Rena	Rena Maeve Williams.
Man	Pretty name.
Rena	I know you.
Man	Is that a fact?
Rena	You come from near where my Gran lives.
Man	Where's that then?
Rena	Balvicar Street.
Man	Nice view of the park.
Rena	You do though, don't you?
Man	If you say so.
Rena	I never forget a face.
Man	There's a club I like down there.
Rena	I called you.
Man	Gonnie get Rhiannon for me?
Rena	It's her sister I called you for.
Man	She's o'er young for me.
Rena	But you must. You must do it.
Man	Do what?
Rena	Noelle. She's going to tell me something that I don't know. And once she's told me I'll know it. And I'll not be able to unknow it. And my whole life'll change. I don't want that. You've got to stop her. Please Mister. Please, please.
Man	How am I to stop her?

Beat.

Rena	See her. See her way down there. Noelle's a bitch you know.

Man	She looks alright to me.
Rena	She's very far away. You wait till you see her up close.
Man	I'll take your word for it.
Rena	That's my Dad in the grass with my Auntie Doe. He's in love with her. He always has been. See her voice now. That's what he loves. You've only got to have the one beauty. It's supposed to be a secret. Their love. We all know. Doesn't make things too easy between Noelle and me. See. She blames my Dad. And I blame her Mum. And neither of us says what we mean.

Beat.

	Don't you think Noelle's just the swankiest awfullest name?
Man	Who's the boy?
Rena	Martin. I like him.
Man	What's your Mother doing?
Rena	God knows. She tells a lot, Noelle. But she always knows more than she tells. Feel my heart. I'll die it's beating so fast. You've got to shut her up. You are Manning aren't you? You've got to be him.

In the cove the primus roars. A kettle boils.

Ailsa	Hot and sweet for shock.
Rhiannon	I don't like it sweet.
Ailsa	You'll drink it whether you like it or not.
Rhiannon	You're a bully Auntie Ailsa.
Ailsa	It's not my fault you know.
Rhiannon	What?

Beat.

Ailsa	You hope that you're not going to be alone. That's what I hope anyway. Circumstances are such that I find myself to be . . .
Rhiannon	My mother loves my father.
Ailsa	She should tell my husband that.
Rhiannon	Whose child am I?
Ailsa	The bleeding's stopped.
Rhiannon	Please Auntie Ailsa. Please.

Beat.

Ailsa	Will we play another round, Rhiannon? I'll give you another chance.

Rhiannon	What?
Ailsa	How do you keep that body in trim?
Rhiannon	What?
Ailsa	It's not absolutely natural. The way you look. Show me what you do to help it.
Rhiannon	I exercise Auntie Ailsa, that's all.
Ailsa	Teach me the exercises.

Beat.

Close your mouth Rhiannon. Nobody looks quite the thing with their mouth agape be they ever so pretty.

Rhiannon	Don't you care at all how I feel?
Ailsa	I care about my own child. You've enough people caring about you. If I can do what you do I tell you nothing. If I can't, you get to know what I know. May it do you more good than it has me.
Rhiannon	This isn't a game.
Ailsa	How come we're all playing it?
Rhiannon	You can't do what I do.
Ailsa	You've nothing to lose then.
Rhiannon	I've been dancing all my life Auntie Ailsa.
Ailsa	We've all heard about your dancing Rhiannon.
Rhiannon	You can't just spread your legs and put your head on the sand.
Ailsa	Yes I can. I've been doing Canadian Airforce exercises since the Canadian Airforce came into being. We'll swop. You show me what you do and I'll show you what I do.
Rhiannon	You'll hurt yourself Auntie Ailsa.
Ailsa	I can't hurt more than I do already.

The wind in the long grass. Dora's delighted laughter.

Dora	Don't John. What are you doing?
John	Stopping.
Dora	Not now.
John	'Don't,' you said.
Dora	I've changed my mind.

From the path.

Gareth	Oh my God.
David	Move. Move, move, move.
Gareth	Dad!

He pulls his son round the corner.

David	She see you?
Gareth	No.
David	Sure?
Gareth	Dad, for God's sake.
David	Did she see you?
Gareth	She didn't see me. / She didn't see me. Alright?
David	Come on son.
Gareth	You're not even shocked.
David	We're walking / aren't we?
Gareth	What's going on?
David	With you or without you, Gareth.

He walks away.

Gareth	Dad.

The wind blows in the hollow. Dora laughs.

John	Say you've missed me.
Dora	Don't stop.
John	Say it.
Dora	John.
John	Not till you say it.
Dora	I've missed you. I've missed you. God damn you John. How could I not?

A bird screams.

Gareth	What are you going to do?
David	I'm doing nothing.
Gareth	Jesus Christ, Dad.
David	We don't know. / We didn't see.
Gareth	That's your wife.
David	If they'd wanted us to see they'd have done it in front of us. Now let it be.

Gareth	Do something. Do anything.
David	I'm walking up this path Gareth. I'm looking down at the ocean. I'm watching the waves break on the shore. And I'm asking you to walk with me.

Wind. A bird cry.

Smoke?

David flicks open a cigarette case. He dunts a cigarette on the metal. Lights Gareth's cigarette and his own. Drags deeply.

Gareth	How long's it been going on?
David	I'd add this to the marriage vows. Keep your secrets. Never breathe. Never hint. Don't tell at the moment of a parting or on the day of a death. Don't let a fight pull it out of you. If you sin. It's your sin. Never cast your sin on another for their forgiveness and your relief. Bear your guilt yourself forever. Confession only injures the hearer. Lock it up. Lock it all inside you. See that? That back there. Who's to say that's not my fault? If that's what your mother needs to give me fifty weeks of her year. So be it. I don't want her to tell me about it. Don't want that ever. The day she tells me's the day I lose her. The longer the time that passes and her silent the more sure I am that she'll never speak. That I'll keep her.
Gareth	You can't live with this.
David	I can. I have.
Gareth	I don't have to.
David	You speak and I'll have nothing left. You've your own life Gareth. This is mine.
Gareth	Where are you going?
David	Going on up. Feel the wind. Coming? Gareth?

Rhiannon counting in the cove. The grass creeps with heat. A bird cries. A small groan.

Rhiannon	Two, three, four, five, six, seven, eight.
Ailsa	That's a split isn't it? That's a split Rhiannon.
Rhiannon	Box split.
Ailsa	You didn't bloody think I could. Admit it. Come on.
Rhiannon	I didn't think you could.
Ailsa	Well I can. I bloody can. What now?
Rhiannon	Lay your upper body flat on the ground.
Ailsa	What?
Rhiannon	Arms out. Bust on the sand.
Ailsa	Still in a split?

Rhiannon	Don't do it if you feel any strain.
Ailsa	There's bound to be some strain isn't there?
Rhiannon	Take it slowly.
Ailsa	My God it's not possible.
Rhiannon	Watch. Five, six, seven, eight.

A slight exhalation of breath.

Ailsa	You're allowed to turn your face sideways are you.
Rhiannon	Cheek on the sand.
Ailsa	Not nose?
Rhiannon	Your nose is bigger than mine. Auntie Ailsa. You wouldn't have as far to go.
Ailsa	Cheek then. Arms out?
Rhiannon	Oh God, Auntie Ailsa.
Ailsa	Nothing to it.*
Rhiannon	Wait.
Ailsa	* You watch Rhiannon. Just you watch.
Rhiannon	Auntie Ailsa please.
Ailsa	Just takes concentration. Five, six, seven, eight.

A grunt of effort. An awful sound. The noise of a tendon snapping. The littlest sound from Ailsa.

Ailsa	Oh.
Rhiannon	Oh God.
Ailsa	Oh.
Rhiannon	Auntie Ailsa?
Ailsa	Rhiannon!
Rhiannon	Get up Auntie Ailsa.
Ailsa	Oh Rhiannon. I'm an awful fool.
Rhiannon	Get up. Get up. Please.
Ailsa	A bloody, bloody fool.

She wails.

Looking down from the cliff.

Man	Your mother's in trouble.
Rena	I don't care.

Man	Go on down.
Rena	I will not.
Man	That's your mother. It's the only one you'll ever have. Now you go on down to her. Or you'll get a skelp from me.
Rena	No man lifts his hand to me.
Man	I'll count to three.
Rena	I thought you'd be different.
Man	One.
Rena	You're not the least bit what I expected.
Man	Two.
Rena	You're a hell of a disappointment do you know that?
Man	Go on. Go on. Get.

Rena runs down the cliff path past Martin and Noelle.

Martin	Look out Rena.
Noelle	Be careful.
Martin	Where are you going?
Rena	Are you deaf?
Noelle	It wasn't your Mum screaming?
Rena	Uh huh it was.
Noelle	Oh Jesus. I'm coming Rena.
Martin	Can I come?
Noelle	This is family.

The sound of running feet.

Martin	I'll see you later. Rena? Noelle?

His voice fades as they run.

	I'll see you later won't I?

There's a dry heat in the cove.

Rhiannon	They're all coming Auntie Ailsa. Tell me. Tell me quick. Which one of them's my dad?
Ailsa	How can I tell you what I don't know?
Rhiannon	What?

Ailsa	I know nothing. I surmise that's all. I know no more than you.
Rhiannon	You're a cheat Auntie Ailsa.
Ailsa	I'm punished for it then. At my lowest I've thought I was the richer for all of it. I've lived I told myself. And I watched other women with their cosy lives and I didn't envy them. 'What's the worst that can happen to you?' I'd ask myself. 'Nothing,' I'd answer. 'Nothing's the worst that can happen to you.' I'd tell myself that for comfort but I'd be lying. The tales I've spun to myself. One Easter he was down here working in Cardiff. I thought I'd lost him to your mother then right enough. And with each tale I told myself. I treated him different. I drove him further and further away. Whatever he's done. I paid him out. My pride made sure I did. You're some man's daughter Rhiannon. That's the only certain thing. I would guess you must be some good man's daughter. For you've turned out fine. Let that do you.

She shouts.

Jooooooohn.

The sound of the shout fades from near to far. The cry of a bird rising from the long grass.

Dora	She's got you on a string.
John	She's hurt.

John gets up.

Dora	Stay with me.
John	I'd go to a cat if it yowled like that Dora.

Rena's shifting from foot to foot on the stones.

Ailsa	For God's sake Rena, stand still.
Rena	Does it hurt?
Ailsa	I've snapped a tendon. Of course it hurts.
Rena	Are you comfy?
Ailsa	What do you think?
Rena	Will I get a cushion?
Ailsa	Don't keep on Rena. Stop gawping at me.

Pause. John comes down the cliff path.

John	Don't you lash out at her Ailsa. She's done nothing.
Ailsa	You took your time getting here.
John	Poor wee girl.
Ailsa	I need your hand on me. I hurt my leg John.

John lays his hand on Ailsa's leg.

John	Better?
Ailsa	I dream of your hands John. Long . . . cool.
John	Rest.
Ailsa	I still dream of him, my son. Yours and mine, John. Our wee boy. I dream of him in his grave and I'm standing by the side of it and I throw myself down and I'm trying to dig him up. So I can hold him. So I can tell him I love him. I never held him John. They should have let me hold him. So I'm down there on my knees and I'm crying and I'm digging in the earth and I'm worrying about my nails John, that I'll break them. And I feel bad because I'm thinking about the state of my damn nails and not just about my wee boy. They should have let me hold him John before they took him away. They should have let me hold him.
John	You're my own love. My own heart. Shhh. Shhh. Shhh. Alright?
Ailsa	Nice.
John	Need anything?
Ailsa	My stomach thinks my throat's cut.
John	What do you want?
Ailsa	Some of your curry John. That's what I've a yen for.
John	Your wish is my command.

He walks away over the stones to the cove.

Ailsa	This is a hell of a holiday so far.
Rena	I know.
Ailsa	Look at your Auntie Doe wobbling down that cliff path.
Rena	You're a bitch.
Ailsa	I'm allowed to be. How can he like a fat woman?
Rena	Who?
Ailsa	Your father for God's sake Rena. Use your intelligence. What did God give it to you for? Your father. Your father. Your father and your Auntie Doe. Tttt. Beware of women Rena. No matter what they look like. They're dangerous. Fat or thin. Beware of friendship. For between women there's no such thing. We're powerful God help us. Every last one of us. And what we do to each other. My God Rena. My God. Don't you be a woman when you grow up.
Rena	Don't cry.
Ailsa	Why not?
Rena	I don't like it.
Ailsa	You'll have to lump it then. Oh God, Rena. I can't stop.

Rena pats her mother's bare shoulder.

Rena   Sorry.

Ailsa   Don't you ever let what's happened to me happen to you. You be strong. Do you hear me? Never love a man. Take what you want from them. A passing warmth that's all they've got to give. Sex? You can do that better for yourself. I'll have you know that you're alone. Here and now. We're born alone. We die alone. And in between, believe you me, we're alone then too. Live without illusions. For if you haven't got them no one can take them from you. Can they? Can they?

Rena   No.

Ailsa   I can't hear you.

Rena   No. I said. No.

Ailsa   I spend all my waking hours thinking of your father. All my waking hours. He is the one and only love of my life. Tell me. How could it happen that I am not the love of his? You tell me. How could such an awful thing occur? When I lost your brother. All I could think was I'd killed his son. I never once thought that it was a part of me gone. God help you I didn't think of you at all.

Silence.

This is going to be a long two weeks and a long long life to follow.

She sniffs.

Curry.

She sniffs again.

Feel the smell of that curry. Your father's curries. Curry and tears, eh? Curry and tears.

The roar of the primus. The clang of a pail. The scrape of metal on metal.

John   Hands off Rhiannon.

Rhiannon   I can cook.

John   I make the curries.

Rhiannon   You want a bit of help don't you?

John   No other hand but mine.*

John slaps Rhiannon's hand.

Rhiannon   Ow.

John   * Be told will you? What age are you?

Rhiannon   Old enough to go barefoot in some man's kitchen.

Beat.

John	I'm not so easily impressed.
Rhiannon	Wasn't trying to impress you.
John	What then?
Rhiannon	Uncle . . .
John	Drop the Uncle, shall we? I'm sure you're old enough for that.
Rhiannon	What will I call you?
John	I think we'll make do with John, don't you?
Rhiannon	I've got a boy-friend then, John.
John	Not so very hard to come by for a girl with average looks. Most men have their tongues hanging out. The surprise would be if you didn't have something sniffing at your heels.
Rhiannon	Was that supposed to be an insult?
John	Oh I can do better than that with insults if I just set my mind to it.
Rhiannon	I want to live with him.
John	Give me the cloth. I don't want to burn my hand.

John holds the pail steady while he gives the curry a turn with a wooden spoon.

John	I gather we're not talking about marriage.
Rhiannon	I want my father to wish me luck.

The pail handle scrapes down the side of the pail.

John	You want to go off and be some man's whore?
Rhiannon	I'm going to London today.
John	In your bathing suit?
Rhiannon	I took him a case last night.
John	You'll break your mother's heart.
Rhiannon	I thought my father might comfort her.
John	Your father's the man who brought you up. He may be quiet but he cares.
Rhiannon	There's a tone in my father's voice that I hate. I hear it in my own voice. For I take after him. There's a light in his eyes that I love, that I'm glad to see in mine. Will you not wish me luck?

Beat.

John	That your friend up there?
Rhiannon	He's a nice man.

John	'Nice' puts on a suit and walks up to the altar.
Rhiannon	He loves me.
John	He'll live with you. He'll take what he wants. He'll never marry you. One day you'll have lines around your eyes. Rhiannon. And he'll find someone younger. I'm warning you.
Rhiannon	Not all men are like you.
John	What kind of bastard do you think I am?
Rhiannon	He's already married, John. He married a Pape.

Pause.

John	If there's any trouble. I'll come running to you. Conversely. You know where I am. You come to me. And if you're barefoot and pregnant in his kitchen let me know the child you give birth to. Will you do that?
Rhiannon	I will always keep in touch with you.
John	That's my own girl.

The sound of the waves. Footsteps on stone.

Dora	You alright?
Ailsa	All the better for seeing you.
Dora	Don't start.
Ailsa	Och well.
Dora	Don't you want us to take you to hospital?
Ailsa	It's a torn ligament.
Dora	Bad enough.
Ailsa	It's my own damn fault.

Rhiannon's walking up the cliff path.

Dora	Where's Rhiannon going?
Ailsa	You've had your mind on other things, Dora. She's been watching that cliff top all day.
Dora	What for?
Ailsa	That's what for.
Dora	Who is he?
Ailsa	He's a stranger to me Dora. But by her greeting I'd guess Rhiannon knows him well enough.
Dora	She's only a baby.

Ailsa	He doesn't seem to think so.
Dora	What's she playing at?
Ailsa	Go and ask her that yourself.
Dora	I can see me puffing up that cliff. I can just see me.
Ailsa	You should diet, do you know that?
Dora	She's not going Ailsa. She's not leaving. Oh my God. She should come here to me. She should say goodbye to me.
Ailsa	David's there.
Dora	That's my child. She'd never have been born but for me. He can't say as much. She says goodbye to him though. Girls and their fathers. I should have had sons.

Dora starts up the path.

Ailsa	For God's sake Dora you can't run up there. You'll have a heart attack.
Dora	'You want another child find someone else to sire it.' That's what he said after Gareth. David. French letters. My God I hate the things. I thought I could get him lost in passion. Not him. We'd be making love, he'd stop and out they'd come. He never forgot. Not once in the three years between Gareth and Rhiannon. My husband is utterly dependable. My good, good man. I was thin then. All my days went on devising ways to make him lose his head. My God practically acrobatic I was. I hurt with thirst for another child. I made love to his brother. Not that I loved John. Never did. Never have. Don't now. Children I had a passion for. They are the loves of my life.
Ailsa	My poor John.

Pause.

	I have passion in me that's not been touched yet. I have such a wealth in me. I'll die when all my passion's spent. That's your daughter walking up that path and she didn't say goodbye. I don't blame her. I'd walk away from you if I could.
Dora	You should have stopped coming here years ago.
Ailsa	It's my fault now is it? For God's sake, Dora, don't cry. If I'm not I don't see why you should.
Dora	I've lost my beautiful daughter.
Ailsa	She'll be back. Don't you worry. She'll be back bearing a child in her arms that she'll ask you to look after. For God's sake. Stop your greeting. We've two weeks to dig a hole on this beach and bury the past in it. We'll communicate by letter after that. We'll take Rena abroad next year. After all she's my only child. It's high time she saw the advantage of that. Maybe we'll ski at Christmas. We've the Cairngorms on our doorstep. I've a good job. I make the most of the limited talent God's granted me.

Dora   I envy you your work.

Ailsa   Dry your eyes for God's sake. / Reach me a cushion for my leg hurts.

The wind and the grass and the cry of the birds. Rena's private voice.

Rena   Dear Mr Manning. Come down from the roof of the world. Please, please Mr Manning come down here and kill them all.

Noelle's eating curry with a spoon from a china bowl.

Noelle   Who're you talking to?

Rena   The murderer on the cliff top.

Noelle   I met him.

Rena   You can't let me have anything to myself can you? You've always got to stick your nose in.

Noelle   You can have Martin.

Rena   I don't want Martin.

Noelle   Just because he's English.

Rena   I like him. I don't want him.

Noelle   My mother says never marry a Welsh man. They don't know how to pay a compliment.

Rena   What does your mother know about the English?

Noelle   Just because she's fat, Rena Williams, doesn't mean she hasn't travelled.

Rena   He's coming down from the top of that cliff and he's going to murder the whole lot of us.

Noelle   It's Rhiannon's boy-friend.

Rena   Don't talk shite.

Noelle   I like knowing things. It's special. I like being special. I'm very good at it. I'll be special all my life.

A guitar.

This is rare good curry.

Rena   I don't like it.

Noelle   You depress me do you know that? Give it here.

Rena   Look at them, Dora and Ailsa. They could almost be friends they're so close.

Noelle   Know what they're talking about?

Rena   Shut up.

Noelle   My Mum / and your Dad.

Rena   Shite.

Noelle   You're like an / ostrich you are.

Rena   Shite / shite shite.

Noelle   Ostrich. Ostrich. Bowl's empty. Go and get me some more curry.

Rena   Get it yourself.

Noelle   My Mum stuck holes in French letters to get Rhiannon, though she was ashamed of doing it. And when the holes didn't work she got your Dad to do the necessary. Which was quite considerate of her because it kept it all in the family. Do you believe me?

Rena   She's very pretty, Rhiannon.

Noelle   Say you believe me or I'll tell you something else.

Pause.

Rena   There's no more to tell.

Noelle   Is there not?

Rena   Is there?

Noelle   It's there in front of you. It's there inside you. You only have to reach for it.

Beat.

          Easter's a movable feast, Christmas is not. The year I was born Easter was early and your Dad came down to Cardiff. Work out the rest yourself. You're too big to be spoon fed.

Rena   Where are you going?

Noelle   Maybe I'll swim with Martin.

Noelle walks away across the stones.

Rena   I like Martin. Noelle. Noelle. We better take the bowls back.

Beat.

          You're my sister too are you? Noelle?

Noelle's laughing as she walks down to the sea's edge.

          Noelle. Mr Manning. I've got her for life now. You could have prevented this. You only had to lift your hand. Never trust a man. Never trust a woman. Trust your own self that's the only one you can be sure of. I've learnt a lesson this day. You've let me down badly do you know that? Do you hear me Mr Manning? Are you listening to me? Sod you then.

She runs along the beach. Noelle shouts.

Noelle	See him. See Rhiannon with him. One day somebody'll kiss me like that. After all I've got breasts.
Rena	You can't swim straight after curry.
Noelle	I don't know what's in store for me Rena. I don't know and I don't want to know. But I'm telling you this. Death by drowning isn't it.

A voice begins to sing 'Good Morning Blues'.

Gareth	I laid down last night Turning from side to side* I laid down last night Turning from side to side But I wasn't sick Just dissatisfied.
Noelle	* Listen to him. Gareth. Pity your father has no son.
Rena	I'll be good one day. I'll be good at something anyway. Maybe I'll be an engineer. He'd like that, my dad. If I was an engineer the guitar wouldn't matter.*

The waves break. The birds cry.

Gareth	I woke up this morning Blues sneaking round my head I woke up this morning Blues sneaking round my head I couldn't eat Blues all in my bread Good morning Blues* Blues how do you do?

Other voices quietly join in the song, Ailsa and Dora and John.

	Good morning blues Blues how do you do? I'm doing alright Good morning how are you?
David	With me Doe Doe. With me now.
Dora	Drifting and dreaming While shadows fall Softly at twilight I hear you call.

The pebbles ebb and flow with the pull of the waves. Martin shouts.

Martin	Rena! Noelle!

Dora's singing in the distance.

Dora	Love's old sweet story Told with your eyes*

> **Drifting and dreaming**
> **Sweet Paradise.**

The sound of splashing water. Screams and shouts and laughter. A wave breaks.

Rena	* It's a mystery. Jesus.
Noelle	What?
Rena	Life. Noelle!
Noelle	You just tell it to wait right where it is. Life? I can't wait to get my hands on it.

The waves break and break. The guitar plays on. There's laughter at the water's edge.

The End.

Activities

Family Relationships – page 176
Diary Entry

Rena is having difficulty coping with her parents. As the Williams family approach she takes the time to write an entry in her diary.

Once everyone has completed the diary entry ask them, in turn, to read out the sentence that best sums up Rena's situation. Discuss her relationship with her parents, Martin and Mr Manning.

Love Triangle – page 180
Hot Seat

After Ailsa and Dora's exchange, hot seat the two women together.

If both participants wish to enter into a role play dialogue as the hot seating progresses, allow this to happen.

The discussion afterwards should include the role of women, family gatherings and rivalry.

Secrets – page 200
Role Play

Rena falls asleep. In her dream she has a conversation with Noelle and she tells Rena what the dark secret is. In groups of twos, ask the students to perform a role play. One is Rena and the other Noelle.

If there is time during the reporting back session after the role play, choose one or two conversations to listen to.

Discuss all the ideas and if possible record some of the most popular.

Morality – page 209
Conscience Alley

John and Dora have gone off together. Ask the group to form the conscience alley and then, one at a time, have Dora and John walk down the alley.

Discuss the words used by the group and the opinions formed as a result of the alley.

Cuckold – page 211
Hot Seat

David and Gareth have seen Dora and John together. Hot seat David.

Afterwards, ask the group to give their opinion on the situation and their reaction to David's answers.

Character Studies

The play revolves around two brothers and their families: David Williams, his wife Dora and their three children Gareth, Rhainnon and Noelle; John Williams, his wife Ailsa and their only daughter Rena. John and David are Welsh. John and his family live in Scotland whereas his brother and family live in Wales. Each year John, Ailsa and Rena make a pilgrimage to Wales where the whole family meet up.

We can all identify with family gatherings and the kind of things that occur, the arguments, rituals or gossip perhaps. The Williams clan are no different. We see clearly that there is a secret to be told and, rightly or wrongly, this year it is going to come out.

Rena

Rena is the central character. She is 11 years old. She is clever, cheeky, amusing and tough, but she lacks confidence and self-esteem. She doubts her own ability at times and is jealous of Noelle. She likes Martin when she meets him and there is the usual boy/girl stand off; neither want to admit they like each other but through teasing and sarcasm they strike up a friendship. She knows there is a family secret but she is bound by a mixture of fear and intrigue. She knows that when she finds out it will change things for ever.

Cheeky

Rena doesn't make her meeting with Martin easy but she does like him.

JOHN [calls]
> *Shift, Rena.*

Martin yells after her.

MARTIN

> *What's your name?*

RENA

> *You stupid or what are you?*

JOHN [calls]

> *Rena!*

RENA

> *The whole of bloody Wales knows my name.*

Easily embarrassed

Rena is probably typical of an 11 year old. She is embarrassed about her parents.

Ailsa begins to sing. Her voice embraces the whole coastline *(page 167)*.

RENA [whispers]

> *Christ, don't sing.*

Lacking in confidence and self esteem

(page 175)

RENA

> *I'm no good at the guitar.*

We also see this later with her Uncle David *(page 179)*.

RENA

> **I can't play.*

DAVID

> *No such word.*

RENA

> *I'm useless Uncle David. You know that better than anyone.*

She runs. John calls after her.

Tough

She shows this when Martin gives her a hanky *(page 180)*.

RENA

> *Jesus. The bloody thing's clean. Mammy's boy. Won't ever say shite. I hate Mammy's boys. You can't trust them.*

Jealous

She is jealous of Noelle and frightened of her.

MARTIN

>   *What were you crying for?*

RENA

>   *My cousin's imminent. Noelle, for she was born on Christmas day. So she started out special. Doesn't that make you sick. If you like me. You mustn't like her. Promise.*

Fear

She fears what Noelle is going to say because she knows it will change everything *(page 220)*.

RENA

>   *Look at them, Dora and Ailsa. They could almost be friends they're so close.*

NOELLE

>   *Know what they're talking about?*

RENA

>   *Shut up.*

She talks to Mr Manning by way of dealing with her anxieties. In this way she gets relief from the traumas of growing up and also the tension between her parents.

She has many moods throughout the play and she takes these 'out' on Martin, Noelle and Mr Manning.

Ailsa

Ailsa is Rena's mother. She is Scottish. The annual pilgrimage to Wales is a trial for her. We see this when Rena begs her to say that she is enjoying the holiday *(page 171)*.

RENA

>   *Say you like coming here.*

AILSA

>   *I come here for him. [John]*

RENA

>   *Say it. Please.*

She obviously loves her husband. She indulges him in all of his notions.

She has her suspicions about his relationship with Dora and she hints very strongly throughout the play. John talks about dying happy if he knows his only daughter has his cherished guitar *(page 176)*.

AILSA

>   *Rena Maeve'll be left will she? Rena Maeve and your Gibson Kalamazoo.*

JOHN

> *Enough, Ailsa.*

AILSA

> *Is that all that'll be left?*

JOHN

> *I'm warning you.*

AILSA

> *You are not the clean potato John Williams.*

Again she passes comment, this time on Rhiannon *(page 179)*.

AILSA

> *She is growing into the family look. I see my husband in your eyes Rhiannon. She's John's eyes Doe. God help us all. You see your age in the young ones Dora.*

She has a love–hate relationship with Dora

AILSA

> *It's always good to see you in the flesh Dora.*

DORA

> *I look forward to your visits.*

AILSA

> *There's a masochist in all of us then.*

At the end of the play the women come to terms with one another *(page 219)*.

DORA

> *You should have stopped coming here years ago.*

AILSA

> *It's my fault now is it? For God's sake, Dora, don't cry. If I'm not I don't see why you should.*

DORA

> *I've lost my beautiful daughter.*

AILSA

> *She'll be back … We've two weeks to dig a hole on the beach and bury the past in it. We'll communicate by letter after that.*

She loves her husband but wishes she could do as Rhiannon has and walk away from him, but she can't. She loves her daughter too much and won't leave her with John. Ailsa's sadness is also for the son she lost. She has great love and passion that she feels her husband has never reached.

Dora

Dora is plump and feels she is passed her best. She loves children and when her husband didn't want any more, she went to great lengths to have another child – with her brother-in-law. She also finds this fortnights holiday trying and has to give as good as she gets to keep up with Ailsa's onslaught. She and John still have an attraction for each other.

He takes her in his arms *(page 196)*.

DORA

> *We're old for kisses.*

JOHN

> *No such thing.*

DORA

> *I'm fat.*

JOHN

> *You're like a river salmon.*

She laughs.

> *Lush.*

She doesn't leave him. She lets him coax her down into the grass.

She wants their secret to stay that way but knows deep down that the truth must come out. She finally makes her peace with Ailsa. They know they will always have their differences but agree to try to bury the past and get on with their lives.

David

David appears to be the strong silent type. He knows exactly what his wife and brother have been 'up to' for years and he has chosen to look the other way, even when he and his son come across the pair in the meadow *(page 210)*.

GARETH

> *What are you going to do?*

DAVID

I'm doing nothing.

GARETH

Jesus Christ, Dad.

DAVID

We don't know. / We didn't see.

GARETH

That's your wife.

DAVID

If they had wanted us to see they'd have done it in front of us. Now let it be.

This could make David look weak or perhaps even stupid, but it doesn't. It lets us see he is a deep, thoughtful man who has over the years weighed up this problem and come to a decision to ignore it unless Dora speaks about it to him.

Noelle

Noelle is the youngest daughter of David and Dora. She was born on Christmas day, hence her name, and has been led to believe that she is special because of this. We get the impression she is spoiled. She is Rena's worst nightmare. She has always got an answer. She is cruel and spiteful. Her jealousy is at the route of all the torment she inflicts on Rena *(page 203).*

NOELLE

She's an evil cow.

MARTIN

What does that mean?

NOELLE

Means she's my cousin. She's got red hair and green eyes and everybody turn their heads to look at her when she walks by. That's fine most of the time. Now and then it gets to me ...

Noelle and Rena's relationship mirrors that of Dora and Ailsa and we see the same thoughts and emotions being conveyed through both pair's encounters.

Rhiannon

Rhiannon is the second child of Dora and David. She has a secret of her own. She is going to leave with a stranger from Glasgow and begin her own life. She has spent all of her childhood holidays in this strained atmosphere. Before she leaves she wants to know the truth, having had her suspicions for a long time. She tackles her Aunt Ailsa to try to find out the truth but Ailsa plays hard to get. They have a very easy relationship though, much easier than that of Ailsa and Dora *(page 199)*.

RHIANNON

> *You know who my father is. Why shouldn't I?*

Finally she find out the truth and confides in her biological father that she is going off with a married man.

RHIANNON

> *I will always keep in touch with you.*

JOHN

> *That's my own girl.*

John

John is Rena's father and as the play unfolds we discover he is also Rhiannon's father. He is a moody man, which is reflected in his guitar playing and the exchanges he has with his wife. He returns each year with his family to Wales to visit his brother and his family. He is a selfish man, having carried on a long affair with his sister-in-law. He hurts his wife constantly, making comments about his death and saying he will be happy if his guitar is left in the good hands of his daughter Rena. This may also be seen as his declaration that Rena is his favourite daughter. He has a special bond with Rena *(page 175)*.

RENA

> *I won't marry.*

JOHN

> *You will.*

RENA

> *I won't leave you.*

He and his wife survive together. Neither appear to be happy but do nothing about it. John is unaware that Dora and Ailsa have made a pact that this will be the last year they meet. He doesn't realise that his wife and lover have ended his affair.

Gareth

Gareth is David and Dora's son. He is shocked to find his mother rolling about in the grass with his uncle. He wants his father to take immediate action but instead learns a lesson from him. Gareth's part in all this is the quietest child who watches and learns.

CHAPTER SIX

GUIDELINES FOR STUDENTS

English and Communication

This section is designed first and foremost to help you achieve the learning outcome for the Literary Study Unit. However, it will also help students studying at Higher and Intermediate 2 prepare for the Critical Essay in the written examination, which is part of Paper II: Analysis and Appreciation. All students studying at Intermediate and Higher must attempt Textual Analysis in the written examination. In this part of the paper you will be required to demonstrate your ability to **understand**, **analyse** and **evaluate** a previously unseen piece of poetry, prose or drama, and so apply the skills that you have already practised in responding to texts as part of your Literary Study.

It is your performance in these key areas of understanding, analysis and evaluation that will be assessed in both the Literary Study Unit and the written examination. It is important to remember that these areas don't fall neatly into separate categories that can be dealt with in isolation. However, as a general rule, the kinds of questions you will be asked will invite you to establish what you know about a particular aspect of a text first, and then ask you to develop your response through analysis and evaluation of its form and content. What will be required of you in each area is outlined below.

1. Understanding

Your response should demonstrate that you know what the text is about and that you understand its key ideas and themes. You should be able to refer to significant details in the text in your discussion of it.

2. Analysis

Your response should demonstrate that you are able to explain and give examples of how aspects of the text, such as its structure and use of language, contribute to meaning and create a particular effect or impact.

3. Evaluation

Your response should demonstrate that you have engaged with the text and are able to evaluate, or judge, how effective the text is in making an impact. You should link your evaluation of the text to your understanding and analysis of it, using the points you have made and the examples you have given to back up your judgement of it.

Finally, *all* responses are assessed on their **expression.** This means they are judged on how effectively they communicate your ideas. In order to produce a well-written response that answers the question asked, you need to be able to stick to your line of argument and use critical terminology appropriately.

What follows are some sample questions on each of the plays and some advice on how to produce an extended response to them. You should be able to apply the same set of guidelines to different kinds of questions on the plays in this book, and to other plays that you might read. All the questions are examples taken from English and Communication examination papers, Paper II: Analysis and Appreciation.

Your written response to the plays needs to be well-structured and models of how to do this are given for each of the questions that follow.

There is also reference made to the activities based on each play. This is to remind you of what you know about the play and to help you connect relevant aspects of the text and your ideas on it to appropriate points in your critical essay.

Higher

Choose a play in which the deterioration of a marriage or a relationship is important. Show how the dramatist presents the deterioration, and why it is, in your opinion, important to the play as a whole.
In your answer you must refer closely to the text and to at least two of: characterisation, theme, dialogue, plot, conflict, or any other appropriate feature.

This question is well suited to *Medea*.

Introduction

You should begin by stating that:

☐ the deterioration of Medea's and Jason's marriage is very important, in fact central, to the action of the play and is established as such from the opening speech;

☐ the consequences of the deterioration and its impact on the central character is developed as soon as Medea is on stage through her speech and interaction with Jason;

☐ it is 'discussed' and considered by the chorus in their commentary throughout the play.

Basically, what you do in your introduction is demonstrate that you understand two things: what is being asked of you in the question and what some of the key ideas and themes are in the play.

You could consider some of the ideas that arose from the first role on the wall (ROTW) exercise on the play where you considered the characters of Medea and Jason. Here you established from a very early point in the drama that the deterioration of the marriage is the central issue.

Development

Now you should consider aspects of the text which deal specifically with the deterioration of a relationship. In *Medea* the whole play is centred round this, so you should select aspects of the drama that you particularly engaged with. It is important that you cover at least two of the named aspects listed in the question (characterisation, language, conflict). The deterioration is established through:

- [ ] What Medea says and does;
- [ ] What Jason says;
- [ ] What the chorus says.

In your analysis and evaluation of how the dramatist presents the deterioration, you should focus on key parts of the play. You will need to refer to the text closely and this means including direct quotes.

You have already put Medea in the 'hot seat' as part of your revision of the text where you've scrutinised her motivation. Also, in the character studies you have already explored in depth the characters in the play, including their emotions and motivations. This will provide you with the kind of detail that you need to discuss the deterioration of Medea and Jason's relationship. The background information section of the play also provides other relevant details, in particular relating to how language is used in the play. There are also examples of how bits from the text are used to back up a point being made. Here's how to do this.

"The words of the chorus as they address Medea and the audience on the subject of her broken marriage switch in register and style. On the one hand they can be sneering commentators on Medea's plight:

> 'marriage over? shame that's the end of it
> so get on with it'

On other occasions, when they sympathise with her situation, their language is much more poetic:

> 'salt and bitter are those tears
> as the seas you sailed with him'

The effect of these 'switches' on the audience is to continually remind them of the different responses that are possible to Medea's situation. In particular, a quite cynical female viewpoint is presented, which sounds very contemporary and also connects the setting of the play in ancient Greece with modern society in a powerful way."

The short extract above contains both analysis, in the part where the use of language by the chorus is discussed, and evaluation, when there is discussion of the effect and impact of this technique on the audience.

You should include a number of analytical and evaluative comments like the one above as you build towards your conclusion. What you select for discussion should always be relevant to the question: this is the key to responding appropriately. What you select should then be shaped into a coherent response that reinforces your particular view of the text.

Conclusions

The closing scenes of the play provide a suitable focus for pulling together your ideas on the deterioration of the relationship between Medea and Jason. As you have explored in the drama activities and character study, Medea is a very strong personality who feels wronged and wreaks her revenge in a terrible way. You should both judge the impact of the ending as an extreme portrayal of a marriage gone wrong, and discuss how effectively Liz Lochhead builds up the drama to its final, terrible climax through her use of language. You're not introducing any new ideas at this point. Your task is to conclude by highlighting how the deteriorating relationship stays central to the play until the very end of story. In this way you stay true to the question asked.

Intermediate 2

Choose a play in which an important character is in conflict with another character or characters in the play, or with herself or himself.
Describe the conflict and show in what way it is important to the development of the plot and theme of the play.
In your answer you must refer to the text and to at least two of: theme, plot, characterisation or any other appropriate feature.

This question is very well suited to *Heritage* because the conflict between Sarah and her parents over her relationship with Michael is central to the drama of the play. As this conflict arises primarily from the different religious backgrounds of the main characters, you will be able to discuss some of the wider issues and themes of the play that arise through conflict.

Introduction

You should establish Sarah as the central character to be discussed. Highlight how the theme of conflict and violence is established in the opening scene before anyone speaks, and is then linked directly to Sarah, who speaks first. She is described as a 'rebel' by Michael and this further reinforces the idea of conflict. The play ends with Sarah in a state of inner conflict and confusion, uncertain about her future. It is important to state in the introduction that the key source of the conflict is Sarah's relationship with Michael. The conflict arises primarily because they are of different religions.

The character study on Sarah will help you consolidate ideas for the introduction. The diary entry and the ROTW activities on Sarah and Michael should remind you of the kind of relationship they have.

Development

The drama activities on *Heritage* explore in some depth the relationships between the various characters in the play. The character studies are useful for thinking about the attitudes and behaviour of Sarah's parents and Michael's father. Ruth's walk down 'conscience alley' will also help you think in-depth about her deeply held beliefs and her actions. It's worthwhile reflecting on this before you write about Sarah's conflict with her parents over her relationship with Michael. You need to demonstrate, too, how Nicola McCartney uses the troubled relationship of Sarah and Michael as a focus for exploring wider issues of conflict in the world around them and links them to religion, history and politics, as well as events in the drama. The background information section and the timeline of events will be helpful here.

You should work through key scenes with Sarah and her mother, her father, Emer and, finally, Michael himself. For example, Sarah is often in conflict with her mother, not only over Michael but also in general over her attitudes and beliefs.

SARAH

> *The story of Deirdre of the Sorrows. Do you know it?*

RUTH

> *I do not? Where did you hear that?*

SARAH

> *At school once …*

RUTH

> *I don't want to hear it.*

When you analyse and evaluate the writer's craft you could deal with how the playwright not only uses *Deirdre of the Sorrows* as a parallel story to that of Sarah and Michael, but also uses it to add poetry and theatricality to the play.

Conclusion

As with *Medea*, the death at the end of the play is a result of earlier conflict. You could focus your ideas around the circumstances of Michael's death. This will allow you to bring the key ares of conflict together, yet still keep Sarah at the centre of your discussion.

Intermediate 1

Choose a play that deals with family life. How are the relationships between members of the family portrayed and to what extent do you find these relationships convincing?
In your answer you must refer to the text and to at least two of: characterisation, key scene(s), conflict, dialogue or any other appropriate feature.

This question is well suited to *Sea Urchins*.

Introduction

In your opening paragraph you should describe the set up between the two families. Focus on particular relationships within the family. These could include:

- [ ] Rena and her parents;
- [ ] John and Ailsa;
- [ ] John and Dora;
- [ ] Rena and Noelle;
- [ ] David and Dora;
- [ ] Ailsa and Dora.

Don't try to cover all the possible relationships in the play in-depth. Pick two or three as your main examples and mention any others in passing when you need to.

The first 'diary entry' by Rena and the joint 'hot seating' of Ailsa and Dora will be useful sources of information here because these activities are set up so that characters 'reveal' things about their relationship with other members of the family.

Development

Use the character studies plus activities on characterisation, conflict and dialogue in the play to help you discuss the particular relationships on which you want to focus. The role play between Rena and Noelle about the 'dark secret' will remind you of the tensions and jealousies between the two girls. Other activities like 'conscience alley', relating to the relationship between Dora and John, are very helpful too. In fact, all the activities are largely based on exploring family relationships, so you can select what you want to discuss from a wide range of possibilities. Make sure, however, that you include some discussion of Rena, because she has a central role in the play.

Describe how popular songs are used in the play. There are comments on this in the background information section. Refer to some particular parts of the drama where characters like John use song as a way of communicating their feelings about their relationships:

> *'She's driving me crazy / What am I going to do?'*

You can also analyse the use of slashes and asterisks in the text by highlighting how this technique, when 'acted out' gives a sense of the communication difficulties among the various characters. Pick some specific examples to discuss. Model your approach on the fully worked out example of this in the background information of the play. The 'family secret' and its impact on particular family members should also be discussed.

Conclusions

Finally, you need to evaluate how convincing you think the relationships are? Does Sharman Macdonald succeed in presenting an entertaining yet realistic view of family life?

Specialist Study in Literature

If you have selected the Specialist Study in Literature as one of your areas of study, you might choose to use one or more of the plays in this collection for your review. As with the critical essay, you will be assessed under the same headings of understanding, analysis, evaluation and expression, but you will be expected to write more (up to 1800 words).

You should aim for a detailed study of one aspect of the play(s), such as the role of a character or how a particular idea or theme is worked through. The character studies and some of the activities will be helpful here, as will the background information section for each play. These sections establish key ideas, themes and aspects of each play and so you could develop quite a focused argument around which to structure your review.

Alternatively, you could compare aspects of two of the plays in the collection. For example, you could discuss how family relationships are explored in *Sea Urchins* and *Heritage* or you could consider how playwrights explore gender issues in *Medea* and *Sea Urchins*. The way that Scottish drama represents marriage would also be a worthwhile topic and all of the plays could be used to explore this. The advice offered in the following Drama section is also relevant to the Specialist Study in Literature.

Drama

The guidelines provided in the previous section for English and Communication students will be useful, up to a point, in helping you achieve learning outcome one in the unit on Contemporary Scottish Theatre: demonstrate knowledge and understanding of contemporary Scottish theatre. However, there is an extra dimension to the learning outcome in Drama, which involves analysing *three* plays and using these texts in *two* responses. Furthermore, the analyses demand that the plays are discussed in relation to a particular issue or trend. This means that not only do you need to know each text well, but you also need to have some understanding of the issue or trend on which you've chosen to focus.

It is worthwhile thinking about how the three plays in this collection 'fit' the specified trends and issues of the Unit Study.

1. Social, political and religious dimensions

Heritage fits all three of these categories with its focus on religious tension between Catholics and Protestants. Its setting provides potential for discussion of the social dimension as it deals with the challenges facing new immigrant communities in Canada.

Sea Urchins, too, has a strong social dimension with its focus on family life, and *Medea* has as a central idea the social pressure that arises from the 'mixed' marriage of Jason and Medea.

2. The use of history, nostalgia and popular tradition

Again, *Heritage* is a text that can be explored in relation to history and nostalgia. *Sea Urchins* also links here with its use of popular song.

3. Issues of gender

This issue is central to all three plays although *Medea*, in particular, provides a very strong core text for discussion and analysis.

Written Response

Discuss the representation of marriage in Scottish drama. You should illustrate your answer with reference to at least two plays you have read or seen.

The question on *Medea* in the earlier English and Communication section, asks students to explore a play in which a deteriorating marriage plays a central role. All the material discussed there can be used to provide key ideas and textual examples for your written response. Similarly, the example included for *Sea Urchins* can be used with a particular focus on the married couples in the play, as well as reference to the views of Rena and Noelle on marriage and future relationships.

As you discuss the representation of marriage in each play, you could consider the following points. Is there a positive or negative view being represented? In both plays, conflict seems to be a defining feature, betrayal, too. How are conflict and betrayal handled in each? How do the endings differ? What can you conclude about the way marriage is represented in Scottish drama?

CHAPTER SEVEN

COMPONENTS OF A PLAY

In theatre, everything has a symbolic meaning because the medium is symbolic.

Character

Plays cannot exist without characters. So much of a story is told through their actions, motives and relationships.

Medea

MEDEA

> *right out of the blue*
>
> *humiliation!   I was the last to know*
>
> *the man who was more to me than my own life*
>
> *is now the vilest man alive   my faithless husband*

In these few lines we know exactly what the relationship between Medea and Jason is. We can also see that she is bitter and will seek her revenge.

Heritage

MICHAEL

> *If we don't pray in the same church together we can't marry.*

SARAH

> *I think we've done worse than pray together, Mike.*

Here we begin to see the change in Michael. He is beginning to put up barriers.

Sea Urchins

RENA

> *See that song. She sings it for my father. I'm never going to be a woman.*

In this line we get a real sense of Rena's immaturity but also her deep perception of her parents situation.

Setting

As important as character. All the sounds, silences and components of the scene, and the way that a character relates to them create the context and affect the meaning.

Medea

The characters make a very powerful entrance.

NURSE

> *away in you go my bairnies   watch them man*
> *keep them away from their mother   her hurt eyes of hate*
> *what would she no do?*
> *harm   all harm*
> *to your enemies   Medea   no those you love!*

The first primal cry from Medea inside.

NURSE

> *there there wheesht my wee loves my bairnies*
> *your poor mither   she's no right   run*
> *keep away from her   thon's no your mother*
> *the state she's in*

The Manservant hurries them indoors.

From off Medea cries out in a voice that is not Scots but a foreigner speaking good English – an 'incomer voice'.

Heritage

Scene One

A dream: The stage is lit by the fire. A boy dances slowly at first to the beat of a drum. The dance grows more frenzied as the beat quickens and a flute comes in. The sound of people shouting and running in alarm.

Fire consumes the boy dancer.

A scream.

Blackout.

Silence.

The sound of a woman weeping.

This is the beginning of the play. It leaves a strong image in our minds.

Sea Urchins

JOHN

> *Rena!*

MARTIN

> *That your / dad?*

RENA

> *Your brother's breaking his / heart.*

MARTIN

> *Aren't you / going?*

The use of the (/) and (*) in the play creates an effect and sets the atmosphere of the scene.

Language

How do the characters speak? A dramatist uses language as a psychological means of exploring the character.

Medea

KREON

> *frankly I'm feart of you   why no?*
> *feart you hurt my daughter   why no?*

What kind of king is Kreon? What kind of man is he? We can tell a lot from only one or two lines.

Heritage

SARAH

> *Can I come again?*

EMER

> *B'fhearr e mura dtiocfadh se' anseo aris coiche.*
> [Translation – It's better she doesn't come here again.]

The use of a different language again tells us a lot about a character, and in this case makes us ask why Emer doesn't use English.

Sea Urchins

AILSA

> *You drive that girl too hard.*

JOHN

> *She's my harp of joy.*

AILSA

> *Is that what she is?*

This is a good example of John using unusual words, words that tell us where he comes from.

Plot

The plot emerges from the action on stage. Establishing character, setting and language is often where the dramatist starts as a way of developing the plot. Dramatic conflict is the essence of a play.

The following are examples of conflict seen throughout the plays. There are various conflicts between individuals, groups, religions and nations.

Medea

MEDEA

> *. . . we women are too weak   they say   for war*
> *wrong us in bed though   oh man*
> *we'll have your guts for garters.*

CHORUS

> *we promise you we are women Medea*
> *we know men   we know who is in the right*
> *punish him for us Medea*

Heritage

RUTH

> *You go up to that woman's house? . . .*
> *. . . and never ever go there again, d'you hear me ? There's an end to it.*

Sea Urchins

JOHN

> *Who knows what the future holds.*

AILSA

> *We've a long way to go yet, you and me.*

JOHN

> *Not so long as we've been.*

AILSA

> *Planning on leaving me?*

Structure

Time and space have a different meaning on stage. They might not be linear.

Heritage is probably the best example of this. Sarah starts in the present then takes us back in time. Throughout the play she goes between the present and past to tell her story.

Rhythm

The tempo of a play is very important. It is the bringing together of all the above in a particular way. Diversity is necessary to avoid one tone for too long. If the rhythm does not shift there must be a reason why.

Examples of this can be easily found in *Sea Urchins* with the use of the (/) and (*). These symbols are used to draw our attention to the script, making us look more closely at what the characters are trying to say. And in performance, the actors will be speaking in competition with, and at cross-purposes to one another, disrupting the flow of dialogue.

Staging

A play was written in order to be seen. The playwright lays the words on paper but relies on the actor to make it come to life. The role of the director is to guide the actors through the play and to assist in presenting the visual aspects of the work to an audience unless, of course, the play is meant for radio.

Often when reading a play we have a visual picture of the locations where the action takes place.

We have to think of the constraints of staging a play in a theatrical space. With modern technology a lot more can be achieved in the space but still there are constraints. When thinking about this aspect try to be as imaginative as possible.

Firstly, does the play lend itself to the proscenium stage, theatre in the round, arena, traverse or promenade?

What kind of set will you have? Will you use a box set, flats, trucks or cyclorama? Will it be realistic? Will it be symbolic? Does the play rely heavily on the time and place to make the story work or can it be an abstract setting?

Think of plays that you have seen. What was their visual impact? Did you like it? Did it detract from the story? Did it add atmosphere? You don't have to have a technical mind to think about how the stage will look but it is helpful if you can use your imagination to capture the essence of the play and convey this to the audience.

CHAPTER EIGHT

TEXTUAL ANALYSIS

The examples of Textual Analysis which follow replicate the format used for this question in the Higher Still exam. Each example can be used in two ways: as revision of the text being studied and as practice for the exam itself. Each extract and questions have been pitched at the level of study designated for each play. However, this should not limit their use with students. The extract from *Sea Urchins* is aimed at students attempting Intermediate 1 but would be appropriate, too, for students aiming at Intermediate 2, or even Higher, as general practice in the skills required for the exam. Similarly, *Heritage* could be used with students studying at Higher level, particularly in the earlier stages of their course. *Medea* is the most challenging of the three, largely because of its use of dramatic conventions.

Medea, by Liz Lochhead (After Euripides)

The play is a modern version of Euripides' play originally performed in Athens in 431 BC. The drama centres around the main character Medea who has fled into exile in Corinth with her husband, Jason. Medea is a very powerful woman, in Euripides' orginal she was a sorceress, who has helped Jason gain the Golden Fleece and even murdered to support his cause. She has just learned that he now intends to wed the daughter of Kreon, King of Corinth. The chorus, who provide a commentary on the events of the play, were typically part of the drama of ancient Greece.

> *Another – the second – primal cry from Medea inside.*

> *Enter Chorus of women of all times, all ages, classes*
> *and professions. (The Nurse does not see, or react with,*
> *the Chorus, their initial communication is to each other*
5   *and also in unison direct to audience.)*

Chorus   That cry   we heard it
                knew it in our bones   it curdled our blood too

> *Medea cries from inside again – for the third time.*

Chorus   we are sorry for your sorrow   sister
10   is that how they cry in Kolchis   Medea?

Nurse   this house is a ruin   ashes
                a cold hearth and the fire put out in it
                for ever

he's lording it lolling in bed with his royal bit
15 she lies in cold ashes inconsolable.

Medea calls out from inside.

Medea I wish to all the Gods that I was dead and done with it

Chorus oh daft to wish for death
when it comes soon enough
20 without you tempt it
so your man fucks another?   fuck him
loves her?   tough   love him do you?
you'll grow out of that

we were not born yesterday
25 we are all survivors of the sex war
married women   widows   divorced
mistresses   wives   no virgins here
marriage over?   shame   that's the end of it
so get on with it

30 **Medea** justice   Gods
look down on me and see my pain
I killed my own brother for you Jason
now I'll see you dead and that damned royal poppet too

Chorus bring her out and let us convince her
35 we're her friends   we can help her

Nurse I'm in terror even to approach her
I know her
her cunning   her spells   her power
how far she'll go   and I'm feart o her
40 more even than I fear for her
she nurses her rage
like a lioness suckling her last living cub
claws at me   bull glares
would gore me   gash me
45 I'm anathema
that blank stare!

The Nurse goes inside.

There is silence from within. Chorus are listening, tense, for something that doesn't come.
Very softly at first –

50   **Chorus** that cry!
it was a cry we've heard
from the woman
opening the door to the telegraph boy in wartime

the cry from   the unquiet wife
55   opening the door
to the chequered hats of two policemen
late late on a foggy night

the cry from   the mother in the hospital corridor
when she sees the doctor's face

60   the cry from   the woman
whose lover's eyes have not quite lied
when she asked him
'tell me is there someone else?'

that cry
65   we have heard it
from our sisters   mothers   from ourselves
that cry
we did not know we knew how to cry out
could not help but cry
70   and we say

we are sorry for your sorrow   sister
is that how they cry in Kolchis   Medea?
rage yes rage at that traitor in your bed
salt and bitter are those tears
75   as the seas you sailed with him

Enter Medea – not a girl – but dignified, beautiful, calm and utterly reasonable. Somehow exotic.

Medea graciously approaches the Chorus.

Questions

1. *Enter Chorus of women of all times, all ages, classes and professions.*

   Explain what meanings a contemporary audience might make from this stage direction. *(2)*

2. a) In what ways does the language of lines 8–15 evoke sympathy for Medea? *(2)*

   b) Gives examples of contemporary language used by the Nurse and comment on the effect of this in her speech. *(2)*

3. Read lines 18–29.

   The Chorus express strong opinions about Medea's circumstances and how she should deal with her situation.

   a) Explain their views of her predicament.

   b) Discuss how effectively they put these views across. *(4)*

4. How does Medea's response to the Chorus suggest her strength of character? *(2)*

5. In lines 36–46 the Nurse reveals a very dark side to Medea. What is revealed and how does the poetic language of this speech do this effectively? Select some examples from the text and explain their effect in detail. *(4)*

6. Read the closing section of the extract from where the Chorus listens and Medea arrives on stage. Explain how the stage directions build up tension, climaxing in Medea's entrance. *(4)*

7. Discuss in detail the content of the speech delivered by the Chorus and explain how it could have a very powerful impact on an audience.

   You should focus on;

   a) the examples of suffering highlighted in the speech;

   b) the language used to express the suffering; and

   c) the connections that are made between past and present. *(10)*

   (Total 30 marks)

Heritage, by Nicola McCartney

The play is set in Canada in 1914. Sarah McCrea, a Protestant has emigrated there with her family from Ulster where they own a farm. Sara meets and falls in love with Michael Donaghue, a Catholic boy on a neighbouring farm. Their relationship becomes a source of conflict for the two families. In this extract, Sarah starts to tell the story of Deirdre of the Sorrows, a tale of old Ulster that Michael has told her.

	Sarah	It happened many years ago. One stormy night, after a fierce Battle, Conor the King was feasting at the house of his poet, Felimidh. A child was born to Felimidh's wife.
	Ruth	What story's this?
5	**Sarah**	The story of Deirdre of the Sorrows. Do you know it?
	Ruth	I do not? Where did you hear that?
	Sarah	At school once.
	Ruth	I don't think so.
	Sarah	It's about Ulster.
10	**Ruth**	I don't want to hear it.
	Sarah	Why not, ma?
	Ruth	Because it's not in our heritage, Sarah.
	Sarah	But we're Irish.
	Ruth	Our ancestors were Scottish. We're Irish but British too.
15	**Sarah**	And now we're livin in Canada, so what does that make us?
	Hugh	We're Scots Irish Canadian British subjects, Sarah. That's what we are.

Scene Nine

	Sarah	Heritage
20		A brand burned in deep
		Through skin of centuries.
		Scarring forever
		The soul
		The land

25	The memory
	The future.
	Carried across deathbeds
	Across oceans
	To far away land.
30	Running deep into the soil
	Blood in the veins
	And fire in the blood
	What fire!
	Sixty thousand miles from here
35	Big guns go
	Boom Boom
	Boom Boom
	At Ypres
	Canadians
40	French
	British
	Irish
	All
	Defending the Empire
45	Boom Boom
	Sixty thousand miles away
	They harvesting and reaping
	And counting the dead
	Sixty thousand miles from
50	Planting and harvesting and profit.

Scene Ten

Late summer 1915. The McCrea Farmstead. They are building
a barn. Sarah remains on stage throughout. Hugh enters.

	Sarah	Ten cows now
55		Twenty sheep
		And one hundred and ninety acres
		Planted
		Corn, oats
		And wheat
60		Farm laid out neat now in strict rectangle
		Wooden frame house at the one end
		Stable here
		Outhouses on this side
		Here
65		Orchard that will grow apples, plums, cherries
		And peaches
		There
		Vegetable garden
		Leeks, beets, carrots, potatoes, cabbages

70		Grapes, melons, squash
		In front
		Orange lilies in the memory walk
		Sown from crease of the letter seeds
		From home.
75		And now
		The barn

Hugh   Here we go! One, two, three – lift!

Sarah   Progress.

Hugh   I need two more men on the back wall. Two I said – you and
80   you. Come on, let's go!

Sarah   Men from Italy
   Doukhobours and Ruthenians
   Irish men
   Orange men
85   To build the new barn
   Log on log
   Plank on plank
   Up and up
   Tower of Babel

90   **Hugh**   You! Get me two ropes!

Sarah   Ready for Harvest
   Ready to hold the wheat of
   Boom Boom
   Wheat Boom

95   **Hugh**   No. Ropes, man. Ropes! Does anybody here speak English?

Sarah   Tap tap tap
   Whistle of saw through wood
   Rhythm of the future

Hugh   No, no, no. Jays! Does anybody speak English here? All
100   hands to the pump! Sarah! You know how to drive a nail
   home, don't you?

Sarah   Yes, Daddy.

Hugh   Well, get to it! John, reach me my claw hammer. Hurry up!
   I'm tellin ye, no one's raised a barn so quick as this.

105   **Sarah**   My nail goes in
                     Bang
                     South wall
                     Facing
                     America

Questions

1. Read lines 1–17

   a) Select two things that Ruth says which indicate her hostility to Sarah's story. *(2)*

   b) Explain why she feels this way. *(2)*

2. a) How does Sarah react to her mother's hostility? *(1)*

   b) What do Sarah's questions reveal about her as a character? *(2)*

3. How does Hugh's answer to Sarah's question link to the title of the play? *(2)*

4. Read Scene Nine carefully.

   a) Describe how the form and content of this scene differs from the first 17 lines of the extract. You should refer closely to the text in your answer. *(4)*

   b) Explain what you think Sarah means when she says,

   'Heritage
   A brand burned in deep
   Through skin of centuries.' *(2)*

   c) Why is it an effective image? *(2)*

5. Read Scene Ten, including the stage directions.

   a) If the play was being performed, how might the action and the words being spoken by Sarah work together on stage? *(3)*

6. Compare Sarah's speech in Scene Nine with her opening speech in Scene Ten. What are the similarities and differences between them? *(3)*

7. What is revealed about Hugh's character in Scene Ten, and how is this done? *(2)*

8. Hugh and Sarah are on stage at the same time but do not speak to one another. What might this suggest about their relationship? *(2)*

9. Explain how this extract as a whole could be considered important in relation to the title of the play, *Heritage*? *(3)*

(Total 30 marks)

Sea Urchins, by Sharman Macdonald

It is June 16 1961 and the two branches of the Williams family have met up for their annual holiday in Wales. Ailsa and John Williams have arrived with their daughter Rena, aged eleven, from Scotland and David and Dora Williams, who live in Wales, have brought their three children. Noelle, the youngest, is also eleven. John and Dora have been having a long-running, on and off, extra-marital affair.

The / indicates an interruption. The * indicates that the dialogue runs from * to *.

Ailsa's singing drowns out the sound of the waves.

	Ailsa	Then one lonely day the stranger sailed away
		With a parting kiss that came too soon*
		And now the Trade Winds sigh
		As ships go sailing by
5		Underneath a blue Tahitian moon
	David	* Back to back. Come on now. / Noelle. I'm talking to you.
		Come on Rena.
	John	We'll tell you who the tallest is but for the
		bonniest we'll leave you to fight it out between you. As
10		for the sweetest natured we'll leave that for the future to
		decide. I've never met a sweet natured woman yet. Not
		after I've married one.
	Ailsa	Been married often then have you?
	John	There's married and married.*
15	**Ailsa**	What's that supposed to mean?
	Dora	* That's enough John.*
	Ailsa	I don't need you to fight my battles Dora.
	Noelle	* I'm the tallest see. Don't have to / stand back to
		back to tell that.
20	**Ailsa**	I may not be the first woman in your life John Williams.
		But I'll make damn sure I'm the last.
	John	Is that a threat?
	Ailsa	It's a promise.

	John	Don't I have a say?
25	Ailsa	You had your say when you married me. You've said a couple of things since that haven't been so hot but I'm prepared to overlook them.
30	John	Here, Noelle. Here's a fried egg roll. Of my making, mind. Nice and hot and fresh out of the pan. One for you Rena. Now. My advice to you. Take yourselves away. Don't let your sweet young selves be contaminated by this witch I married. Gareth don't you marry. Don't you ever marry.

He sings. David's guitar picks him up.

35	John	Oh I've got those mean mean woman blues
		I've got those mean woman blues
		She treats me so bad
		I've got nothing left to lose
		I work * hard to keep her
40		But she throws my care away.

The guitar keeps the twelve bar going.

	Ailsa	* I work, I might paint my nails red but I work
		my fingers to the bone. You show me a smarter woman
		when I leave the house in the morning. There isn't a
45		smarter woman in our street. Nor any house with
		cleaner windows. * My windows shine. My baking tins
		are aye filled with gypsy creams and Empire biscuits.
		My stovies are unrivalled. You're living with a miracle
		John Williams. You're living with a miracle and you
50		don't even know it.

	John	* Oh I work so hard to keep her
		But she throws my care away
		The Lord will judge me willin'
		When I come to him on judgement day.

55	Ailsa	Tell me you don't love me John Williams. Tell me
		that and I'll leave this cove and I'll leave this beach and
		I'll take my daughter and you'll never have truck with
		either one of us again. My God, sometimes I wish you
		would tell me. Tell me before I lose my looks John.
60		Do me that favour. Then I can go out and I can find
		someone that'll appreciate me.

	Dora	You'll never learn will you.

Ailsa	What the hell does that mean?

65

Dora	There was the wicked one and there was the good one. You got the wicked one.

Ailsa	And you got what you deserved isn't that right Dora?

Questions

1. Read lines 1–21

   Quote a line that suggests there is rivalry between the two girls? *(1)*

2. a) From what they *say* to one another, how would you describe the relationship between John and Ailsa? *(2)*

   b) If the text was being performed, how would the stage directions, / and *, be used? Pick an example from lines 1–19 to explain your answer. *(2)*

   c) When the stage directions and words combine, what more might an audience conclude about the relationship between John and Ailsa? *(2)*

3. Why do you think the word 'married' is repeated several times in lines 1–21? *(2)*

4. Read lines 28–33, John's speech.
   a) What is John's advice to the girls? *(1)*

   b) How does he emphasise his point in his speech? *(2)*

5. Read lines 35–40 and lines 51–54, John's song.
   a) How do the words of the song John sings connect to what he has said so far? *(2)*

   b) If John believes the words of the song apply to him, what does it say about the role he plays in his marriage? *(2)*

6. Read lines 42–50, Ailsa's speech.
   a) Describe the kind of woman she thinks she is. *(2)*

   b) *'I might paint my nails red … My windows shine.'*

      What is the effect of using these phrases in Ailsa's description of herself? *(2)*

7. Read lines 35–50, paying special attention to the stage directions, / and *.
   a) Describe how the playwright uses the / and * in this part of the play to direct the way the lines are spoken. *(3)*

   b) Why do you think they are used in this way at this point in the drama? *(2)*

255

8. Read lines 55–61, Ailsa's speech.

    a)   From what you have read so far, how would you describe Ailsa's feelings for John? *(2)*

    b)   Ailsa is very emotional at this point. How is this made clear through her choice of words? *(2)*

9. Read lines 62–67.

What do we find out about the relationship between Ailsa and Dora in these lines? *(1)*

(Total 30 marks)

Acknowledgements

Medea by Liz Lochhead

This version of *Medea* first published in Great Britain in 2000 as an original paperback by
Nick Hern Books Limited, 14 Larden Road, London W3 7ST, in association with Theatre Babel,
Glasgow.
Copyright in this version of *Medea* © Liz Lochhead 2000.
Liz Lochhead has asserted her rights to be the author of this work.

CAUTION All rights whatsoever in this version of the play are strictly reserved. Requests to
reproduce the text in whole or in part should be addressed to Nick Hern Books.

Amateur Performing Rights Applications for performance in excerpt or in full by non-professionals
in English throughout the world (excluding stock productions in the USA and Canada) should be
addressed to Nick Hern Books, 14 Larden Road, London W3 7ST, *fax* +44 (0) 20-8735-0250,
e-mail info@nickhernbooks.demon.co.uk
Professional Performing Rights Applications for performance by professionals in any medium and in
any language throughout the world (and for stock productions in the USA and Canada) should be
addressed to Rod Hall Agency Ltd, 7 Goodge Place, London W1P 1FL, *fax* +44 (0) 20-7637-0807.

The publication of this play does not imply that it is necessarily available for performance by
amateurs or professionals, either in the British Isles or overseas. Amateurs and professionals
considering a production must apply to the appropriate agents for consent before starting
rehearsal or booking a theatre.
No performance may take place unless a licence has been obtained.

Heritage by Nicola McCartney

Heritage was first published in Great Britain by Traverse Publishing (Traverse Trading, trading as
Traverse Publishing), Traverse Theatre, 10 Cambridge Street, Edinburgh, EH1 2ED.
Heritage copyright © 1998 by Nicola McCartney.
Nicola McCartney has asserted her moral right to be identified as author of this work.

CAUTION All rights in this play are strictly reserved. Requests to reproduce the text in whole or
in part should be addressed to the author c/o Traverse Theatre, Cambridge Street, Edinburgh,
EH1 2ED.

Sea Urchins by Sharman Macdonald

Sea Urchins copyright © 1998 by Sharman Macdonald.
Sharman Macdonald is hereby identified as the author of this work.

CAUTION All rights in this play are strictly reserved. Applications for permission for any use
whatsoever, including performance rights, must be made in advance, prior to any such proposed
use, to MacNaughton Lord Representation Ltd, 200 Fulham Road, London, SW10 9PN.
No performance may be given unless a licence has first been obtained.